Higher Education

Higher Education

Open for Business

Christian Gilde, editor

LEXINGTON BOOKS

A division of
ROWMAN & LITTLEFIELD PUBLISHERS, INC.
Lanham • Boulder • New York • Toronto • Plymouth, UK

LEXINGTON BOOKS

A division of Rowman & Littlefield Publishers, Inc.
A wholly owned subsidiary of The Rowman & Littlefield Publishing Group, Inc.
4501 Forbes Boulevard, Suite 200
Lanham, MD 20706

Estover Road
Plymouth PL6 7PY
United Kingdom

British Library Cataloguing in Publication Information Available

Library of Congress Cataloging-in-Publication Data

Higher education : open for business / Christian Gilde, editor.
   p. cm.
Includes bibliographical references and index.
ISBN-13: 978-0-7391-1847-4 (cloth : alk. paper)
ISBN-10: 0-7391-1847-1 (cloth : alk. paper)
ISBN-13: 978-0-7391-1848-1 (pbk. : alk. paper)
ISBN-10: 0-7391-1848-X (pbk. : alk. paper)
1. Education, Higher—Finance. 2. Commercialism in schools. I. Gilde, Christian,
1973–
   LB2342.H492 2007
   338.4'3378—dc22   2007006294

Printed in the United States of America

♾™ The paper used in this publication meets the minimum requirements of American
National Standard for Information Sciences—Permanence of Paper for Printed Library
Materials, ANSI/NISO Z39.48-1992.

To all of you,
I dedicate this book

Contents

Preface

Christian Gilde

I was fortunate that an extraordinary group of scholars with distinct skills, abilities, and expertise agreed to participate in this project. Each of these individuals contributed an integral part to this book in the area of his or her expertise in which he or she works, teaches, researches, or publishes. It is this diverse array of experiences that assigns this text its unique flavor, accessibility, and mass appeal.

The aim of the book is to create awareness for the commercialization/ overcommercialization of higher education and set out for change. While composing this book I was driven by the notion to help students to consciously navigate through a system of higher education that is over-stimulated by commercialization. Furthermore, when assembling this text many questions crossed my mind, some of which were as follows: What does is take for a university to morph from a knowledge seeker into a profit seeker? Doesn't the development of commercialization undermine the academic integrity and identity of an institution? Do students, parents, and educators really care about the commercialization issue in higher education?

The way my coauthors and I address this topic is to allow the readers to enjoy a comprehensive discussion of the subject at hand and familiarize themselves with the problems associated with this issue. In addition, this information can help our readers to make crucial academic decisions. Parents can more easily prevent children from becoming overexposed to a college culture that is penetrated by commercialism when making the decision where to send them to take up higher education. College administrators are aided in drafting and enacting more student-centered policies instead of courting and worshipping the corporate givers. Government officials can pause, for once in their lifetime, from being so busy on making policies and actually implementing them, which helps everyone involved in academia to return to what they are supposed to be doing—focus on learning.

Many educators and administrators have lost sight of this primary reason for an academic institution's being (the focus on learning) and have forsaken education to make way for commercialization.

Acknowledgments

I WOULD LIKE TO ACKNOWLEDGE AND THANK a few individuals and organizations who made it possible to publish this book. My heartfelt thanks are extended to my parents, my grandparents, and all my former and current professors and the people I know at Santa Monica College, The University of California at Los Angeles, Eastern New Mexico University, Boston College, and The University of Bath, who instilled me and always supported me in my efforts to strive for higher grounds and create something that transcends time. Especially, I would like to thank David, Erin, Eve, Fred, Juliet, Liz, Markus, Mike, and Sal for their amazing patience during the long hours it took to complete this book and for their contributions, guidance, and advice. Furthermore, many thanks are also extended to Steven Miller, Liane Berardino, Tom Lemon, Sue Barrett, Eydie Tesdahl, and Kit Mahoney for their research assistance and helpful comments. I also wish to express sincere appreciation to my publishing team at Lexington Books, a division of Rowman & Littlefield Publishers, and their acquisition editors, T. J. MacDuff Stewart, Mr. Patrick Dillon, and NT Ngo, as well as their Assistant Production Editor, Paula Smith-Vanderslice.

Christian Gilde

Introduction

Christian Gilde

It is disturbing to see that today's cafeteria conversations do not center around topics such as Shakespeare or international affairs. Due to the overcommercialization of higher education, college and university students sadly start paying attention to issues such as the following: Are we a Gateway or a Dell campus? Are we a Coca-Cola or a Pepsi campus? Are we a Nike or an Adidas campus? These matters should not be a primary concern to students in an environment in which the main focus rests upon learning. It is not to say that the much-needed financial benefits of commercial ventures should be denied to institutions of higher education. It would be foolish to do so. However, commercialism has gotten too close to certain aspects of academia, and this dangerous development is addressed in the forthcoming book.

A serious issue that needs to be taken into consideration while writing and assembling such a book is to locate the areas of higher education that are most widely affected by overcommercialization. After surveying the applicable literature on commercialization (overcommercialization), one will discover that four areas which are vulnerable to commercialization emerge in this literature over and over again; the classroom, the campus environment, research, and college sports. These are vulnerable areas that relinquish their academic territory and independence to the commercial world. Guided by this discovery the authors of this book make a concerted effort to write in these four areas and group their contributions accordingly.

Through this structure the flavor of the text and its chapters have been created; a flavor that alerts consumers of higher education about wrongful behavioral tendencies in tertiary education that are associated with commercialization and that, to a certain extent, allow to answer the question one will eventually ask himself or herself while reading this book: What is the price at which universities start selling out? If universities morph, more and more,

1

from knowledge seekers into profit seekers, than we are faced with a development that will change the landscape of higher education—how we think, how we work, and how we approach things—and undermine what academia stands for, learning.

Furthermore, this book is a well-argued critique of the emergence of business values in a system reserved for learning and scholastic inquiry from a diverse host of authors from all parts of the educational spectrum. This text points out that many businesslike routines are not fashioned to work in and be adopted by universities and colleges. This book stresses a commercial independence and decision-making power that should not only rest with the administration of an institution, but also with the students and their parents and provides helpful information as well as controversy. Furthermore, since it is a multi-authored work, the following introduction provides a roadmap through this book to be able to enjoy more fully the selected contributions this effort has to offer.

In the introductory chapter 1, Elizabeth Miller familiarizes the readers with the market of higher education. Miller asks: who are the primary stakeholders that contribute to and/or are affected by commercialization? Chapter 1 explores this and other related questions as well as the various techniques used to market to college students, thus setting the stage for later chapters to examine the effects of commercialization on the overall institution of higher education. In addition, by highlighting the various techniques that students are likely to encounter and how marketers view the student market, this chapter will provide students (and other stakeholders) with the tools and knowledge to better utilize (or ignore) such information.

In chapter 2, I provide a sense for the gravitate of the problem of commercialization that besets higher education by presenting short but plausible pieces of evidence for the dilemma at hand and set the stage for upcoming chapters. Furthermore, my chapter introduces an unexposed framework that this text follows and which frequently emerges in the contemporary literature related to this topic. This framework identifies four vulnerable areas that are the academic domains most likely to be exposed to commercialization—the classroom, the campus environment, research, and college sports. This structure enables a logical progression through this topic. My chapter closes by pointing out that not all aspects of commercialization are bad. However, it cautions that institutions and their stakeholders have to be careful when walking the fine line between knowledge seeker and profit seeker.

Catherine O'Neill presents in chapter 3 how commercialization can be found in classrooms; a disturbing sign of our time that educational experts are signaling. However, while these experts in student learning have called for a recommitment to quality undergraduate learning, many campuses have ignored complaints from students, parents, legislators, and employers, who accuse them of a lack of focus when it comes to "bread and butter" general education courses. O'Neill points out that adjunct faculty are overused and underpaid, and the Total Quality Management philosophy often encourages excessive downsizing that keeps students from getting their money's worth. Even worse, some campuses seem to have abandoned ethical standards in the quest for corporate dollars. The chapter stresses that organizations like the American Association of University Professors and the National Institute of Health have worked against the growing problem of conflict of interest in some of the United States's best graduate research programs. Then again, the sell-out of faculty and administrators has threatened the reputation of the academies and the validity of university research.

The second part of Catherine O'Neill's contribution to this text is chapter 4, in which she focuses on online education. Online universities are probably the largest commercial force with which contemporary institutions must reckon; a commercial development that has sparked a rush for easy online money from hopeful students. O'Neill mentions that in this rush some for-profit universities have earned the reputation of snake oil salesmen, making promises of almost instant success to students who would never meet entrance standards for a typical college or university. In spite of the many lawsuits and the stiff fines imposed on profligate online shops, Wall Street seems to consider the violations to be business as usual. The chapter argues that, while many online programs and courses do in fact offer students a good chance to earn a quality degree, minority students are most commonly at a disadvantage when it comes to spotting the telltale signs of a digital sweatshop. O'Neill advances that when higher learning is reduced to the "widget" model, and online for-profit websites are heavy on enticement and lean on actual information, when it is assumed that courseware can replace seasoned master teachers without a loss, it seems that the hegemony of the dollar has seriously damaged the academy's ability to foster tomorrow's generation of bright, young scholars once and for all, at least those who don't have strong parental support and/or a hundred thousand dollars or more tucked away for the pursuit of knowledge.

Chapter 5 reflects on the business activities in online learning, branches out to discuss the online hybrid developments of intranets and Web-enhanced classes, and provides insights into the pedagogical dynamics that are behind distance learning. In this context, Fredrick Chilson and David Rutledge emphasize that the amicable relationship between institutions of higher education and online education companies has flourished over the past decade. Yet, as time passed this relationship has shifted its focus from "knowledge pursuit" to "profit pursuit," often sidelining educational needs. Additionally, this chapter focuses on the fact that within these commercial-technological alliances, the pedagogical component has to enter the online teaching equation; more specifically, the authors stress that the distance learners' needs are to be at the center of this knowledge conversation. Both Chilson and Rutledge convey to the reader that taking an online course, as well as teaching one, is much more than just a point-and-click experience. Appropriate management and assessment of online learning are essential tools to ensure students receive a decent return on their monetary investment. However, this relatively new form of course delivery still has many flaws that need to be worked out.

College sports today are a major economic driver in the commercialization of higher education. In chapter 6, Michael Malec shows the extent and severity of the problem of college sports as a business and introduces this issue from a historical and contemporary perspective. The ongoing debate about the conflict between the amateur and professional being of sports is highlighted. Emerging from these issues are the primary corporate commercial pressures of company takeover, increased collegiate professionalism, and academic integrity infringement college sports face today; these pressures are explored in the second part of the chapter. The conclusion presents some possible solutions to the aforementioned collegiate dilemmas.

By analyzing the "privileged role of consumption," Juliet Schor raises in chapter 7 the question of "whether the expansion of consumerism, as a way of life, constitutes a threat to liberal education?"[1] "On the face of this, this may seem an odd question. After all, isn't consumerism merely the logical extension of the liberal paradigm that elevates individual rationality, choice and freedom? Perhaps. But even on those terms one might wonder if the essence of the contemporary consumer stance is at odds with the context in which liberal discourse and action must take place, such as full information, deliberate and planning activity, and a community of equals."[2] Additionally, Schor introduces some other aspects of this expansion of consumerism that concern liberal education. She takes a closer look at what impact this entire commercialization development has on the campus, the nation's need for active citizens, and the ethical and moral responsibilities of liberal education. As will be revealed, in the end consumer denial and the privileging of the consumer model are easy ways to disengage ourselves from the critical (self-reflective) stance liberal education is encouraging us to take.

In chapter 8, Eve Spangler highlights that not only commercial but also political pressures threaten the relative autonomy of the university and attempts to fashion a case study out of her own institution's response to these pressures. Like many other schools, this institution in the Northeast is trying to increase its prestige and research reputation under challenging circumstances. The chapter points out that when faced with an aging faculty, the absence of mandatory retirement, the shrinkage in research overhead formulae and the competition for foundation dollars, financial considerations are becoming an increasingly important criterion in university decision making. Yet, this college is also struggling to maintain its identity as a Jesuit and Catholic institution with particular pedagogical and ethical commitments (education of the whole person, men and women in service to others). Standing at the intersection of these difficult and contradictory forces, Spangler shows that several institutional efforts are launched at this school to respond to corporate demands on academia. By holding a Fair Trade Holiday Sale, the exercise of social justice values and practices at this particular school are emphasized. A joint vocational program with independent business partners exemplifies a socially just, corporate-university collaboration around personnel training. Finally, the attempt at socially responsible university purchasing (sweatshop-free university insignia merchandise, and sustainable agriculture coffee) represents this college's response to creating a socially legitimate market system.

Eve Spangler and I conclude the discussion on overcommercialization in chapter 9. In this chapter, Spangler and I revisit some of the classical sociologists who help the readers to think about the overcommercialization of academic life. Inspired by these scholars' critical approach to the businesslike administration and standardization of school operations on a domestic and global basis, we pose the question: why do the current guardians of the university, who are supposed to shelter the academic community from corporatization and commodification, fail to do so? In addition, we present a list of commercially vulnerable areas that need safeguarding; a list to which those who are entrusted with guarding academia should give some serious consideration. The conclusion challenges the readers and scholastic institutions to reflect on whether present-day universities are capable of striking the proper balance between necessary financial concerns and overcommercialization?

By addressing a wide spectrum of commercialization issues in higher education, it is the sincerest hope of the authors that the following book creates awareness for the problem of commercialization/overcommercialization in tertiary education and helps present and future generations of students, parents, and educators to make more rational decisions when it comes to embarking on the right career path and choosing the right college or university.

NOTES

1. Juliet B. Schor, "Spending Nation: Liberal Education and the Privileged Place of Consumption," in *Higher Education: Open for Business*, ed. Christian Gilde (Lanham, MD: Lexington Books, 2007).

2. Juliet B. Schor, "Spending Nation: Liberal Education and the Privileged Place of Consumption," in *Higher Education: Open for Business*, ed. Christian Gilde (Lanham, MD: Lexington Books, 2007).

BIBLIOGRAPHY

Schor, Juliet B. "Spending Nation: Liberal Education and the Privileged Place of Consumption." in *Higher Education: Open for Business*, edited by Christian Gilde. Lanham, MD: Lexington Books, 2007.

Chapter One

The Market of Higher Education

Elizabeth G. Miller

"In an age when the college demographic is no longer easily reached via television, radio, or newspapers . . . a microindustry of campus marketing has emerged."[1]

Sarah Schweitzer, "Building a Buzz on Campus: Companies Enlist Students to Pitch Products to their Peers" (2005)

Commercialization has become embedded in American life. The university has not been immune to these effects. This chapter examines the stakeholders who contribute to and/or are affected by commercialization, focusing in particular on the student market and the characteristics that make this segment attractive to marketers. In addition, this chapter looks at a number of techniques used to market to college students in order to enable students (and other stakeholders) to recognize and respond to such persuasion attempts.

WHO CONSTITUTES THE MARKET OF HIGHER EDUCATION?

The university is a complex entity consisting of numerous stakeholders. These stakeholders include the administration, faculty, students, alumni, parents, and companies themselves. Each of these stakeholders contributes to the university culture and may impact consumption decisions. As such, many of these stakeholders contribute to commercialization on college campuses and/or are affected by commercialization.

There are 4,326 colleges and universities in the United States.[2] Currently, there are approximately 17.7 million students enrolled in these colleges and universities, and this number is expected to rise to 19.5 million students by

2014.[3] Of these students, ten million study at four-year and graduate institutions, with the remaining students studying at two-year colleges and other academic entities.[4] International students comprise approximately four percent of the student population.[5]

Students constitute the core of the educational institution. They are the key recipients of the services the university offers (education, cultural activities, housing, dining, etc.), and they make large numbers of consumption decisions each day. Indeed, estimates suggest college students account for $26 billion in discretionary spending.[6] Students are affected by commercialization in a number of ways. First, they are constantly exposed to advertising and marketing messages. In fact, the average consumer in the United States receives about three thousand marketing messages per day.[7] These messages appear on billboards and flyers posted around campus, in the school newspaper, on products in the campus store, and in the dining halls. Students may also be exposed to marketing messages through on-campus promotions, direct mail, examples in their textbooks, and recruiters. Second, students are affected by commercialization through a narrowing of choice options. For example, if a university has a beverage contract with Coca-Cola, it may be very difficult to find other beverages on campus, often leading students to have to consume (or purchase) a less preferred beverage.

However, not all effects of commercialization are negative. Students benefit from campus improvements and programs which are funded via dollars obtained from corporate sponsorships. For example, Baylor University used funds from their sponsorship agreement with the Dr. Pepper Bottling Company of Texas to fund a new student center,[8] while the University of Ottawa started an alumni-student mentoring program with funds from MBNA Corporation.[9] Such improvements and programs benefit not just the students, but other stakeholders, such as the university as a whole and alumni, as well.

Indeed, the administration is a key player in the creation of the university culture and plays a large role in the degree of commercialization on campus. With respect to commercialization, the administration can be viewed as a gatekeeper. The administration controls which companies receive contracts and which are allowed to advertise on campus billboards, displays, and at athletic events. They also choose whether or not to co-sponsor events with other entities (including corporations). In this way, the administration helps to create the limited-choice environment that students face, implicitly endorses some products over others (through allowing special promotions and offering certain products, such as computers, for sale through the university), and shapes the advertising messages to which students are exposed.

However, as noted previously, the administration also uses corporate sponsorships to directly benefit students. Through corporate sponsorships, the university receives money which it can use to build new facilities and create academic or sports programs. For example, after signing a multi-year contract with Pepsi, the University of Minnesota reported that it intended to use the money for scholarships, academic programs, student activities, and other university initiatives.[10] Such money can also be used to attract star professors (through increased salaries, research funds, and/or equipment and facilities) and students (through scholarships and improved offerings). Indeed, many of the improvements made to the university as a consequence of increased funding become selling points the university can then use to attract students. Thus, the administration contributes to commercialization by acting as a gatekeeper who controls which companies and messages are promoted, and it benefits from commercialization through increased funds, which can be funneled toward school-wide improvements.

Other constituents of the university also benefit from commercialization. Increased funding from corporate sponsorships may allow universities to increase faculty salaries and/or provide monetary resources for research, including lab equipment and facilities. Corporate sponsorships also often enable increased funding for athletic events and schools may even contract with athletic companies, such as Nike, to provide them with sports equipment and clothing. TV and radio contracts for athletic events also contribute to the university's coffers.

Alumni may also benefit indirectly through commercialization. In general, alumni play a vital role in the university system. They often contribute money to the university and may serve as ambassadors for the university, encouraging future students to apply. Improvements to the university, which increase the university's reputation indirectly benefit alumni by increasing the value of their degree. Many universities also offer special promotions, including credit cards, which donate a small percentage of purchases back to the universities, to their alumni. Thus, alumni are affected by commercialization both directly through special offers sent to them from the university and indirectly through campus improvements, which may affect the school's overall reputation.

Finally, it is also important to consider the role of parents in the overall market of higher education. Parents contribute to the university environment by providing advice, help, and support to their children (the current students). They are indirectly affected by commercialization to the degree they help their children make consumption decisions. Thus, they also experience the limited-decision environment that confronts college students, and may be influenced by the university's tacit endorsement of certain products.

This chapter's discussion of the various stakeholders in the university highlights the far-reaching effects of commercialization and the diversity of players who contribute to and are affected by commercialization. While each of these stakeholders is important, many of these stakeholders and their role in commercialization are discussed elsewhere in this book. Therefore, the remainder of this chapter will focus its attention on the student market.

CHARACTERISTICS OF THE STUDENT MARKET

In order to understand students as a target market, it is crucial to understand their demographic, psychographic, and usage profile. The "traditional" age of college students is 18–22 years of age. However, the number of nontraditional students is growing. Indeed, the average age of students attending community colleges is 29,[11] and the US Census Bureau reports that only 53 percent of undergraduate students are aged 18–21, with an additional 28 percent aged 22–29. Of these, 66 percent attend college or university full-time,[12] and approximately 58 percent are women.[13] Fifty percent of undergraduates consider themselves dependents, and of these, 32 percent come from families whose income is less than $40,000 per year, 35 percent come from families whose income is between $40,000–$80,000, and 33 percent come from families whose income is greater than $80,000 per year.[14] The majority of undergraduate students are white (63 percent), with an additional 14 percent identifying as African American and 13 percent identifying as Hispanic.[15]

The majority of students fall into a segment of consumers known as Generation Y. This group of consumers, sometimes also called Generation Nexters or Echo Boomers, consists of all people born between the years of 1980 and 1994. Many marketers believe that groups of people who come of age at about the same time (known as "cohorts") tend to have common preferences and attitudes because they have lived through many of the same experiences. The experiences they have shared shape how they think, what becomes important, and how they might react in the future. These generational commonalities tend to cut across racial, ethnic, and economic differences, and thus in order to best understand the student market, it is useful to understand the values and consumption behavior of this segment.

Generation Y grew up in the digital age and are consequently extremely media and technologically savvy. They use a large number of high-tech products, such as computers, the Internet, cell phones, and DVD players, to communicate with each other, play games, do homework, and shop.[16] Indeed, 92 percent of students report owning a computer and 69 percent report owning a cell phone.[17] Many college students do not own another phone besides their cell phone, which is perhaps why this segment accounts for over $16 billion in annual revenue for the cell phone market.[18] Their exposure to videos and computers growing up has also led students to process information faster. This facility with information and expectation of quickly changing environments contributes to this group's reputation as a "notoriously fickle consumer group [that demands] the latest trends in record time",[19] as well as their reputation as consummate multi-taskers. Indeed, according to a Student Monitor survey, 77 percent of college students report eating while watching TV; 58 percent report talking on the phone while watching TV; and 56 percent report doing homework while watching TV.[20]

In general, Generation Y has been described as confident, achievement-oriented, sociable, valuing morality, civic-minded, street smart, and optimistic about what they might be able to finesse. Since September 11, 2001, the values of Generation Y have tended to shift back to more conservative core values such as family, saving for a rainy day, religion, and civility. Indeed, this generation has been reported to be less brand loyal and more accepting of purchasing generics than other generations,[21] and is generally thought to value price more than brand loyalty or particular advertising messages. Consistent with these values, 66 percent of college students report that they "hunt for bargains" and only 27 percent consider it important to stick with certain brands.[22] Findings from the Student Monitor Survey also support this return to traditional values.[23] Eighty-nine percent of students report life goals that emphasize having a happy marriage, while 81 percent have life goals which include a fulfilling career or good friends. Only 23 percent indicate that money is a necessity for having a good life.

These values are largely a function of the events, such as heightened concerns over terrorism, presidential scandals, and corporate scandals, that transpired while these individuals were coming of age. Such events have also contributed to these individuals having a particularly skeptical and mistrusting outlook which influences their responses to marketing messages. Generation Y does not like a hard sell. They are particularly wary of blatant attempts to influence them and dislike ads which "smack of derision."[24] They want advertisers to talk *to* them, not *at* them, and they tend to process messages carefully, caring less about company boasts and more about what benefits the product can offer to them.

Thus, the student market is largely composed of individuals aged 18–30 who fall within the generational cohort known as Generation Y. This segment is technologically savvy and price sensitive, with traditional values, such as family and civility. They tend to be fickle in their tastes and desire the latest trends. They are also skeptical of advertising and wary of attempts to influence them. Given these characteristics, what makes this segment attractive for marketers?

THE STUDENT MARKET: FROM THE MARKETER'S EYES

Although college students can be a particularly difficult group to market to, it is also a very attractive segment for marketers. According to a Harris Interactive survey, the student market spends nearly $200 billion a year, and they spend an average of $287 per month on discretionary items.[25] Much of this discretionary income is spent on beverages and snack food ($11.4 billion) or entertainment and leisure activities (over $12.2 billion). In addition, college students tend to have greater earning power post-graduation compared to those without a bachelor's degree. This difference in earning power peaks when the college graduate is 50–54 years old.[26] College graduates have above-average expenditures on alcohol, entertainment, personal care, and food away from home.[27]

Thus, college students are an attractive market for both their current spending habits and their potential future spending. College is often the first time that students are away from their parents and making independent consumption decisions.[28] As such, they may not have well-developed brand preferences yet. They are also at a time in their life when they are open to experimenting with new products.[29] Thus, preferences may be malleable, and once formed, may result in lifelong purchasing habits. Indeed, Vickers reports that college students keep their first credit card for an average of fifteen years.[30] In addition, because college students frequently share their opinions with peers, there is a great opportunity for generating positive word-of-mouth which can help a new product spread through the population more quickly. Indeed, much of the success of the movie *The Blair Witch Project* has been attributed to word-of-mouth,[31] and a majority of students report listening to friends when purchasing movies (78 percent) or video and computer games (58 percent).[32]

Given these potential benefits for marketers, it is not surprising that marketers aim so much of their marketing at this segment. However, given students' known skepticism toward advertising, marketing towards this segment can be quite challenging. What techniques do marketers use to target this segment and what techniques are likely to be effective?

COMMON MARKETING TECHNIQUES

Given our discussion so far, it should be clear that traditional marketing tactics and traditional media are less likely to be effective at persuading the student audience. Results from a Student Monitor survey suggest that most college students (90 percent) only watch ten hours of television per week, and much of the time spent in front of the television is shared with other tasks, such as eating and talking on the phone.[33] Thus, traditional television ads are unlikely to be seen or processed.

However, marketers can improve the effectiveness of their television ads by truly understanding their target market's values and behavior. Effective advertisements will often incorporate symbols, issues, and language to which this group can relate.[34] For example, Virgin Mobile USA has successfully used creative television ads which cater to word-of-mouth to attract the student market.[35] Companies should be careful when using slang in commercials, however, as phrases can become out-of-date by the time an advertisement appears, making the product appear "uncool."[36]

In addition to trying to appeal to consumers by using music, humor, issues, or language that appeals to the target market, it is also important to consider the types of message content that will be persuasive and where the target market is likely to "tune in." For example, advertisements on TV networks, such as MTV, or on TV shows, such as *The OC*, which appeal to the student market are more likely to be noticed. In addition, because students are often wary of persuasion attempts, it is important for ads to talk to them, providing reasons why the product will be beneficial for them. Such messages will also benefit from short, snappy phrases, rather than long-winded explanations, as this technologically savvy market is used to having information come at them at a quick pace.[37]

In addition to television advertisements, many marketers have turned to college newspapers to attract students. Data from Student Monitor indicate that most college students read their college newspaper, with 72 percent reporting having read at least one of the past five issues and 42 percent having read three or more of the past five issues. College newspaper advertisements may also be beneficial because reduced clutter increases the chance the ad will be perceived and attended to.[38]

Marketers are also turning increasingly to more nontraditional media and marketing techniques in order to better access the student market. Cosponsorship of recreation or special events and guerrilla or viral marketing are just two examples of such nontraditional media. Some companies are trying new forms of media, such as magalogs (a magazine-catalogue combination that features lifestyle articles interspersed with product information), blogs, and podcasting. Other companies, such as Honda, are going straight to the classroom, embedding their marketing campaign within the curriculum, by having students design and implement an on-campus marketing campaign to reach college students as a class project. The success of such nontraditional media remains unknown. However, preliminary results are encouraging. In an article in *American Demographics*, Tim Hudgens, regional division marketing manager for General Motors, reports that brand and product awareness measures can increase five- to tenfold over the course of a semester with an in-class project.[39]

Another example of an emerging new media that marketers are beginning to use in order to better target students are social networking sites, such as Facebook. Facebook offers three types of ads to marketers: sponsored groups, banner ads, and text announcements.[40] Text announcements are the least expensive of the three options and are typically used to target specific college campuses. Sponsored groups allow users to sign-up, post messages, and get information from the sponsoring company and are typically used to promote products, ideas, or brands. Banner ads typically employ bright colors or flashing icons and enable users to buy a product, sign up for a program, or be linked to a new site in a matter of clicks. Marketers use these ads to promote many products and services, including movies, music, posters, and travel packages, to students. Despite the high cost of sponsored groups and banner ads, this form of marketing is still in high demand.[41] In fact, Yahoo! recently offered to buy the company for $1 billion.[42]

RECOGNIZING AND RESISTING PERSUASION ATTEMPTS

Given the large number of marketing messages from a diversity of sources that students are exposed to on a daily basis, what can they do to avoid being unduly influenced by them? To answer this question, it is useful to consider persuasion tactics in general, rather than specific marketing techniques. Robert Cialdini identifies seven key principles of social influence—automaticity, commitment and consistency, reciprocity, scarcity, social proof, liking, and authority.[43] This chapter describes each of these sources of influence and provides suggestions for recognizing and resisting persuasion attempts based on these sources of influence.

Automaticity refers to an individual's tendency to respond in automatic ways without carefully processing the message.[44] This principle relies on individuals' tendencies to use heuristics, or simple decision rules. With respect to persuasion, people who are asked a compliance question often do not think hard about what they are being asked or what the implication of their response is. Consequently, if a reason is provided for the request (e.g., "because X"), the person is more likely to comply, even if the reason provided is not a very good one (for example, "May I use the photocopy machine because I have to make copies"). The mere presence of the word "because" is enough to make people comply.[45] This technique is more successful for small requests than large ones, because people are more likely to process requests heuristically when they are unmotivated to process the information. To avoid falling prey to such a technique, students should carefully consider the message and think critically about why they are engaging in a particular activity. They want to move from a state of mindlessness to one of mindfulness, that is to a state where they are focused on the information at hand, and motivated and able to process it.

The second principle of social influence is known as "commitment and consistency." This principle relies on our desire to behave in consistent ways. This suggests that once we make a choice or take a stand, we will encounter interpersonal and internal pressure to behave consistently with that commitment. Thus, we respond in ways that justify our earlier decision.[46] For example, once you agree to try a new "free" service, you may feel compelled to continue with that service (beyond the free trial period) in order to seem consistent with your past behavior. A number of marketing tactics are predicated on this notion. For example, individuals often make a small request (e.g., help me with my homework tonight) followed by a larger request later (e.g., regular tutoring sessions); this technique is known as "foot-in-the-door."[47] Car dealerships often obtain an initial commitment from an individual and then change the deal. People stick with the new deal out of commitment to the old deal; it is too much effort to rethink the entire new deal and they feel committed. This technique is known as "low balling." Smoking cessation programs often encourage the smoker to "tell everyone who matters to you that you are going to quit smoking." This public commitment increases the probability that the smoker will actually quit because they now are committed to the action—it would seem embarrassing to seem inconsistent and the person may believe that they really want to quit if they told others about it.

To defend against commitment and consistency influence tactics, students need to ask themselves why they are agreeing to the action. They should listen to their gut if it tells them that they are being taken for a ride and ignore consistency for consistency's sake. They should ask themselves if they could go back in time, knowing what they know now, would they still make the same choice? If the answer is no, then they should decline.

The reciprocity principle relies on the idea of "give and take." When someone does you a favor, you often feel obligated to return the favor. You try to repay in kind what another person has provided you with.[48] Marketers often use this notion to try and persuade consumers to purchase products. For example, many merchants offer free samples in the hopes that once you try the sample you will feel obligated to buy something. Fundraisers (including university development officers) often begin with a large, unreasonable request, and then follow up with a smaller more reasonable request. This technique is often successful because the person feels bad about denying the earlier request, so they agree to the smaller request. To defend against these types of requests, again the students need to remove themselves from a state of mindlessness into a state of mindfulness. They need to consider the request at hand and decouple that request from earlier actions.

The scarcity principle relies on the idea that scarce objects are presumed to be more valuable. Consequently, individuals are more likely to desire an object when they perceive it to be scarce.[49] Marketers play on this notion when they include phrases such as "limited edition" or "for a short time only." Students can defend against this notion by trying to evaluate their true utility for the object. If there were an unlimited number of items available, what would the student be willing to pay for the item? Would they still want to purchase it? By asking themselves questions like these, students can assess their true value for the object and then use this assessment to determine if the purchase should be made.

The principle of social proof refers to the idea that the perceived validity of correctness of an idea increases as the number of people supporting the idea increases.[50] Examples include peer pressure for conformity or presenting a list of other people who have already purchased or donated money. Students can defend against this influence technique by trying to assess their individual utility for the item. If nobody else would ever know whether they had purchased the item or not, would they still buy it? Do they truly desire the item or are they only interested in the item due to peer pressure? By answering questions such as these, the student should be able to assess their true value for the object and thus reach a more unbiased decision about whether to purchase it.

The last two principles—the liking principle and the authority principle[51]— relate to characteristics of people that we want to comply with. That is, we tend to want to comply with requests made by people we like because we desire their respect or want them to like us too. Similarly, we often comply with people in authority because we want their esteem or because we do not perceive that we have any other option. When the university promotes a particular product, we may be more likely to purchase it because we view the university as in a position of authority. When a friend recommends a product, we may be more likely to purchase it due to our feelings for the friend. Marketers often consider these two principles when choosing spokespeople for their products or models to use in their ads. For example, www.Studentcity.com identifies students to serve as "campus representatives" based on the number of friends these students recruit to travel on spring break together. Once the campus representative has been identified, the company sends the representative flyers to pass out on campus to continue to recruit other students. These flyers contain a promotional code that corresponds to the representative. When these recruited students use the code to sign up for trips, the representative's trip gets credited, reducing his cost as compensation for his efforts.[52]

To defend against persuasion techniques based on liking or authority, students again want to remove themselves from a heuristic processing mode to a more effortful processing mode. They need to ask themselves about the benefits of the product and the reasons they are choosing to purchase the product. Does the product have real, rational benefits for the student or is the student being unduly persuaded by more intangible aspects of the marketing message, such as how similar he perceives himself to be to the spokesperson or how much he likes the spokesperson? What other options are available and how do these options compare to this alternative? By asking questions such as these, the student can more carefully determine his true utility for the item, leading to a more optimal decision.

CONCLUSION

The college market is attractive to marketers. Students are often making purchases for the first time and are open to trying new products. The products they develop preferences for now may become their product of choice for years to come. This potential revenue stream combined with revenues from current purchases make students an attractive target market.

However, college students are known to be skeptical of marketing attempts and they do not acquire information from the same media sources as their parents. As such college students can be a difficult market to target. This difficulty has led marketers to seek alternative media such as college newspapers, special events, exhibitions, college fairs, and the Internet to communicate their message. In addition, college campuses often provide a unique opportunity for marketers to reach this difficult to reach market, leading to an increase in promotional material and commercialization on campus. College students should be aware of the sources of these promotional messages and the potential impact of commercialization on their consumption behavior. By recognizing promotional messages and biased information sources, as well as various influence techniques, students can be better prepared to make informed decisions. This chapter attempted to assist students in these goals by highlighting the stakeholders in the university who contribute to and are affected by commercialization, techniques used by marketers to target and influence students, and strategies for defending against common persuasion techniques.

NOTES

1. Sarah Schweitzer, "Building a Buzz on Campus: Companies Enlist Students to Pitch Products to their Peers," *Boston Globe*, 24 October 2005.

2. National Association of College Stores (NACS), "Higher Education Retail Market Facts and Figures 2006," 2006, <*www.nacs.org/public/research/higher_ed _retail.asp*> (13 October 2006).

3. Chronicle of Higher Education, "Projections of College Enrollment, Degrees Conferred, and High-School Graduates, 2004 to 2014," *The Chronicle of Higher Education* 52, no. 5 (23 September 2005): A46.

4. NACS, "Higher Education Retail Market," 2006.

5. National Center for Education Statistics (NCES), "Digest of Education Statistics Tables and Figures, 2005," 2005, <*http://nces.ed.gov/programs/digest/d05_tf.asp*> (14 October 2006).

6. Harris Interactive, "College Students Tote $122 Billion in Spending Power Back to Campus This Year," 2004, <*www.harrisinteractive.com*> (14 October. 2006).

7. John Hagel III and Marc Singer, *Net Worth: Shaping Markets When Customers Make the Rules* (Boston, MA: Harvard Business School Press, 1999).

8. Kent Steinriede, "Pouring Wars," *Beverage Industry* 88, no. 10 (1997): 10–11.

9. Marcia Vickers, "Big Cards on Campus," *Business Week*, 20 September 1999, 136–38.

10. Steinriede, "Pouring Wars," 10–11.

11. American Association of Community Colleges (AACC), 2006, <*www.aacc .nche.edu*> (14 October 2006).

12. AACC 2006.

13. NCES, "Higher Education Retail Market," 2005.

14. NCES, "Higher Education Retail Market," 2005.

15. NCES, "Higher Education Retail Market," 2005.

16. Wayne Hoyer and Deborah MacInnis, *Consumer Behavior,* 4th ed. (Boston: Houghton Mifflin Company, 2007).

17. Harris Interactive, "College Students Spend $200 Billion Per Year," Spring 2002 Wave of the 360 Youth/Harris Interactive College Explorer Study 2002, <*www .harrisinteractive.com*> (14 October 2006).

18. Hoyer and MacInnis, *Consumer Behavior*.

19. Charles Lamb, Joseph Hair, and Carl McDaniel, *Marketing,* 8th ed. (Thomson-Southwestern, 2006), 80.

20. Sandra Yin, "Degree of Challenge: College Students Present Daunting Challenges," *American Demographics*, (1 May 2003): 20–22.

21. Lamb, Hair, and McDaniel, *Marketing*.

22. Yin, "Degree of Challenge," 20–22.

23. Jane Rinzler, "Beyond Body Piercing," *Brandweek* 38, no. 36 (1997): 20–22.

24. Yin, "Degree of Challenge," 20–22.

25. Harris Interactive, "College Students Spend," 2002.

26. Yin, "Degree of Challenge," 20–22.

27. Yin, "Degree of Challenge," 20–22.

28. Steinriede, "Pouring Wars," 10–11.

29. Yin, "Degree of Challenge," 20–22.

30. Vickers, "Big Cards," 136–38.

31. Richard Scheib, "The Blair Witch Project," *Science Fiction, Horror, and Fantasy Film Review* 1999, <*www.moria.co.nz/horror/blairwitch.htm*> (6 November 2006).

32. Harris Interactive, "College Students Tote $122 Billion in Spending Power Back to Campus This Year," 2004, <*www.harrisinteractive.com*> (14 October 2006).

33. Yin, "Degree of Challenge," 20–22.

34. Hoyer and MacInnis, *Consumer Behavior.*

35. Yin, "Degree of Challenge," 20–22.

36. Hoyer and MacInnis, *Consumer Behavior.*

37. Hoyer and MacInnis, *Consumer Behavior.*

38. Yin, "Degree of Challenge," 20–22.

39. Yin, "Degree of Challenge," 20–22.

40. Angela Manese-Lee, "Companies Use Facebook to Target Customers," *Roanoke Times*, 7 November 2005.

41. Manese-Lee, "Facebook."

42. Kevin J. Delaney and Rebecca Buckman, "Yahoo's Talks with Facebook Get Bogged Down," *Wall Street Journal*, 12 October 2006, A3.

43. Robert B. Cialdini, *Influence: Science and Practice, 4th Edition* (Needham Heights, MA: Allyn & Bacon, 2001).

44. Cialdini, *Influence.*

45. Ellen Langer, Arthur Blank, and Benzion Chanowitz, "The Mindlessness of Ostensibly Thoughtful Action: The Role of 'Placebic' Information in Interpersonal Interactions," *Journal of Personality and Social Psychology* 36, (1978): 635–42.

46. Cialdini, *Influence.*

47. Jonathan L. Freedman and Scott C. Fraser, "Compliance Without Pressure: The Foot-in-the-Door Technique," *Journal of Personality and Social Psychology* 4 (1966): 195–202.

48. Cialdini, *Influence.*

49. Cialdini, *Influence.*

50. Cialdini, *Influence.*

51. Cialdini, *Influence.*

52. Liane Berardino (Boston College student), personal communication, November 2006.

BIBLIOGRAPHY

American Association of Community Colleges (AACC). 2006. <*www.aacc.nche.edu*> (14 October 2006).

Chronicle of Higher Education. "Projections of College Enrollment, Degrees Conferred, and High-School Graduates, 2004 to 2014." *The Chronicle of Higher Education* 52, no. 5 (23 September 2005): A46.

Cialdini, Robert B. *Influence: Science and Practice, 4th Edition*. Needham Heights, MA.: Allyn & Bacon, 2001.

Delaney, Kevin J., and Rebecca Buckman. "Yahoo's Talks with Facebook Get Bogged Down." *Wall Street Journal*, (12 October 2006): A3.

Freedman, Jonathan L., and Scott C. Fraser. "Compliance Without Pressure: The Foot-in-the-Door Technique." *Journal of Personality and Social Psychology* 4 (1966): 195–202.

Hagel, John III, and Marc Singer. *Net Worth: Shaping Markets WhenCustomers Make the Rules*. Boston, MA: Harvard Business School Press, 1999.

Harris Interactive. "College Students Tote $122 Billion in Spending Power Back to Campus This Year." 2004. *<www.harrisinteractive.com>* (14 October 2006).

———. "College Students Spend $200 Billion Per Year." Spring 2002 Wave of the 360 Youth/ Harris Interactive College Explorer Study. 2002. *<www.harris interactive.com>* (14 October 2006).

Hoyer, Wayne, and Deborah MacInnis. *Consumer Behavior.* 4th ed. Boston, MA: Houghton Mifflin Company, 2007.

Lamb, Charles, Joseph Hair, and Carl McDaniel. *Marketing.* 8th ed. Thomson-Southwestern, 2006.

Langer, Ellen, Arthur Blank, and Benzion Chanowitz. "The Mindlessness of Ostensibly Thoughtful Action: The Role of 'Placebic' Information in Interpersonal Interactions." *Journal of Personality and Social Psychology* 36, (1978): 635–42.

Manese-Lee, Angela. "Companies Use Facebook to Target Customers." *Roanoke Times*, 7 November 2005.

National Association of College Stores (NACS). "Higher Education Retail Market Facts and Figures 2006." 2006. *<www.nacs.org/public/research/higher_ed_retail .asp>* (13 October 2006).

National Center for Education Statistics (NCES). "Digest of Education Statistics Tables and Figures, 2005." 2005. *<http://nces.ed.gov/programs/digest/d05_tf.asp>* (14 October 2006).

Rinzler, Jane. "Beyond Body Piercing." *Brandweek* 38, no. 36 (1997): 20–22.

Scheib, Richard. "The Blair Witch Project." *Science Fiction, Horror, and Fantasy Film Review,* 1999. *<www.moria.co.nz/horror/blairwitch.htm>* (6 November 2006).

Schweitzer, Sarah. "Building a Buzz on Campus: Companies Enlist Students to Pitch Products to their Peers." *Boston Globe*, 24 October 2005.

Steinriede, Kent. "Pouring Wars." *Beverage Industry* 88, no. 10 (1997): 10–11.

Vickers, Marcia. "Big Cards on Campus." *Business Week*, (20 Sept. 1999): 136–38.

Yin, Sandra. "Degree of Challenge: College Students Present Daunting Challenges." *American Demographics*, (1 May 2003): 20–22.

Chapter Two

The Overcommercialization
of Higher Education

Christian Gilde

"Making money in the world of commerce often comes with a Faustian bargain in which universities have to compromise their basic values—and thereby risk their very souls—in order to enjoy the rewards of the marketplace."[1]

Derek Bok, *Universities in the Marketplace: The Commercialization of Higher Education* (2003)

"Being again where frosts and tests were hard. Find yourself or fold. Here, imagine a spirit moves. John Harvard walks the yard. The books stand open and the gates unbarred."[2] These idealistic words spoken on a streaming video tour of Harvard University seem to become more and more faint in an academic world that has struck a "Faustian bargain" with commercialism.[3] I cannot imagine that John Harvard would approve of this development. He didn't leave "half of his estate and 400 books" to a pioneering institution such as Harvard in order for his investment in higher education to be sold to the highest commercial bidder.[4] He believed in education and not the commercialization of education and knew that if society wanted to have the capacity to educate and train people, it would need the necessary facilities and qualified people to do so. He was aware that if the younger generation wants to get anywhere, they would have to do it through education for education sake and not through its commodification.[5]

Books that are sold on campus in a bookstore that is operated by Barnes & Noble; tests and test-preparations that are administered by companies such as the Educational Testing Service (ETS); or unbarred gates that allow, for instance, entrance to the McDonald's Liberal Arts Building or the Dell Technology Laboratory. When did we come to a fork in the road and take the wrong way? When did we enter a (Faustian) bargain that enslaves rather than empowers higher education? When did we redefine our bottom line and let commercialization take over?

When looking at the historical development of education, who would have thought that institutions of higher education would, one day, morph from knowledge seekers into profit seekers? Universities have survived for centuries and maintained and upheld their knowledge-seeking mission throughout generations. Only in recent decades has this mission been infringed upon and universities pressured to yield to the forces of the commercial age.

Formal university life and the institutionalization of academia began with the University of Bologna, Italy, in around 1100 A.D.[6] When formal higher education was still in its infancy, students were educated in the three major academic areas which were prevalent at the time: theology, medicine, and law. During the middle ages, the clergy had a strong hand in the scholastic well-being of students and the day-to-day operations of the academy. However, the message that academia is supposed to follow was always clear: seek knowledge.

In the Anglo regions another university was established around 1200.[7] This was at Oxford in the United Kingdom, where students were able to engage in advanced scholarly work and be educated in the arts, humanities, and sciences. Cambridge, a rival institution, was founded in 1209.[8] Oxford was, in later years, to become more the humanities center of university inquiry, whereas Cambridge became the locus for the sciences.

The Renaissance and Enlightenment in the sixteenth and seventeenth century introduced new ideas to an antiquated system of higher education. The ideas of Isaac Newton, Thomas Hobbes, and Charles Darwin, together with a strong liberalist movement that was strengthened by the French and American Revolution, brought new challenges to the intellectual life and literally exposed the then archaic university to a renaissance. However, even during these daring times the university never lost sight of its primary mission—to seek knowledge. Not even the increased professionalization and rationalization of trade and colonial expansion could persuade higher education to adopt profit seeking as its primary goal.

From the early years of the university until the end of the nineteenth century, university life was a privilege mainly reserved for the upper class, and in particular for a male audience. With the rise of the German University in the nineteenth century and the changing of the guard from English to German domain, a concerted effort was made to make higher education accessible to a wider audience, which allowed women to enter the realm of tertiary education.[9] More and more students were processed (mass-schooled) rather than educated to cope with the increasing demand for well-educated people, a demand that was sparked by the industrial revolution, mass production, and consumption.

In the beginning of the twentieth century a new higher education power-house emerged. As the commercial power of the United States grew stronger and stronger, so did this nation's system of higher education. The freedom of academic inquiry, together with an enormous influx of intellectual potential, enabled the United States to assume the number one position in university education. Nonetheless, money, lots of money, was needed to fuel this intellectual machine. With the government having limited resources, colleges and universities had to turn to alternative sources, such as private businesses, that were willing to feed this insatiable industry. In the late 1970s a liberalization of laws concerning profits derived from patents took place and the close relationship between higher education and the commercial world began.[10] More profit-focused thinking penetrated the, up to this point, relatively pristine and independent grounds of university life. The dependability on corporate funding grew out of proportion, disabling colleges and universities to stop this frightening development. Initial commercialization of higher education evolved into overcommercialization, a development that will prevail in higher education for the foreseeable future.

Overcommercialization takes place when the lines between the scholastic and the commercial are blurred and when the business side penetrates academic areas where it does not belong. This, to a certain extent, is true for the classroom, curriculum development, research, and specific areas of student and faculty life. It is an open secret that the majority of the academic community is against too much commercial penetration. However, efforts of certain members of academia (e.g., Ernest Boyer, American Association of University Professors) to resist commercialization seemed to have been in vain and were unable to stop big business from getting a foothold in the realm of higher education.

So, what can be done then to resist the commercial encroachment of big business? This is a challenging question that might be better approached by examining the forces that make universities commercialize. When taking a closer look at the synergy between commercializing and being commercialized, the reasons that drive schools to overcommercialization can be assigned to one of three categories: consumer choice, business influence, and stakeholder power.

The first reason why institutions of higher education are exposed to overcommercialization is based on consumer choice. The consumer choice approach reveals that the actors in a free market economy are assumed to be rational. Being rational means that consumers seek to maximize their payoff, and thus, make choices (consumer choices) that enable this maximization.[11] The main actors in this market are the students, and to a certain degree their parents, who are offered a wide variety of educational services at different institutions, ranging from extension classes to research education. Colleges and universities have to have and provide the necessary resources to make these curricula offerings and the settings in which they are delivered appealing to the students. However, in order to have the necessary resources, very often, institutions of higher education depend on the support of private companies. These companies are driven by rational decision-making processes (consumer choices) as well and want to have, next to a decent return on their investment, certain ownership privileges which can make their presence felt in form of access to student information or a request for work-ready employees.

The second reason why universities and colleges are vulnerable to over-commercialization is the fact that influential individuals as well as corporations want to have a say in education. They want to have people who will stroke their status egos or who will be potential future consumers for their company products. In this context, it is hard to believe that David Geffen just donated $200 million dollars to the UCLA School of Medicine to enjoy tax advantages.[12] This generous gesture allows him to improve his status in society (e.g., David Geffen School of Medicine) and gain a certain degree of prestige among his peers. Under certain circumstances, such individual generosity might even help the donor to acquire an influential position in an academic institution. In addition, corporations are involved in giving either because they want to exert a certain amount of influence on the curricula offerings of schools or because they want to place their key people on university boards and, thus, shape the institutions from the inside.

The third reason why overcommercialization takes place is the power stakeholders—such as university administrators, companies, competitor institutions, and the government—can exercise within the university realm. These internal and external stakeholders enable as well as constrain an institution to operate and achieve its organizational goals. These internal and external powers are present in the social, cultural, political, economic, and technological fabric of university life. The administration that oversees and executes university operations and regulations could prevent an institution from suffering commercial overexposure. However, since the administration is one of the primary expense items on a school's income statement, money is needed to maintain its operations. Thus, this university entity will not bite one of the hands that feed it. Similarly, the current structure of the educational market system places peer pressures on institutions to fiercely compete for every educational dollar and outscore one another in magazine (e.g., *US News and World Report*) and newspaper (e.g., *The Financial Times*) rankings to attain a respectable and powerful position among their peers. Government complacency is another factor that can subject higher education to commercialization. This happens when the government is reluctant to design and implement the appropriate legislative regulations to keep commercialization confined.

Admittedly, until a couple of years ago I was a mindless victim of corporate exposure myself, sitting in the university cafeteria, or "dining experience" as it is called nowadays, and consuming food served by Sodexho Marriott Food Services while taking in the content offered by the College Television Network (CTN)—CTN has "6,500 television monitors on 800 campuses nationwide, which broadcast a proprietary mix of information" and entertainment and is sponsored by such companies as ESPN, Nintendo, and Clairol.[13] One could say, "I'm guilty as charged!" But not anymore. Becoming actively aware of your environment and realizing what is actually happening in this milieu is maybe the single most important step in dealing with the overcommercialization issue; an environment that consists of many different scholastic areas.

The following paragraphs introduce the most vulnerable academic areas—education, the campus environment, research, and sports—that can be subjected to profitability thinking; all will be discussed in greater detail in the upcoming chapters. However, examples such as crucial research findings delayed to please corporate donors, college sport departments run like corporations, or education purely fashioned for the propose to attract commercial funding, are only a few of the indiscretions that show the vulnerability of these areas and cause the public to question the academic integrity and independence of America's schools.

EDUCATION: THE CLASSROOM

Education is one of the areas that are vulnerable to commercialization. In this realm, curricula offerings, administrative appointments, and lecture delivery are particularly vulnerable to becoming corporate prey. Imagine the following not so unrealistic scenario:

Sometimes private businesses come along to save the day. If this business is a bank and is even willing to invest into the local community, what more can an educational institution ask for.

Let's assume that an economically disadvantaged public university in upstate New York was fortunate enough to find a generous bank donor. The school, located in a run-down neighborhood, was strapped for cash. The president of the university approached the local bank and encouraged the business to sponsor the school. Since the bank director was a far-sighted man who believed in youth, he arranged that, during the start-up phase, a steady stream of money would pour into the local university. Over time, that sponsorship grew into something much bigger: a financial commitment that provided the university with millions of dollars. In return, the bank requested and got a say in the management of the school as well as in its daily operations.

The bank placed its people on the school's board of trustees and began a massive restructuring program. At first, the owner of a local supermarket chain was hired as the new vice president for business affairs. The bank's reasoning for this move was that the institution needed someone who possessed the proper tools to turn this run-down educational place around. Secondly, the key administrative positions were restaffed to improve the academic environment while, at the same time, directing the educational goals more towards the needs of the local business community. Finally, new equipment was purchased from companies that owed the local bank money to improve the desolate facilities of the school.

As a result, a number of poorly populated educational programs such as social work, literature, and early childhood education were cut. In contrast, more banking and accounting courses were introduced. The English and math core-course offerings were reduced to the minimum, barely enabling the university to make it through the next accreditation. The bank's logo was placed on the students' Internet portals. The bank prided itself that all this was accomplished in just one and a half years. When interviewed, both the university and the bank were pretty confident that the venture had worked out well.

This might be one possible example of how education is infringed upon by commerce. Here private investors and institutions of higher education work hand-in-hand to the benefit of . . . whom? The university got financial resources and a business-like managed environment, in return for what? The already diminished general education and social science curriculum was cut to a minimum, jeopardizing a future accreditation and survival of this institution. New courses were offered to satisfy the bank's vocational needs for skilled labor. Key positions in the organizational structure were taken over by bank-selected officials. The bank openly displayed its dominant sponsorship position on the electronic classroom platforms used by the university.

This is not an uncommon scenario in today's world of higher learning. Private businesses are taking over, clearly showing that higher education, in its current state, is too much commercialized. However, the classroom as an educational venue that needs to be rescued from business encroachment is explored in much more detail in Chapters 3 and 4.

THE CAMPUS ENVIRONMENT

The campus environment is a complex, interdependent system that consists of many variables—such as stakeholders, organizational structures, and administrative procedures—that influence its being. One area where the commercial penetration of the campus environment makes itself felt is textbooks. According to an article in the *Toronto Star,* companies might be able to buy advertising space in textbooks in the near future.[14] This unwanted intrusion of advertising would contribute to the problem that more and more peripheral information is finding its way into these schoolbooks, at the expense of basic and essential information. However, what is needed are textbooks that present the information in a more accessible, nonglorified, and inexpensive manner. Concerning the high costs of textbooks, nowadays the situation has progressed so far that certain schools offer their students the option to rent rather than purchase books.

In addition, during the textbook frenzy in the beginning of the semester when students are buying their books at the campus bookstore, a sizable number of flyers promoting everything from shampoo brands to credit cards make their way into the plastic bags in which the schoolbooks are carried. This stack of junk pamphlets and brochures is slipped into the plastic bags by store clerks when they are ringing up their customers. In this context, another disturbing development is that more and more campus bookstores are operated by a limited number of companies, one of which is Barnes & Noble. According to Kevin Kniffin in his paper "The Goods at their Worst: Campus Procurement in the Global Pillage," Barnes & Noble "operates [bookstores] on approximately 350 campuses, having increased at a steady rate of fifteen to twenty colonies in each of the last ten years."[15]

Sometimes commercialism sneaks in by the back door, unnoticed by well-meaning students and faculty. The food services at universities and colleges are more and more subject to outsourcing to professional hotel or catering chains which take advantage of this service area. In the book *Campus, Inc: Corporate Power in the Ivory Tower,* Kevin Kniffin reports that the market share of the Sodexho Marriott Group in this area is estimated to be "somewhere around 24–40 percent."[16] Very often exclusive contracts are handed to these companies by administrative officials with licensing agreements spanning over several of years, thus creating monopolies on campus food and catering operations. What either side forgets to mention is that these firms provide food for an already (financially) starving student population at prices that are frequently higher than those at off-campus dining facilities or regular inner-city restaurants.

Another disturbing development is that computer and software companies are also busy taking over the campus environment. Such brand names as Dell, Apple, or Gateway and Microsoft, Adobe, or Linux are conquering and dividing the college and university market. There is no shortage of examples for these kinds of commercial endeavors on campus. At all the institutions where I have worked—from America to Europe; from California to Massachusetts—there was always one preferred brand of computer and the software that came with it. What was for one campus Apple and its operating system OS, was for another campus Dell and its operating system Microsoft. Alternative product offers were not on the menu as far as the campus computer store was concerned. Some of these operations looked like corporate branches of Apple or Dell rather than a campus service that should offer its students a range of product choices with which to enhance their learning experience.

Only a couple of years ago, when the cell phone was still a bulky communication device, pagers roamed the college grounds. At Californian universities communication companies tended to literally shower their freshmen with great deals before, during, and shortly after the school year had started. But what Los Angeles-based Loyola Marymount University (LMU) did in 1999 made it stand apart form other campuses. The Southern California campus provided its freshmen with pagers during the orientation season. The reason reported for this move was to "combat the impersonalization of college culture and its bureaucratic image; [therefore,] Loyola Marymount officials have sent pagers to each of the university's 1,000 incoming freshman."[17] In all fairness, this electronic messaging device could be employed to provide the university with an opportunity to remind students about school dates and deadlines while, at the same time, supplying them with information on administrative issues as well as data on the school itself. However, it was reported that "students will have free use of the alphanumeric pager until classes begin in August. Afterwards, they have the option of keeping the pagers at a discounted rate."[18] This confirms that whatever company was behind that effort, its intention was to create long-term customers for this service. It is obvious that this was one of many promotional ploys in the beginning of the school year to get students to purchase something—along with the magazine subscriptions, car-installment plans, and two-for-one deals at local food or drug stores.

RESEARCH

Medical, engineering, and business schools are often the willing prey of big-name companies, open to receiving what money these companies can give. Therefore, it should not be surprising to hear that in the midst of high ranking institutions, one of the University of California Medical Schools sold off parts of dead bodies to other outside entities without permission of the relatives of the deceased. "The criticisms started in 1996, when families of donors filed a lawsuit claiming that UCLA had mishandled cadaver remains for several decades after it started the world's first donation program in 1950. They continued three years later, when the director of UC Irvine's cadaver-donation program was fired after allegedly selling six cadaver spines to a Phoenix research company."[19] It is hard to believe that this was done to help out fellow institutions with their shortage of body parts for medical research. That one can make some money without having to produce major results is a convenient side effect of this venture. In another case, the University of Michigan, Ann Arbor, reported that in 2004 John Ross, a real estate mogul, made a $100 million donation to the University's Business School.[20] This was the biggest single donation ever to a school of business in the United States to date.[21] The Business School's dean announced that this generous gift will enable this school to build its "future as the top business school in the nation" and "significantly expand its endowment."[22] The keywords that go together with this generous gesture are "top" and "significantly." Even though this gesture is undoubtedly helpful to advance research, especially in the business realm, people have to think one step further and ask themselves where this focused generosity leaves other schools and their research. Big money buys state-of-the-art equipment and creates publicity, thus attracting even more generous donations. In addition, this monetary infusion allows the school to court high caliber faculty and students to join it. However, other institutions could have equally valuable research and a need for quality scholars but lack the connections and resources to attract such big monies in order to advance their business area.

The engineering field is not clean from commercial pollution either, as Jennifer Washburn, the author of *University, Inc.,* reports in a 2006 *Los Angeles Times* article. Washburn takes a look at the relationship that Stanford University entered into with Exxon Mobile and writes, "In 2002, Stanford signed a 10-year, $225 million deal with Exxon and other energy companies to fund a Global Climate and Energy Project, or GCEP. At the same time, Exxon Mobile was pushing the U.S. government to reject any mandatory curbs on greenhouse gases; it also continued to question whether human use of fossil fuels causes global warming."[23] It is amazing that deals between the academic and commercial sphere have to be based on such hypocrisy.

An article in the *New York Times* reported on the link between medical research and drug companies and the strings attached to these liaisons. In an anonymous survey conducted by researchers from Harvard University and the University of Minnesota and published in the *Journal of the American Medical Association,* over half of the university scientists questioned revealed that in exchange for gifts from biotechnology or drug companies they were expected to relinquish some control over their work such as allowing pre-publication paper reviews or patent right ownership.[24] Forty-three percent of the 2,167 scientists that responded to the survey indicated that they had received gifts.[25] "One-third of the 920 scientists who received gifts said their corporate benefactors expected to review their academic papers before publication. . . . 19 percent said that the donors wanted the patent rights to commercial discoveries stemming from use of the gift."[26] Furthermore, the article mentions an incident involving Dr. Petty Dong, a pharmacology professor at the University of California at San Francisco. Dong's study findings that a thyroid drug had the same effects as cheaper generics were suppressed by her sponsor Knoll Pharmaceutical Company.[27] However, after a while the company had to repeal itself due to negative public sentiment.

Such instances are a sad display of a dangerous marriage between the commercial world and the world of higher education. This development should be even more alarming due to fact that not only members of the educational community but also medical patients suffer.

The preceding discussion attempts to show that research is a major target of commercial endeavors in the scholastic realm—this is because the rewards can be so lucrative and research is one of the most powerful areas in academia. Due to the central position of research, this area is especially prone to misconduct hidden from the public which poisons the social fabric of the educational system. Sponsored university research should be part of the public record and should be conducted under the banner of the pursuit of knowledge. However, the details of commercial agreements and corporate and other private giving rarely leave the confines of the administrative ivory tower. This is especially true when the commercialization of research is undertaken with the intent to turn schools from knowledge seekers into profit seekers.

COLLEGE SPORTS

The contemporary literature identifies college football and basketball as the primary commercial drivers of today's college sports. One of the works that presents a fairly complete picture of college football is Keith Dunnavant's book *The Fifty-Year Seduction*.[28] The story told by Dunnavant shows that the epic struggle for football money began in around 1950, when the then National Collegiate Athletic Association (NCAA) Executive Director Walter Byers allowed the major television networks to have a stake in college football. Allegedly, he viewed TV as the enemy; however, it was the enemy with whom he struck a "Faustian bargain" that placed the NCAA at the center of regulatory power.[29] ABC was the member of the TV aristocracy most closely tied to college football. In the early years, ABC secured itself exclusive broadcasting rights that were, in the later years, expanded to include a lucrative five-year deal for college Bowl Championship Series (BCS) events—the Rose, Sugar, Orange, and Cotton Bowl were the honey pots of the latter deal.

However, over the years the NCAA seemed to morph from an organization that was supposed to protect collegiate sports and athletes into a monopoly, led by Walter Byers, that exercised its powers in an absolute manner (e.g., television rights). In March of 1984 this empire was brought down in a landmark ruling by the Supreme Court which exposed the NCAA as what it had been all along, a monopoly.[30] Yet, the College Football Association (CFA) and other stakeholders in college football celebrating this victory did not consider the law of unintended consequences: with this ruling and the subsequent deregulation of television safeguards the entire world of college football plunged into a turf war over television rights and money that lasts to this very day. Language was introduced to college football that no longer "centered around pride, achievement, and honor, but branding, business synergy, and new streams of revenue."[31] The people "once called fans are, nowadays, called customers."[32]

Another defining work that covers the realm of basketball is Walter LaFeber's book *Michael Jordan and the New Global Capitalism.* Who would have thought that a simple school game invented 115 years ago would evolve into something that spans the globe and produces unparalleled figures such as Michael Jordan, a former University of North Carolina student, or Magic Johnson, a former Michigan State undergraduate? These figures were and are surrounded by infrastructures which support the rise of individuals (e.g., Phil Jackson, David Stern) and corporations that back them (e.g., Nike, News Corp.).[33] These multinational companies and media outlets leverage the commercial potential of this sport and its college ties to the fullest. One cannot help but notice that the global village seems to have turned into a village called Nike Town with a mayor called Michael Jordan.

Sadly, professional basketball was not the only arena targeted by firms hoping to increase profits. Multinational companies and media outlets utilized the commercial potential of college sport as well. Among those multinationals that employ foreign labor, view the world as one big market, and embrace the bottom line is Phil Knight's Nike Corp. Primarily a producer of sport shoes, Nike was able to find the right advertising icon in Michael Jordan and was aided by such developments as a profit-oriented NCAA and the proliferation of television technology. Nike, a company which was already well-seasoned through its professional sponsorship experiences, showed no restraint when it came to promoting its products through collegiate avenues. However, the path from the free-throw line to the basket should be "better marked," not "marketed," especially for college basketball.[34]

College basketball is one of the longest standing areas in academia that was and is exposed to commercialization. This commercialization can range from exclusive school contracts to trademark licensing. Which college or university does not want to place their logo on athleisure wear or become a Nike-School when it can expect hundreds of thousands of dollars in return for entering such a deal?[35] Yet, the disturbing element in striking such a dangerous bargain is that, as Sheila Slaughter argues: "Corporations such as Nike and Adidas are aiming not simply to sponsor the university but to be the university."[36] This aggressive strategy is also reflected in the way how Bill Friday, the former president of the University of North Carolina, so insightfully observed the corporate doings: "Nike influences the coach's salary. They influence who wears what, and they prescribe what logo is worn."[37]

One topic that surfaces and resurfaces when the literature mentions collegiate athletics is contracts. Contracts are regarded as an integral part in this competition for money, power, and prestige. These contracts govern how university logos are used, what kinds of fees are paid to the universities, and what commercial exposure institutions and their sponsors will have. In essence, these written agreements, literally, tell athletes what to wear, whom to represent, and where to play. The "college nation" seemed to have become a "college corporation" in which learning assumes second place to profit seeking. This notion is supported by a study that was conducted by Putler, *et al.* in 1999 and published in the *Sociology of Sport Journal*. The research indicates that "ethics and winning, and education and revenue, tend to be competing athletic program priorities."[38]

The existing literature also points out the degradation of academic standards for the sake of college sport success and even acknowledges this problem. However, no sincere efforts are undertaken to really change this dilemma, rather resorting to lip service and precautionary measures such as: half-hearted academic quality standards for college athletes; academic policies against commercialization for which the administration has the ability but lacks the willingness to enforce; and university controlled trademarking and licensing.

The need for organizational growth is another pertinent issue associated with college sports, a need that supports an ever-growing administrative apparatus and quest for prestige. This growth is most apparent in joint ventures struck between major corporations such as Nike, Toyota, and AT & T and megaversities such as the University of California Los Angeles, the University of Michigan Ann Arbor, and Duke University.

Sponsorship, licensing, and syndication are the major revenue generators in today's professional and college sports. Making the big bucks by selling tickets is a relic of the past. A sponsorship commitment such as a college coach receiving "$200,000 per year to outfit his team in specific shoes" is not that uncommon.[39] Another example of the lavish display of academic commercialism is the annual salary Kevin Stallings receives as the basketball coach of Vanderbilt University. This coach gets $981,046 per year, thus by far, outstripping high-paid university officials and Nobel Prize winning faculty members.[40]

College athletes turn, more and more, into walking billboards and the infrastructures supporting the sports make these men and women to humble servants of corporate America. Building naming rights, commercial displays in sports facilities, and athletes to be used for commercial promotions, bear witness to this disturbing development. In addition, through these engagements universities relinquish some, if not all, control over their sports to outside businesses and open the door for student and alumni exposure to commercialism. *The Lombardi Program on Measuring University Performance* at the University of Florida reports: "To manage [the increased pursuit] of universities for high-visibility of intercollegiate sports, almost all colleges and universities transferred substantial portions of their institutional control into the hands of outside organizations."[41] *The Lombardi Program* goes on to say that "sports are about winning above all" and that "universities would do almost anything imaginable to gain an advantage in the competition because it is by winning that sports deliver value to their university investors."[42]

Since corporations discovered that college sports reach a staggering number of people beyond the college community, college sports have morphed from collegiate events into the commercial events. Where does this leave the Olympic spirit of *citius-altius-fortius* (faster-higher-stronger) that should prevail, especially in university settings, which ask for amateurism and not professionalism? At present, college sport seems to be the most vulnerable academic area that can be subjected to profitability thinking.

THE COSTS AND BENEFITS OF COMMERCIALIZATION

Let us assume, for a moment, that a big company selling personal computers would approach a large university in the West with an offer to change its long-standing motto from "Eternal Light and Wisdom" to a commercial slogan such as "The Portal to Your Future" on a permanent basis. In return, the computer company would place $1 billion into the university's endowment, increasing the endowment's principle value by approximately 25 percent. This would provide the Western school with a lead in many academic and student service areas and would allow the university to substantially increase its annual scholarships. Furthermore, fundraising efforts would be advanced for at least a decade. Yet, this "Faustian bargain" would require the institution to give up what it stands for and conveys with its time-tested university motto.[43]

Up to this point, institutions of higher education have been reluctant to go that far and sell their "very souls."[44] But, who knows what developments will take place in a couple of years. Maybe institutions will be forced to sacrifice their own souls in order to guarantee their financial survival in a system where the concern for competition has overtaken the concern for education.

Returning to the hypothetical proposal brought before the Board of Regents of the University in the West by the computer company: the University is faced with weighing the costs and benefits of this offer to render a decision. When extending this seemingly irresistible offer this scenario assumes to all institutions of higher education, in his book *Universities in the Market Place: The Commercialization of Higher Education,* Derek Bok suggests that the following cost and benefit items should be carefully examined:[45]

Costs
• Undermining the academic status
• Damaging the academic community
• Risking an institution's reputation

Benefits
• Monetary profits
• Incentives to produce better results

One should not lose sight of the fact that a cost-benefit analysis is not a clear-cut procedure that provides clean and precise solutions; especially not as far as commercialization decisions are concerned. Rather, this analysis is to be employed as a tool that emphasizes red flags and furnishes its users with a suggestion of which direction to take.

Even though institutions of higher education have to be watchful when engaging in commercial ventures, commercialization is not all bad. As has been stressed in the introduction of this text, it would be foolish to deny colleges and universities the benefits they can derive from these commercial endeavors. When talking a closer look at the advantages that can be derived from such enterprises, at least four of these benefits are especially conducive to modern institutions of higher education: profits, inducements, human resources, and equipment.

The most obvious among those is profit, or the bottom line, as it is referred to in the financial world. It goes without saying that "money attracts more money." Money has many friends, and if money is at one place its friends will follow it there. Money is either generated through tuition income, donations, or through the sale of educational products such as course materials, patents, or online education. In recent history, especially online education has proven to be a goldmine for institutions of higher education. If properly managed or even, as in the case of Columbia University and The University of Chicago, sold to an outside business, great benefits can be reaped. Columbia and Chicago sold their online education to an outside provider for sizable amounts of money while retaining licensing and other fees of their course products.[46] Now their educational services can be enjoyed all over the world via distance education by students on various continents.

Another benefit can be found in the nature of inducements. In this case contributions can function as incentives to mature research discoveries into useful products for ordinary consumers, extend the enthusiasm for college sports from big schools to small schools, and last but not least, initiate the creation of new knowledge. Without a doubt, medical advancements such as penicillin, psychoanalysis, or the prevention of cholera or discoveries in physics such as gravity, weather forecasting, or the rings of Saturn could not have been possible without the support of universities. Nowadays, many small schools enjoy a spillover effect from big institutions as far as the excitement for college sports is concerned. Who has not heard a story such as the success of Villanova University in basketball—Villanova is a small university in suburban Pennsylvania? It is the entertainment and the fact that a small-town boy (small-college team) succeeds in the big city (NCAA Division I) that rallies the crowds and puts this school on the map. Another area that can be stimulated with incentives is knowledge generation, which benefits the students and the general public, at large.

Very often, people forget that a university is not only made up of buildings and grounds but also the people that are part of this scholastic enterprise. Human resources allow the place to exist and give it its distinct flavor. The more financial means a school has to support its human resources, the better students and faculty it will attract. The fact is that the best students and faculty and capable administrators can be found at institutions of higher education that have the means to support them and their work.

Another benefit would be that increased financial resources enable institutions of higher education to purchase more sophisticated equipment. This can be in the form of new and better computers in the learning laboratories or faster Internet connections. This added benefit can also be materialized in a way that provides better equipment for medical and engineering schools or new space (buildings) for already overcrowded classrooms and lecture halls. More money for equipment can also translate into improvements of the personal spaces of students and faculty, such as dormitories, offices, or lounges.

So, despite all the dangers that lurk in business ventures for colleges and universities, there are still plenty of good things to be said about considering the commercial in higher education.

It is always easy to criticize the status quo without suggesting actions to improve or solve the existing problem. It has to be mentioned though that attempts to improve the current situation have been undertaken before (e.g., initiatives of the AAUP against conflicts of interest). However, these attempts seemed to have been stifled when the Bayh-Doyle Act was passed in Congress in 1980. This Act affords universities, and thus, indirectly corporations, to "control their [own] new patents and innovations created through university-based research."[47] This Act was supported by the Carter Administration to provide American businesses with the necessary advantage to compete successfully on a global basis and sub-sidize expensive corporate research.

Richard Daniles, et al. provide some useful suggestions in their paper "Re-sisting Corporatization of the University," which was published in the book *Campus, Inc.: Corporate Power in the Ivory Tower*. Daniles emphasizes the following points to combat corporatization:[48]

- Increase the presence of organized labor on campus.
- Organize with students, other faculty, and staff.
- Resist the corporatization discourse [e.g., university administrations].
- Teach [e.g., make students aware of the situation]
- Speak out against corporatization.
- Write articles and letters [in high-powered publications].
- Read and become informed in order to act.

Although the suggestions I list above sound promising and even sus-tainable, I'm aware of the fact that I cannot build an academic Camelot. This undertaking would be a utopian adventure or scholastic dream rather than an achievable goal. However, it would be nice if we could move to-ward an academia that preserves scholastic integrity and independence and abstains from letting the commercial world rule the university and college environment.

NOTES

1. Derek Bok, *Universities in the Market Place: The Commercialization of Higher Education* (Princeton, N.J.: Princeton University Press, 2003), 200.

2. Harvard University, "Harvard Virtual Tour—Movie The Yard," Harvard Uni-versity: Harvard Virtual Tour, streaming video, <*www.post.harvard.edu/ath/video/ yard.ram*> (26 February 2002).

3. Bok, *Universities in the Market Place,* 200.

4. Harvard University, *Harvard Virtual Tour.*

5. Harvard University, *Harvard Virtual Tour.*

6. William Boyd and Edmund J. King, *The History of Western Education 11th Ed.* (London: Adam & Charles Black Ltd., 1975), 130–31.

7. T. L. Jarman, *Landmarks in the History of Education* (London: John Murray, 1970), 101.

8. Boyd and King, *The History of Western Education,* 141.

9. Boyd and King, *The History of Western Education,* 333–36.

10. Sheila Slaughter and Gary Rhoades, *Academic Capitalism and the New Economy* (Baltimore, MD: The Johns Hopkins University Press, 2004), 36.

11. Theodore L. Turocy and Bernhard von Stengel, "Game Theory," *CDAM Research Report LSE-CDAM-2001-09,* 8 October 2001, 3. (This was a draft of an introductory survey of game theory, prepared for the *Encyclopedia of Information Systems,* Academic Press).

12. University of California Los Angeles, "Spotlight: David Geffen Gift to School of Medicine," <*www.ucla.edu/spotlight/archive/html_2001_2002/spec0502_geffen.html*> (12 December 2004).

13. Dale Buss, "Big Brand on Campus," *Brandspeak. Brandchannel,* 27 January 2003, <*www.brandspeak.com*> (3 March 2005).

14. Rick Westhead, "Publisher Pushes Textbook Ads: McGraw-Hill Target Students; Critics Warn Plan Could Backfire," *Toronto Star,* 7 June 2005, D01.

15. Kevin Kniffin, "The Goods at the Worst: Campus Procurement in the Global Pillage," in *Campus, Inc.: Corporate Power in the Ivory Tower,* ed. Geoffry D. White (Amherst, MA: Prometheus Books, 2000), 39.

16. Kniffin, "The Goods at the Worst," 41.

17. Nancy Trejos, "Bonding with Beepers," *Los Angeles Times,* 9 June 1999, Metro Part B, 2.

18. Trejos, "Bonding with Beepers," 2.

19. "Dishonoring the Dead," *Los Angeles Times,* 12 March 2004, Metro Part B, Editorial Pages Desk.

20. University of Michigan, "New York City Real Estate Developer Stephen M. Ross Gives $100 Million to University of Michigan Business School," <*www.business.umich.edu/RossB-SchoolGift/story_1.html*> (3 March 2005).

21. University of Michigan, "New York City Real Estate," 2005.

22. University of Michigan, "New York City Real Estate," 2005.

23. Jennifer Washburn, "The Best Minds Money Can Buy," *Los Angeles Times,* 21 July 2006, California Metro, Part B, B13.

24. Sherly G. Stolberg, "Gifts to Science Researchers Have Strings, Study Finds." *New York Times,* 1 April 1998, A17.

25. Stolberg, "Gifts to Science Researchers," A17.

26. Stolberg, "Gifts to Science Researchers," A17.

27. Stolberg, "Gifts to Science Researchers," A17.

28. Keith Dunnavant, *The Fifty-Year Seduction,* (New York: St. Martin's Press, 2004).

29. Bok, *Universities in the Market Place,* 200.

30. Murray Sperber, *College Sports, Inc.: The Athletic Department vs. The University,* (New York: Henry Holt, 1990), 51.

31. Keith Dunnavant, *The Fifty-Year Seduction,* (New York: St. Martin's Press, 2004), 189.

32. Dunnavant, *The Fifty-Year Seduction*, 189.

33. LaFeber, *Michael Jordan and the New Global Capitalism* (New York: W. W. Norton & Company), 64.

34. Slaughter, *Academic Capitalism,* 286.

35. Slaughter, *Academic Capitalism,* 258.

36. Slaughter, *Academic Capitalism,* 258.

37. LaFeber, *Michael Jordan and the New Global Capitalism*, 147.

38. D. S. Putler and R. A. Wolfe, "Perceptions of Intercollegiate Athletic Program," *Sociology of Sport Journal* 16, no. 4 (1999): 301.

39. LaFeber, *Michael Jordan and the New Global Capitalism*, 128.

40. College Athletic Clips, "Hanging On To Their Own," <*www.collegeathleticalips .com/archives/000419.html*> (23 January 2005).

41. The Lombardi Program on Measuring University Performance, "The Sports Imperative in America's Research Universities," *Annual Report: The Top American Research Universities* (November 2003), 8.

42. The Lombardi Program, "The Sports Imperative," 11.

43. Bok, *Universities in the Market Place,* 200.

44. Bok, *Universities in the Market Place,* 200.

45. Bok, *Universities in the Market Place,* 80–118.

46. Bok, *Universities in the Market Place,* 80.

47. Leonard Minsky, "Dead Souls: The Aftermath of Bayh-Dole," in *Campus, Inc.: Corporate Power in the Ivory Tower,* ed. Geoffry D. White (Amherst, MA: Prometheus Books, 2000), 95.

48. Richard Daniles, "Resisting Corporatization of the University," in *Campus, Inc.: Corporate Power in the Ivory Tower,* ed. Geoffry D. White (Amherst, MA: Prometheus Books, 2000), 72–7.

BIBLIOGRAPHY

Bok, Derek. *Universities in the Market Place: The Commercialization of Higher Education*. Princeton, N.J.: Princeton University Press, 2003.

Boyd, William and Edmund J. King. *The History of Western Education 11th Ed.* London: Adam & Charles Black Ltd., 1975.

Buss, Dale. "Big Brand on Campus." *Brandspeak. Brandchannel.* 27 January 2003. <*www.brandspeak.com*> (3 March 2005).

College Athletic Clips. "Hanging On To Their Own." <*www.collegeathleticalips.com/ archives/000419.html*> (23 January 2005).

Daniles, Richard. "Resisting Corporatization of the University." Pp.72–77 in *Campus, Inc.: Corporate Power in the Ivory Tower,* edited by Geoffry D. White. Amherst, N.Y.: Prometheus Books, 2000.

"Dishonoring the Dead." *Los Angeles Times*, 12 March 2004.

Dunnavant, Keith. *The Fifty-Year Seduction*. New York: St. Martin's Press, 2004.

Harvard University. "Harvard Virtual Tour—Movie The Yard." Harvard University: Harvard Virtual Tour. Streaming Video. <*www.post.harvard.edu/ath/video/yard.ram*> (26 February 2002).

Jarman, T. L. *Landmarks in the History of Education.* London: John Murray, 1970.

Kniffin, Kevin. "The Goods at the Worst: Campus Procurement in the Global Pillage." P. 39 in *Campus, Inc.: Corporate Power in the Ivory Tower,* edited Geoffry D. White. Amherst, MA: Prometheus Books, 2000.

LaFeber, Walter. *Michael Jordan and the New Global Capitalism*, New York: W. W. Norton & Company, 2002.

The Lombardi Program on Measuring University Performance. "The Sports Imperative in America's Research Universities." *Annual Report: The Top American Research Universities*, November 2003.

Minsky, Leonard. "Dead Souls: The Aftermath of Bayh-Dole." P. 95 in *Campus, Inc.: Corporate Power in the Ivory Tower,* edited by Geoffry D. White. Amherst: Prometheus Books, 2000.

Putler, D.S. and R.A. Wolfe. "Perceptions of Intercollegiate Athletic Programs." *Sociology of Sport Journal* 16, no. 4 (1999): 301–25.

Slaughter, Sheila and Gary Rhoades. *Academic Capitalism and the New Economy,* Baltimore, MD: The Johns Hopkins University Press, 2004.

Sperber, Murray. *College Sports, Inc.: The Athletic Department vs. The University.* New York: Henry Holt, 1990.

Stolberg, Sherly G. "Gifts to Science Researchers Have Strings, Study Finds." *New York Times*, 1 April 1998, A17.

Trejos, Nancy. "Bonding with Beepers." *Los Angeles Times*, 9 June 1999.

Turocy, Theodore L. and Bernhard von Stengel. "Game Theory." *CDAM Research Report LSE-CDAM-2001-09*, 8 October 2001, 3.

University of California Los Angeles. "Spotlight: David Geffen Gift to School of Medicine." <*www.ucla.edu/spotlight/archive/html_2001_2002/spec0502_geffen.html*> (3 March 2005).

University of Michigan. "New York City Real Estate Developer Stephen M. Ross Gives $100 Million to University of Michigan Business School." <*www.business .umich.edu/RossB-SchoolGift/story_1.html*> (3 March 2005).

Washburn, Jennifer. "The Best Minds Money Can Buy." *Los Angeles Times*, 21 July 2006.

Westhead, Rick. "Publisher Pushes Textbook Ads: McGraw-Hill Target Students; Critics Warn Plan Could Backfire." *Toronto Star,* 7 June 2005, D01.

Chapter Three

The Impact of Commercialism on the Classroom

Catherine O'Neill

"The strength of the United States is not the gold at Fort Knox or the weapons of mass destruction that we have, but the sum total of the education and the character of our people."[1]

Senator Claiborne Pell

In a 1998 report entitled *Reinventing Undergraduate Education: A Blueprint for America's Research Universities,* the Boyer Commission on Educating Undergraduates in the Research University mapped several recommendations for improving the quality of the undergraduate experience, pointing out that too often our research universities have failed to deliver their promises to students. Universities send out slick advertising brochures and pay for aggressive recruiting; however, once the hopeful freshmen enter the halls of academe, they discover impossibly large sections of foundational courses and have little opportunity to interact meaningfully with the star scholars mentioned in the recruiting materials:

> Again and again, universities are guilty of an advertising practice they would condemn in the commercial world. Recruitment materials display proudly the world-famous professors, the splendid facilities and the ground-breaking research that goes on within them, but thousands of students graduate without ever seeing the world-famous professors. . . . Some of their instructors are likely to be badly trained or even untrained teaching assistants who are groping their way toward a teaching technique; some others may be tenured drones who deliver set lectures from yellowed notes, making no effort to engage the bored minds of the students in front of them.[2]

Ernest Boyer dedicated his career to finding practical ways to improve the quality of American education; he wrote two groundbreaking books on higher education, *College: The Undergraduate Experience*, published in 1986, and *Scholarship Reconsidered*, published in 1991. After serving as Commissioner of Education during the Carter administration, Boyer worked for the Carnegie Foundation for the Advancement of Teaching. He was named Educator of the Year in 1990 by *U.S. News and World Report* and held 123 honorary degrees. Unlike those who call for more testing and accountability, Boyer understood that "to increase test scores or to be world class in math and science without empowering students or affirming the dignity of human life is to lose the essence of what we and education are presumably all about. . . ."[3] During his years as Commissioner of Education, he succeeded in getting a 40 percent increase in funding for education over a three-year period.[4] He was highly committed to offering a quality education to previously disenfranchised groups of Americans. We hear fewer and fewer voices like Boyer's in educational leadership today. He had both vision and practical sense when it came to approaching serious problems within the American educational system; consequently, the Boyer Commission was named in his honor.

David F. Noble, author of *Digital Diploma Mills* and another highly respected mind in higher education today, echoes some of Boyer's sentiments as he explains the crucial distinction between education and training:

> In essence, training involves the honing of a person's mind so that his or her mind can be used for the purpose of someone other than that person. Training thus typically entails a radical divorce between knowledge and the self. . . . Education is the exact opposite of training in that it entails not the disassociation but the utter integration of knowledge and the self, in a word, self-knowledge.[5]

REINVENTING UNDERGRADUATE
EDUCATION: A BLUEPRINT

The Boyer Commission's report charges universities with the responsibility of providing undergraduates with inquiry-based learning opportunities, opportunities to participate in the intellectual pursuits of the finest minds on campus. The report asserts that "learning is based on discovery guided by mentoring rather than on the transmission of information" and that "the traditional lecturing and note-taking certified by periodic examinations, was created for a time when books were scarce and costly."[6] In addition, the point is firmly made that meaningful interaction with students should be a classroom norm, not an exception. The Boyer Commission expressed some concern that technology might distance students from this sort of interaction, asserting that "technology cannot be a substitute for direct interactions between human minds."[7] While technology offers us additional possibilities for intellectual exchanges, students enrolled in online classes may find themselves churning in mazes of automated quizzes and directives, unable to get a prompt response from the actual human being who is "teaching" the class.

The Boyer Commission's report calls for a return to an emphasis on a broad liberal arts education, as opposed to the current preoccupation with preparation for competition in a global market and/or quickly achieving surface measures of success. The commission's report minces no words in faulting the nation's research universities for failing to deal with a "crisis, an issue of such magnitude and volatility that universities must galvanize themselves to respond."[8]

There seems to be consensus that universities have been too complacent and too unwilling to adapt in order to address the needs of their undergraduates: "the record has been one of inadequacy, even failure."[9] Parents and students are spending more and more for tuition, fees, and books, yet they seem to be receiving diminishing returns on this investment. At the turn of the millennium, *Reinventing Undergraduate Education* sounded a loud cry for focus on inquiry-based learning; it made a solid plea against market forces which bring money to schools, but directly compete with students for the time and attention of the most capable professors:

> In a context of increasing stress—declining governmental support, increased costs, mounting outside criticism and growing consumerism from students and their families—universities too often continue to behave with complacency, indifference, or forgetfulness. . . .[10]

These are strong words coming from a highly respected body; although many institutions have responded by creating programs or initiatives that reward excellence in teaching and allow undergraduate students opportunities for rich, inquiry-based learning, there is no question after careful review that the majority of the nation's institutions continue to reel from the unanticipated impact of rapidly changing technological advances, for-profit competition, and dwindling budgets. University administrators have adopted a clear trend of following the dollar without sufficient consideration as to the impact on the quality of student learning. For-profit online universities, the ease with which students may use the Internet in a variety of ways to cheat effortlessly, the TQM movement, and the nation's fascination with popular culture and the prevalent postmodern ethos make it exceedingly difficult for the voices of reason to be heard, let alone respected. The trends are clear, and students might well view their stance as that of consumers who have been "had." Unfortunately, many have accumulated tens of thousands of dollars of debt obtaining a baccalaureate degree without actually acquiring anything of true and lasting value.

According to Mel Scarlett, in his 2004 book *The Great American Rip-Off*, the cost of a college degree has risen quickly; at the same time, today's students graduate with significantly less knowledge and ability than they used to gain in their four years at our nation's colleges and universities. Between 1981 and 1995, tuition went up approximately three times as fast as the median household income (234 percent as opposed to 82 percent).[11] While students are being charged significantly more for their education, they seem much less interested in authentic learning. According to Scarlett, "A number of studies have found that more than two-thirds of college students are guilty of engaging in some form of academic dishonesty, and it is increasing. . . ."[12] A 2004 exchange of emails on the WPA listserve (used by freshman writing program administrators around the nation) explored student motivation for widespread plagiarism; some correspondents seemed convinced that deeply rooted capitalistic beliefs allowed students to buy and sell academic work with no moral conflict whatsoever. After all, anything can be bought and sold in the current climate—why not student work? What is purchased is "owned," and the rights to intellectual and creative work are up for grabs everywhere. It is possible to go onto a publisher's textbook web site to find offers to pay for academic work. An exploration of a university website quickly leads to pop-up invitations to purchase A-grade essays or papers. In such a climate, it is difficult to teach students the intrinsic and long lasting value of a quality general education. The pressure for a high Grade Point Average (GPA), the commodity students exchange for scholarships and promising career opportunities, becomes overwhelming, overriding all other considerations. While many work diligently to offset the damage, these voices seem comparable to the little Dutch boy with his finger in the hole in the dike—they are bound to be too little, probably way too late. The tsunami of consumerism has already taken its toll on the minds and morals of American youth, and there doesn't seem to be an available antidote in large enough supply to remedy such a pervasive and multi-faceted combination of ills.

Professors sometimes view teaching as the necessary evil that supports their research and publication; if the professoriate can be guilty of such moral apathy, should students be held to a higher standard? When universities relate to students as consumers, purchasers of a product, and when more and more of their interactions with students are viewed from this vantage point, it seems logical that the next step would be for students to view their work as a commodity in like kind, one to be manufactured cheaply and sold at the highest price possible. *The Great American Rip-Off* directly addresses the challenges universities face from large numbers of students who are not in class, but instead are engaged in binge drinking, drug abuse, and casual sex.[13] In the equations where educational effectiveness is measured, these factors are seldom taken into account. Perhaps this is because in a customer service environment, the customer is *never* wrong.

THE TROUBLE WITH TQM

The Total Quality Management (TQM) movement has had much to do with a shift in the way legislatures and campus administrators process improvements, and while TQM may be beneficial when it comes to campus services, it has proven to be harmful when its tenets are applied to teaching and the classroom. In a 1996 report entitled *Organizational Paradigm Shifts*, the National Association of College and University Business Officers examine the move toward TQM as an answer to the question of accountability. As an answer toward making universities more economically efficient, the business concept of quality process management has been adopted by many universities. The root of solving problems, according to this model, lies in correctly identifying and then satisfying customer needs: "The trick to being customer driven is to first recognize the customers, then identify their needs, and subsequently, meet or exceed their expectations."[14] TQM is meant to efficiently manage workloads; where workloads are too small, they are made larger. Where workloads are too large, they are left alone or expanded to be yet larger, in a kind of Wal-Mart model of maximizing use of funds while minimizing associated costs. For example, in response to TQM cost efficiency analysis, Kent State had to consolidate programs and eliminate entire programs. Ph.D. options in the School of Business underwent dramatic reductions, and three undergraduate majors were cut. The School of Theater and the School of Dance were merged, probably to cut administrative and clerical positions.[15] All this sounds responsible and prudent; however, someone had to assume the additional workload left by those who might have been downsized out of their jobs. The justification for cutting such programs and positions has nothing to do with the campus's ability to offer quality academics to its students. According to *Organizational Paradigm Shifts,* such changes are driven by "A new, almost hyper-consumer attitude among students" and "technology-based competition."[16] According to TQM principles, the relative value of a program such as, let's say, philosophy, might be easily questioned. Its value would, of course, be impossible to measure. Philosophers aren't known for their money-making abilities; companies don't hire philosophers as consultants (although maybe some should.) Nevertheless, the loss of a philosophy program could have far-reaching implications on the life of the immediate community. Who wants to live and work in a world without Plato? Without the tools for careful reflection on the whys of our culture, we may be

driven on the rocks by the hows, as we listen in the summer of 2006 to news-
casts that simultaneously announce the dangers of global warming and a new
law that will allow drilling for fossil fuels in the central Gulf of Mexico. But
who has time to think about those things, with eight thousand Israeli soldiers
rushing into Lebanon to expand their attack on Hezbollah? A Lebanese diplo-
mat reminds radio listeners of two important distinctions in military reprisal
and war: the principle of distinction and the principle of proportionality.
Should average American citizens be able to understand what he means? How
will our country foster expertise in such areas if our nation's campuses rou-
tinely cut small programs with few graduates simply because they don't produce as much immediate financial gain as larger, more popular programs? As
the saying goes, "Money isn't everything."

The report of the National Association of College and University Business
Officers reiterates Scarlett's concern that "While students are asking for more
from higher education, they are arriving on campus with less to offer." These
same students are "more aware of their role as customers."[17] The palpable
changes in student preparation and attitude make it increasingly difficult to
hold students to high academic standards, even though this would be in the
obvious better interest of all of the stakeholders, or "customers"—parents,
taxpayers, legislators, and even the nation and the world. Students want to
zoom through their chosen courses of study without impediment. After that,
many expect lucrative employment, in spite of an appalling lack of motivation and an inability to demonstrate proficiency in core areas. This report goes
on to make the following observations:

> While one-on-one learning still occurs today in skilled professions such as med-
> icine and in advanced education programs such as the Ph.D. dissertation, it is
> simply too labor intensive for the mass educational needs of modern society.
> The classroom itself may soon be replaced by more appropriate and efficient
> learning experiences. Indeed, such a paradigm shift may be forced upon the fac-
> ulty by the students themselves. Today's students are members of the "digital"
> generation. . . . They approach learning as a "plug and play" experience, unac-
> customed and unwilling to learn sequentially—to read the manual—and rather
> inclined to plunge in through participation and experimentation.[18]

These observations, however accurate they may be, seem to point away
from the Boyer Commission's recommendations for a program of inquiry-
based learning. Should students, as unquestioned consumers, be determining the pedagogy of their instructors? To assume so is to fundamentally
change the nature of the student/professor relationship. Participation and
experimentation sound good, and we'd all agree that the more students are
actually doing as opposed to being passive recipients, the more they'll

learn. Many contemporary academics prefer the role of "guide on the side" as opposed to the "sage on the stage"—even so, it seems wrongheaded to assume that students would be the ones to know how the courses they take should be delivered.

Matthew Delmonico, formerly of St. Petersburg Junior College, cautions against overuse of the TQM approach to management in higher education, pointing out that "higher education is a unique creation and its principles do not often apply to other business enterprises." He warns that "a college's integrity and the quality of its programs may be jeopardized by a complete alteration in philosophy towards a completely market-driven educational system."[19] He worries that the preoccupation with student satisfaction could lead to grade inflation, and that trendier, more popular programs might cause other important programs of study to be phased out. While the Boyer Commission has called for inquiry-based learning and more student engagement, it seems obvious that many students don't know exactly what it is they should be getting in college. Who would the TQM analysts listen to, the students (customers) or the Boyer Commission (experts)? According to Delmonico, some campuses have experimented with instructional guarantees in the hopes of attracting consumer-savvy students.[20] It seems foolish, though, to allow students to have the last word on the quality of instruction, since students do not know enough about a particular course of study to know what should be taught or how it should be taught. Allowing students to make these choices would be unwise. Ignorance is bliss, for a while, but eventually lack of knowledge is bound to have ill effects.

John Aliff, Professor of Biology at Georgia Perimeter College, echoes Delmonico's concerns, worrying that TQM will result in the death of the Socratic method and a watered down curriculum designed by faculty who are primarily concerned with pleasing customers. Eventually, TQM could cause a devaluing of areas without obvious commercial value and the "death of a liberal arts education" as we know it.[21]

It is sobering indeed to see so many experts with such dire predictions. It seems the capital, "the sum total of the education and the character of our people" celebrated by Claiborne Pell, could become a mighty paltry sum indeed, if market forces continue to erode our institutions of higher education. One University of Virginia professor comments on the negative effects of the consumer culture on the campus over the last decade:

> A happy consumer is, by definition, one with multiple options, one who can always have what he wants. . . .The Socratic method—the animated, sometimes impolite give-and-take between student and teacher—seems too jagged for current sensibilities. . . .Students now do not wish to be criticized, not in any form. . . . In the current university the movement for urbane tolerance has devolved

into an imperative against critical reaction, turning much of the intellectual life into a dreary Sargasso Sea.[22]

It seems that the TQM paradigm has led to grade inflation and attacks on tenure, the result of a capitalistic society that views everything as a commodity, even the interactions between students and their professors. Many freshmen are apathetic about their coursework; consequently, the initially inviting "plug and play" distance learning and online course options don't provide these students with the inspiration and interaction necessary for deep learning. The "bean counters" don't seem preoccupied with the issue of quality — just the head count after the first few days of class.[23]

Even though research has proven student evaluations to be unreliable measures of teaching ability, campuses all over the nation continue to rely upon them, thus cheaply fulfilling the imperative "to measure." Data can be printed out in impressive spreadsheets that appear to be objective, scientific. Thus, "instructors are pandering to student customers by inflating grades and increasing the 'entertainment value' of courses."[24] Instead of improving the quality of teaching and learning, many educators worry that student evaluations cause instructors, who are often confounded by their own inability to predict results on the basis of their own impressions of how things went in a particular course, to dumb down their courses. Researchers have identified several factors that can cause bias in student evaluations of teaching, including textbook costs, course policies, grade inflation, learning styles, prior subject interest, sex of instructor, and instructor reputation. Moreover, since instructors can make use of any number of successful teaching strategies, "there is no clear definition of the criterion of effective teaching upon which to develop rating instruments."[25] In one study, a professional actor "performed" convincingly in front of a group of graduate students, who should have been fairly accurate in instructor rating, since they had been in the education system longer than their freshman counterparts. Unfortunately, these students rated the actor surprising well, despite the fact that his lecture was deliberately "devoid of content." Consequently, researchers strongly suspect that "students react more to faculty acting skills than any other factor in their ratings."[26] Even so, administrators and committees often consider student evaluations as significant when making important faculty retention, promotion, and tenure decisions. Apparently, they are more concerned with convenience than with quality or accuracy. All too often, campus decision-making bodies ignore the implications of such research, even when faculty supply them with enough information to know that student evaluations are not trustworthy measures of the quality of instruction.

Some fear that, while TQM has the potential to solve some problems, legislators and administrators are using it to keep faculty in line. Others blame TQM for the reduction in tenure-track faculty, and the subsequent rise in the use of part-timers, who are easier to disenfranchise, exploit, and control, making them more attractive employees under the TQM management model. In 1998, Robert B. Kaplan, Professor Emeritus from the University of Southern California, wrote a letter to the faculty senate concerning their responsibilities with respect to issues of campus governance. In this letter, Kaplan complains that administrators, though they go through the pretense of involving faculty in decision making, repeatedly deny them the facts necessary for good decision making. A former associate dean, he describes the end result of the invasion of corporate culture on American campuses. According to Kaplan, deans and presidents are so preoccupied with raising money that neither has the time to provide the intellectual leadership necessary for solving problems and carrying out responsibilities to students. He exposes serious flaws in the logic of TQM, quoting USC's President Sample as having said, "We must do more, better, with less." Kaplan counters, "Surely he knows that this is a logical absurdity, and surely everyone who has heard it knows that, too. Yet the faculty nodded politely and went along." Kaplan accuses faculty of caving in to capitalistic "narrow self-interest," and points out that he "cajoled, beat and even dragged faculty kicking and screaming, into some involvement in the larger institution." He sees now that this was futile, "because their involvement was resentful and resistant, and as soon as I stopped applying pressure they happily fled back to their respective ivory cubicles."[27] The point Kaplan so convincingly makes underscores much of what has already been said by others with respect to TQM—its negative impact on universities is inevitable, and its oversimplification with respect to rules of supply and demand and merit and reward have fundamentally caused academics to reconstruct their identities within their departments, viewing the sole end of their work as capital, and devaluing work that won't instantaneously produce a reward that can be readily exchanged. Kaplan further expresses frustration in his certainty that professors, being exceptionally bright and resourceful, may well hold the keys to solving institutional ills, if only they were allowed and if only they would once again view themselves as responsible for a deeper mandate.

Thus, it appears that the application of TQM concepts, which are meant to produce the highest amount of customer satisfaction with the lowest investment possible, has harmed our nation's institutions of higher education. By positing students as consumers and devaluing work that doesn't produce instant and obvious capital, we have lost a good bit of the actual value of what our universities were once able to offer to students. The consequences are no doubt being played out in the workplace and the public domain as well. Many students seem to know that they are missing something important in their educational experiences—but one has to possess the riches named by Pell in order to recognize them fully. Without them, the blind will be leading the blind.

This may be why the American Association of University Professors entitled their 2005–06 report on the economic status of their profession as "The Devaluing of Higher Education." In recent years, pay increases for university faculty haven't kept up with increases for other professions requiring advanced degrees, including physicians, lawyers, engineers, and architects. The AAUP points out that the quality of higher education is dependent upon its ability "to attract the nation's brightest scholars." While an overall 6 percent rise in state appropriations for colleges and universities in 2005–06 should bring some help, the AAUP worries that the increase won't be used to raise faculty salaries because campuses have reasons other than fiscal hardship for refusing to adjust faculty pay rates. After all, the salaries of administrators and presidential compensation packages have been steadily increasing.[28]

The AAUP has published facts that reveal a disturbing trend toward an increased use in "contingent faculty," or faculty who are either part-time or are in full-time non-tenure track positions. As of November 2005, 46 percent of all faculty appointments were part-time.[29] These part-time faculty members are teaching mostly core courses, the foundational courses where the Boyer Commission's vision for inquiry-based learning is of particular importance. A recent AAUP fact sheet on contingent faculty asserts that "the excessive use of, and inadequate compensation and professional support for, contingent faculty exploits these colleagues." Further, the fact sheet explains that academic freedom is in general weakened by the overuse of nontenure track faculty, and concludes that "heavy reliance on contingent faculty hurts students," "overuse of contingent faculty hurts all faculty." Many part-time faculty are actually teaching overloads, shuffling from school to school in an attempt to make a decent living. They work hard, long hours, often without adequate office space or institutional support; even though some teach an overload for public institutions within the same university system, they are denied the health and retirement benefits most professionals have come to expect. *Reinventing Undergraduate Education* was published in 1998, yet in the years between 1998 and 2001 full-time, nontenure track positions increased by 35.5 percent. According to the AAUP, this is not because of a lack of money: "many institutions have invested heavily in facilities and technology while cutting instructional spending. Though incoming students may find finer facilities, they are also likely to find fewer full-time faculty with adequate time, professional support, and resources available for their instruction."[30]

The Boyer Commission's report didn't mention problems with poor facilities, nor did it suggest that a huge investment, in fact a poorly considered investment, in technology would result in deeper, more meaningful learning experiences for students. Why is it, then, that our nation's institutions of higher learning (one might reasonably assume their executives or chief academic officers have read the Boyer Commission's report) seem to have largely ignored the urgency of the report's findings? What can account for the fact that medical secretaries earned more per hour than part-time faculty at public two-year colleges in the year 2003? According to the AAUP, "Part-time faculty members with families to support would find their incomes closer to, or even below, the poverty level, which was $12,015 for a family of two in 2003."[31] Auto mechanics earn more than many contingent faculty, leaving these instructors "bitterly disappointed." The presidential call to "do more, better, with less" hasn't applied to everyone at the typical public institution of higher learning; rather, it seems almost exclusively focused on the unseating of tenure track faculty, who are increasingly replaced with part-time faculty faced with the prospect of teaching overloaded courses assigned at the last minute, courses where instructors are hired and handed a text the day class starts. It seems fairly obvious that providing a quality undergraduate education is not close to the top of the list when campus administrators and executives sit down to discuss the budget. According to the AAUP, campuses should strive to limit non-tenure track appointments to 15 percent of all campus instruction. Unfortunately, their advice has been ignored by the typical American university campus.[32] While the American Federation of Teachers deems the heavy use of "qualified but economically and professionally exploited part-time/adjunct faculty" a "deeply disturbing pattern in American higher education,"[33] well-remunerated CEOs and CAOs apparently find this pattern to be business as usual.

A recent article in the *Harvard Education Letter* blames the customer satisfaction model for a steady rise in grade inflation. Student preoccupation with GPAs has shifted their focus from learning to grades, making them liable to opt for the easiest classes in order to avoid anything but the easy A, which is easier and easier to get.[34] Contemporary students don't view their grades as reflections of their comparative performances in their classes, and some aren't interested in a challenge or in the inquiry-based learning that the Boyer Commission report called for. Instead, they view their grades as commodities. The majority of students at Duke have A averages, and some elite colleges don't give Ds and Fs at all. Parents and alumni exert pressure on these institutions to give students high grades; parents want to be sure their big investments pay off, and alumni want to be sure their alma maters' reputations remain untarnished. A dip in GPAs suggests a dip in the quality of the student.[35]

While some researchers postulate that faculty development programs and "mastery approaches" to learning have resulted in more student success,[36] it seems unlikely that these factors account for the higher number of As and Bs earned by contemporary high school and college students. Indiana University's 2004 High School Survey of Student Engagement of over 90,000 students from 103 schools proved that "students do little outside preparation for school, but still receive As and Bs." The survey director concluded, "There's no question, we have some grade inflation"; consequently, she worries that too many students are not prepared for college level work.[37] The rise in Ivy League GPAs indicates a shift in standard brought on by market pressures. This is problematic for students attending less prestigious schools; these students may actually be achieving more, yet they will be edged out in the competition for graduate school or career openings because their transcripts suggest they know and can do less than their Ivy League counterparts. This trend has devalued the baccalaureate degree, furthering the negative impact of market forces on the academy.

A 2002 article in *USA Today* echoes this concern with respect to a disturbing trend toward grade inflation: "Eight out of every ten Harvard students graduate with honors and nearly half receive A's in their courses." This article names student evaluations along with increasing numbers of adjuncts as significant causes of grade inflation. Both of these are directly linked to market factors; the distorted emphasis on student evaluations is a result of the TQM movement, and the increase in the number of adjuncts is the result of legislative and administrative trends toward paying as little as possible for instruction and toward a vulnerable, relatively powerless employee pool. The article raises a perfectly good question: How can it be that, when a third of all college students must take remedial courses, fewer than 20 percent of them receive grades below a B−? The American Academy of Arts and Sciences has tracked grades of Ivy League institutions over the years, and their data confirm the trend toward inflation at Princeton. In 1973, 31 percent of Princeton students got As; in 1997, the number had risen to 43 percent, and another 45 percent got Bs.[38] A cursory glance at Princeton's web site reveals any number of directives or bits of advice on things like seeing professors, avoiding plagiarism, and negotiating school and social realities; it would seem that Princeton's students face the same difficulties as students at any other college in the country, yet their GPAs don't reflect these similarities. True, Princeton has implemented a plan to reduce the number of As to 35 percent in undergraduate classes, and since 2004 the number of As has dropped; even so, the total number of As is still inflated, going from 46 percent in 2003–04 to 41 percent in 2004–2005. The dean of Princeton's undergraduate college checked to be sure lower GPAs wouldn't hurt graduates before enacting the plan,[39] solidly connecting the campus's stance on grade inflation with marketability of graduates.

COMMERCIALIZATION AND
CAMPUS CONFLICTS OF INTEREST

In 1980, the Bayh-Dole Act, or the University and Small Business Patent Procedures Act, was passed along with a couple of other bills that made it possible for universities to profit from patents generated from professional research. This legislation caused a profound shift in the priorities of academic researchers and administrators. Between 1991 and 2000, royalties for new patents went up "more than 520%," and the "business activity associated with the sales of products" in 1999 was more than $40 billion.[40] While the money has certainly proven useful, several disturbing cases of conflict of interest have been identified over the past few years, cases that point to changes in what questions are researched in university labs and classes, as well as what knowledge is made available in professional journals and, subsequently, in textbooks.

One of the most commonly cited examples is the 1998 agreement between the Department of Plant and Microbial Biology at the University of California, Berkeley, and the Novartis Corporation. Over five years, Novartis gave the department $25 million dollars for research, purchasing the right to a proportional share of the licensing rights for research-generated patents, even if the company hadn't funded the research that made the patents possible. In a 2004 report prepared by a subcommittee of the American Association of University Professors' Committee on Academic Freedom and Tenure, the AAUP expressed its concern:

> Where the financial resources of an academic department are dominated by a corporation there is the potential, no matter how elaborate the safeguards for respecting academic freedom and the independence of researchers, for weakening peer review both in research and in promotion and tenure decisions, for distorting the priorities of undergraduate and graduate education, and for compromising scientific openness.[41]

The National Science Foundation and the National Institute of Health have written policies against conflicts of interest that compel researchers to report income that could cause conflict of interest. The American Association for Gene Therapy and the American Association for Human Genetics don't want their members investing in the companies that pay for their research. The National Institute of Health now discourages its researchers from signing agreements that would seriously delay the publication of their research; the NIH felt compelled to do this, since crucial information was being suppressed by companies.[42] The AAUP report cites a study published in *Science and Engineering Ethics* that shows that of 789 journal articles explored, "in 34 percent of the articles one or more authors had a financial interest in the subject matter being studied." Moreover, they enumerate several incidents where conflicts of interests may have caused serious harm, including the death of a clinical trial subject, inappropriate ties between tobacco companies and university researchers, corporate control of endowed chair appointments, and the denial of legal assistance to a whistle-blowing researcher who violated a drug company's gag rule to protect her patients.[43] In spite of attempts of governing bodies to curb researcher conflict of interest, it seems that this trend isn't going to disappear anytime soon.

Leasing the Ivory Tower: The Corporate Takeover of Academia delivers a scathing assessment of the impact of corporate money on universities:

> The story about universities in the 1980's and 1990's is that they will turn a trick for anybody with money to invest; and the only ones with money are corporations, millionaires, and foundations. These investments in universities have dramatically changed the mission of higher education; they have led universities to attend to the interests of their well-heeled patrons, rather than those of students.[44]

According to *Leasing the Ivory Tower,* as of 1995, 30 percent of biomedical faculty at Massachusetts Institute of Technology (MIT) had corporate ties, and close to one in five biomedical researchers from Stanford and Harvard owned corporate stock or receive other money from companies; further, it has been estimated that over half of the National Academy of Science's medical researchers had potential conflict of interest with companies.[45] Worse yet, some universities have deliberately hidden unethical professorial behavior related to conflict of interest for fear of having to pay back the millions they were given by wealthy corporate sponsors. For example, the University of Pittsburgh did all it could to avoid public embarrassment and a reimbursement of $163,000 when Dr. Steven Breuning was convicted of scientific fraud.[46] Business schools on too many campuses are siphoning money away from faculty positions in the arts and humanities to sponsor the industry-related activities of business school professors. While such business professors don't teach very much, they pull in huge salaries, ultimately driving up the cost of tuition:

> . . . Students (and taxpayers at public universities) are subsidizing the consulting, expert testimony, and businesses that professors operate. These tuition in-

creases are used to pay the salaries of newly hired professors who teach the courses that other professors would have taught, if the latter had not abandoned the classroom for consulting.[47]

A 2004 article in *The Chronicle of Higher Education* explains the problems encountered when universities attempt to seduce top scholars in an attempt to likewise attract students. ". . . Stars can create problems. Stars beget jealousy, even if they are of humble mien." On one campus, a faculty member complained that the campus star "spent more time talking on other campuses than teaching on ours." Star scholars usually don't have time for meaningful interaction with students or the department's junior faculty. If the star turns out to be inept at teaching, the campus is going to be reticent to take corrective action—it would be "bad publicity" to openly admit that the expensive star is unable or unwilling to teach as well as his or her lesser-paid colleagues. One star brushed off his dean's concerns about student complaints, "There must be something wrong with your students. Of course, I don't have time to prep anymore. Too busy, you know?" Stars can thus have a powerfully negative impact on departments and programs, described by one faculty member as follows:

> We can't afford stars who just sit around in a holdover glow from past successes or who too frequently fly off to distant lands to further shine. We can't allot a disproportionate share of the wealth just to hang a high-rep name on our marquee. We want a colleague who will work with us, not lord above us, who can be a public intellectual, not an orchid.[48]

Universities have been accused of selling funded professorships, often when department faculty find their new corporate-sponsored chairs and professors "of questionable academic value."[49] *Leasing the Ivory Tower* lists several corporate sponsored "free enterprise" chairs that don't seem interested in careful analysis or reflection when it comes to the economic philosophies they preach. Most students don't realize that many of the endowed professorships on their campuses are actually sponsored by corporations, foundations, and governments outside the United States. In addition, they may not know that more than one hundred "free enterprise chairs" have been put into place by conservative right wing donors who only present one side of their subject, causing a lack of balance in the way the concept of "free enterprise" is taught on American campuses. While university campuses normally pride themselves on being places for the open exchange of ideas, Michael Mescon, former dean of Georgia State University's business school, conceded that chairs such as GSU's Ramsey Chair of Private Enterprise, which he personally held, are "ideologically motivated." The case of Saul Steinberg, who financially supported the Reliance Professorship of Management and Private Enterprise at the University of Pennsylvania, proves that "with big money, even a single person can influence the political environment on campus." Students may not realize that "free enterprise chairs" are "part of a broad network linking on-campus research centers and right wing Washington think tanks." These chairs are using the classroom to "produce and distribute pro-corporate propaganda" instead of teaching and researching like their lesser-paid colleagues in other disciplines. At George Mason University's law school, tenured professors were pushed out of their positions and replaced by extreme conservatives. The changes were prompted by corporate sponsors who wanted new courses and "new directions" in faculty research. The problem was serious enough for the Alliance for Justice to criticize George Mason's new judicial seminars, calling them "conservative efforts to influence the legal system."[50] It seems likely that, should the Association of Private Enterprise Education achieve its goals, future graduates of many prestigious American universities will be denied the typical debate on economic systems needed for the sort of well-rounded education Ernest Boyer hoped all of our country's citizens would have.

According to *University, Inc.*, "from 1980 to 2004, tuition and related charges at public universities have increased at three times the rate of inflation. . . . But few have noted the disturbing paradox of universities simultaneously raising tuition fees and cutting full-time professorships. . . ."[51] The research and appointments companies sponsor alter the curriculum towards their own ends, and raise student costs while offering less qualified instructors than those they advertise when students are recruited. This seems like an undeniable breach in the trust of students, their parents, and the general public.

According to "The Kept University," students on some campuses are starting to express their objections to strong corporate influence. At George Mason, students wore protest buttons at graduation that said, "Stop Dis-Engaging Our Future," a play on words from George Mason's mission statement that mentions "engaging the future." Students were upset about George Mason's plans to further develop corporate ties to expand its information technology and computer science programs. Expansions resulted in cuts of degree programs in foreign languages and other humanities. A campus advocate dismissed student concerns, saying, "We have a commitment to produce people who are employable in today's technology [sic] workforce." Over 1,700 students petitioned against the cuts in Arts and Humanities, and 180 professors made an appeal for the teaching of reading, writing, and thinking skills, pointing out that corporations ultimately want graduates who are adept in these areas.[52]

This same trend has caused a decrease in the number of baccalaureate degrees in the humanities granted over the past couple of decades, and humanities professors are, unfortunately, earning significantly less as a result of the preoccupation with offering degrees that earn money quickly for students, degrees that may not address the broader concerns of educational visionaries like Ernest Boyer and David Noble. The Boyer Commission report, disturbed by such trends, calls for a reconnection between star scholars and students, a redirection of faculty attention to making the connections that distinguish education from training. While some campuses have heard the call and made positive reform, too many have allowed the corporate culture to trespass on what was once considered a sacred trust, the dedication to a genuine quest for truth, as opposed to the grab for a quick dollar. Nelson Kiang, Professor Emeritus at MIT and Harvard, is seriously concerned that university students are "being taught to accept the inhibiting power of money over science."[53]

A Wisconsin watchdog group had serious concerns about conflicts of interest caused by millions of dollars of grant money given by a company named Arjo Wiggins Appleton to the University of Wisconsin. The company was putting unacceptable levels of PCBs into the Fox River and the Green Bay Water system, making it "one of the largest and most serious PCB pollution sites in the world." The local Clean Water Action Council accused university researchers of failing to report negative information about the company, repressing the disturbing truth about the PCBs. Rebecca Katers, Executive Director of the Clean Water Action Council, worried that university scientists were so preoccupied with grant money that they forgot their responsibilities to the environment and the local community. Watch dog groups claim that the researchers did worse than neglect to tell the truth; in some cases, they actually came to the defense of the polluting companies.[54]

It is frightening to think public university researchers might ignore the pleas of citizens in favor of corporate donors, yet the Clean Water Action Council of Northeast Wisconsin had this to say about the lack of data gathering done by University of Wisconsin researchers:

> Inner bay data is desperately needed now, because it would define the level of PCB clean-up needed in the area. The lack of data cripples any planning attempt, leaving PCB-exposed local residents helpless when arguing for cleanup. The lack of data protects the 7 polluting corporations from requirements for bay cleaning, potentially saving them hundreds of millions of dollars.[55]

If this group's allegations are true, these researchers are poor role models indeed for the students and graduate students involved in their research. After all, according to the Council, these professors led their students away from researching the health risks posed by PCBs in Green Bay and the Fox River; consequently, students weren't worried at all about citizens' perspectives on the issue.

The *San Francisco Chronicle* has reported on several cases of corporate intrusion into the academic lives of California university students. The University of California at Berkeley's Haas School of Business accepted a $2 million dollar donation that earned the school's top administrator the dubious title of "The BankAmerica dean." At the University of California of San Diego, students were busy in class designing a cell phone antenna for the Nokia Company, which had given the school some money. According to the *San Francisco Chronicle* article, "The money raised by hundreds of university administrators, faculty members, and professional fundraisers can have an effect on what gets taught. Certain courses and entire degree programs would not exist without private money." Revealing the extent of the problem, eight out of ten University of California department heads and administrators said that "the private sector is involved in the academic life of their department."[56]

A 2002 article published in the *Community College Journal of Research and Practice* seems to champion the Working Connections Program, collaboration between Microsoft and the American Association of Community Colleges. Local companies, college faculty, and administrators work "together" to develop IT curricula and programs. Oddly, though, "There has been no structured evaluation of the courses based upon the subsequent instruction experience." All involved parties seem very satisfied. Unlike most academic programs, there was a "special focus on attracting and graduating people from disadvantaged populations." The community college has had a strong tradition in the United States of providing strong transfer degrees to many students, yet according to this article, the collaboration was in part created because "the demand for skilled workers in this country's diverse and growing high-tech industries far exceeds the supply." True, community colleges often offer certificate programs for skilled laborers, and they do recruit students into these programs—but the idea of a company creating a curriculum and then deliberately recruiting the disadvantaged into that program goes a step beyond. The program's design leads to questions as to who the program serves, the students, or the information technology industry. The article explains that "various strategies for delivering instruction were implemented in an effort to allow students to complete the program as expeditiously as possible." Moreover, the schools are expected to support students where there are "no proficiency requirements in mathematics, computer science, or English for participation."[57] One is reminded of David Noble's distinction between training and education, a distinction determined by the beneficiary of the acquisition of the knowledge, the student vs. the trainer. Clearly, this program represents training, not education. While this production of "skilled workers" may be providing employees for the company, it may not fall under the umbrella of "higher education," not even the community college definition. Microsoft could easily afford to design and house its own training programs. Instead, they decided to make use of public resources to suit their own ends. True, they probably showered campuses with expensive equipment, but they expected their pound of flesh in return. Faculty who teach these courses have been "retrained." One might well wonder what they had been doing on their campuses before this mandatory retraining. Typically, community college advisors are supposed to help students make choices that are in their own better interest. To target disadvantaged students to serve industry needs seems to go against the community college mission. On the one hand, it seems admirable that these companies are extending opportunities; on the other hand, nothing is said about the pay or benefits the laborers earn, or their working conditions or long term job security or promotion possibilities. A degree, rather than a certificate, might have served some of these students better in the long run, not only for employment, but for participation in civic discourse and in life. While companies like Microsoft have a mission to fulfill, community colleges likewise have a mission. That mission should not be compromised to suit the short-term needs of American companies, no matter how much money or equipment they are able to supply.

In *Digital Diploma Mills,* David F. Noble explains that the commoditization of higher education inevitably results in the "disintegration and distillation of the educational experience into discrete, reified, and ultimately saleable things or packages of things." In order to commodify educational processes, the focus has to move from people to products, things like syllabi, tests, and the like. They must be divorced from their producers so that they can be sold by their "owners," those whose ends entail profit rather than the education of students. Noble objects to this process, asserting that bona fide education involves "at its best, essentially unscripted and undetermined process."[58] This is because good professors may change their strategies, assignments, tests, etc. as they interact with students and discern how best to meet educational objectives. While the production of a loaf of bread or an automobile can be reduced to processes that can be repeated in a series of steps to be endlessly reproduced, education cannot work that way simply because each human being, each group of students, possesses a unique body of knowledge and experience and a unique set of attitudes and assumptions that are the starting materials any professor must first inventory as best he or she can before attempting to truly teach.

This is why, as Noble's book outlines, university professors and students alike have organized to argue against the commoditization of university courses. For example, a potential collaboration between the California State

University system and a group of corporations entitled the California Educational Technology Initiative (CETI) was ultimately stopped by strong resistance from both student and faculty groups. Professors strongly resisted directives to put all their courses online, knowing that they would be likely to lose the property rights to their own creations. Students joined faculty in protest marches, and faculty legislatures wrote resolutions against the online commodification of their courses. An AAUP letter to the governor of Washington echoes the words of the Boyer Commission report in its attempt to reinforce their definition of education:

> Education is not reducible to the downloading of information, much less to the passive and solitary activity of staring at a screen. Education is an intersubjective social process, involving hands-on activity, spontaneity, and the communal experience of sharing the learning enterprise. . . . We urge you to support learning as a human and social practice, an enrichment of the soul and mind. . . .[59]

Noble warns that "faculty represent the last line of defense" against the "commercial hijacking of public higher education."[60] He cautions that some online college courses in Canada and the United States are already being monitored by campus or government officials who might intend to curtail academic freedom by policing professorial selections of course materials as well as intruding into professorial interchanges with their students.[61]

In "McDonald's U: Virtual Technology and the Humanities Futures in the Corporatized University," Nancy Knowles and Lina Carro, both university professors, argue that it is anti-intellectual to assume that corporatization of technology is inevitable, "our only option," although they, too, worry that it will cause even clearer divisions between "haves" and "have nots" within the academic disciplines: those with knowledge that can be readily commodified may be strengthened in their positions as "haves," while those with knowledge that is less easily commodified may quickly become the "have nots."[62] Somewhat ironically, there could be a continued rise in professorial "haves" offering packaged courseware to student "have nots" while the professorial "have nots" might still occasionally be made available to actually teach inquisitive students who "have." Knowles and Carro insist that this doesn't have to happen. Interestingly, Congress approved a mandate for face to face instruction for an Army training program funded for minority students because they "view distance education as a degraded, less valuable form of education and have insisted that their constituents receive the genuine article instead."[63]

Knowles and Carro compare the University of Phoenix's step-by-step teaching model, packaged by administrators as "course modules" that can be "replicated easily," to the course development model advocated by Leon Vygotsky, one of the most highly respected learning theorists of the twentieth century. In contrast to the University of Phoenix model, the Vygotsky model "stresses interpersonal learning" and employs instructor teams with "group energy and creativity" to create meaningful student/teacher interchanges. Knowles and Carro point out that if models like Vygotsky's are applied, technology can be used successfully to teach core concepts in the humanities. They call for more critical thought and activism on the part of professors of the humanities, enjoining humanities professors to resist the "multiplicity of force relations" that are pushing the humanities back with a tsunami of fast sales pitches.[64] It is up to experts in these important disciplines to justify their relevance. Without a healthy dose of the humanities, students won't have the tools for meaningful reflection on the way they use technology, the powerful influence of mass media, or the "nature of a capitalistic economy and the power it has to usurp democracy from the governing body which protects and encourages it." Knowles and Carro make a compelling point in the following passage:

> The more universities capitulate to corporate pressures, the less they are perceived as altruistic institutions serving community and nation, and therefore the more the public will resist allocating public money to and valuing government safeguards (such as accreditation standards) of higher education.[65]

Over the past decade and a half, universities have given citizens some sobering reasons to contemplate their motives. Conflicts of interest between corporate sponsorships, individual profit, and the pure quest for truth have caused universities to lose one of their most valuable assets, their credibility.

"The Kept University" lists several cases of unethical expectations of corporations resisted by faculty who were trying to live up to the ideals they were taught in graduate school. For example, four researchers spoke out in a letter to the Journal of the American Medical Association when their corporate sponsor edited passages on the dangers caused by the calcium channel blockers they were researching from their manuscript. Other researchers downplayed the dangers of the drug phen-fen, allowing naïve consumers to do damage to their bodies with the diet pills. Fossil fuel companies have gone so far as to fund studies that made light of a potentially disastrous global warming trend. Too many researchers have benefited from insider trading and other inappropriate financial ventures with companies that have funded their research.[66] *University, Inc.*, by Jennifer Washburn, carefully recounts example after example of academic researchers who allowed corporate sponsors to suppress negative data in the interest of profit, confirming that much of what is written in American medical journals can't be trusted—how can they be, when the articles supposedly written by prestigious academicians were actually written by company "ghosts" whose main interest was to raise the value of company stock? Instead of saving lives, pharmaceutical companies and their university researchers are apparently responsible for the deaths of several patients.[67] If this trend continues, in spite of the admirable risks taken by whistle blowers and academics who organize to protest corporate intrusion into their domain, it won't be long before the public loses all of its faith in those who used to be trusted with the most sacred of American resources, the minds of our youth.

"Universities, a Marriage of Convenience," further explores the negative impact of corporations on American college campuses and quotes Education Secretary Paige as having said, "Businesses should not be policy-makers, but they are. Businesses are one of the most powerful forces in education now." Alan Shaw, professor emeritus of computer science at the University of Washington, comments upon this powerful force: "I think it has affected research in a big way. It used to be that everyone was going after what seemed like the really big, long-term technical issues. It seems much more short-term now."[68] Mildred Dho, a Stanford researcher, echoes this observation when she asks, "What kinds of research questions are being raised? What kinds aren't being raised?"[69] Ignacio Chapela, a professor of microbial ecology at Berkeley, remarked, "Our role should be to serve the public good."[70] It is getting harder and harder to fulfill that role when companies are only interested in funding research that will result in quick profit. This worry, given Ernest Boyer's concerns about the function of education in society, may be the most troublesome worry of all. Andy Gutierrez, an entomologist at Berkeley, emphasized the potential implications of such teaching:

> You can't patent the natural organisms and ecological understanding used in biological control. However, if you look at public benefit, that division [referring to Berkeley's no longer extant Division of Biological Control] provided billions of dollars annually to the state of California and the world.[71]

Gutierrez's research in entomology has helped to save hundreds of millions of people in the third world from possible starvation. Even so, corporations aren't very interested in funding those kinds of research projects; consequently, tomorrow's researchers will be less likely to want to research them.

NOTES

1. Hamilton, Lee H, "What We Owe our Children," (speech delivered at The Third Annual Congressional Conference on Civic Education, Washington, D.C., 25 September 2005) <*http://congress.indiana.edu/speeches/we_owe_our_children1.php*> (9 October 2006).

2. *Reinventing Undergraduate Education: A Blueprint for America's Research Universities* (Stonybrook, N.Y.: Boyer Commission on Educating Undergraduates in the Research University/State University of New York at Stonybrook, 1998), 5–6, <*http://naples.cc.sunysb.edu/Pres/boyer.nsf*> (16 August 2006).

3. Mark F. Goldberg, *Profiles of Leaders in Education,* (Bloomington, IN: Phi Delta Kappa Educational Foundation, 2000), 57.

4. Goldberg, *Profiles,* 55.

5. David Noble, *Digital Diploma Mills: The Automation of Higher Education,* (New York: Monthly Review Press, 2001), 2.

6. *Reinventing,* 15–16.

7. *Reinventing,* 14.

8. *Reinventing,* 37.

9. *Reinventing,* 37.

10. *Reinventing,* 37.

11. Mel Scarlett, *The Great Rip-Off In American Education* (Amherst, NY: Prometheus Books, 2004), 55.

12. Scarlett, *The Great Rip-Off,* 179.

13. Scarlett, *The Great Rip-Off,* 175–78.

14. *Organizational Paradigm Shifts* (Washington, D.C.: National Association of College and University Business Officers, 1996), 4, Book, ERIC, ED 402888.

15. *Organizational Paradigm Shifts,* 60.

16. *Organizational Paradigm Shifts,* 56.

17. *Organizational Paradigm Shifts,* 69–70.

18. *Organizational Paradigm Shifts,* 92.

19. Matthew Delmonico, "Is Treating Students as Customers the Right Move for Community Colleges?" (18 July 2000), 5, Report, ERIC, ED 448838.

20. Delmonico, "Is Treating," 7–10.

21. John Aliff, "Are Students 'Customers' of College Education?" (paper presented at the Annual Meeting of the Georgia Academy of Science, Savannah, GA, April 1998), 4, Speech, ERIC, ED 418748.

22. Mark Edmunson, "On the Uses of a Liberal Education: 1. As Lite Entertainment for Bored College Students," *Harper's Magazine,* 295, no. 1768, Sep. 1997, 7–10.

23. Aliff, "Are Students 'Customers,'" 5–6.

24. Aliff, "Are Students 'Customers,'" 6.

25. Marie-Line Germain and Terri A. Scandura, "Grade Inflation and Student Individual Differences as Systematic Bias in Faculty Evaluations," *Journal of Instructional Technology,* 32, no. 1 (March 2005): 2, <*http://web104.epnet.com/*> (15 May 2006).

26. Germain and Scandura, "Grade Inflation," 3.

27. Robert B. Kaplan, "Death by Mindlessness: Thoughts on Faculty Governance," (a letter to the University of Southern California Academic Senate, The Academic Senate Forum, University of Southern California, December/January 1998), 3–4, <*www. usc.edu/academe/ascen/resources/newsletter/9801/news9801Mindlessness.html*> (14 January 2005).

28. American Association of University Professors, "The Devaluing of Higher Education: The Annual Report on the Economic Status of the Profession, 2005–2006," 24 April 2006, <*www.aaup.org/surveys/zrep.htm*> (17 May 2006).

29. American Association of University Professors, "Background Facts on Contingent Faculty," 2005, <*www.aaup.org.Issues/Contingent/Ptfacts.htm*> (17 May 2006).

30. AAUP, "Background Facts."

31. AAUP, "The Devaluing."

32. AAUP, "Background Facts."

33. American Federation of Teachers, "Standards of Good Practice in the Employment of Part-time/Adjunct Faculty," 2002, <*http:www.aft.org/about/resolutions/2002/standards_ptadjunct.htm*> (20 July 2006).

34. Lisa Birk, "Grade Inflation: What's Really Behind All Those A's?" *Harvard Education Letter,* 16, no. 1 (Jan/Feb 2000), <*www.edletter.org/past/issues/2000-jf/grades.shtml*> (25 July 2006).

35. Elwood Watson, "College Grade Inflation Getting Out of Hand," *Headway,* 9, no. 5 (May 1997). <*http://web34.epnet.com/*> (12 November 2004).

36. Elizabeth Boretz, "Grade Inflation and the Myth of Student Consumerism," *College Teaching* 52, no. 2 (Spring 2004), 2–3, <*http:findgalegroup.com/*> (20 July 2006).

37. Laura B. Weiss, "Little Homework, Yet Reaping A's," *School Library Journal,* 51, no. 6 (June 2005), <*http://web104.epnet.com/*> (16 May 2006).

38. "Ivy League Grade Inflation," *USA Today,* 7 February 2002, A14, <*http://web34epnet.com*> (12 November 2004).

39. Rebecca Aronauer, "Princeton's War on Grade Inflation Drops the Number of A's," *Chronicle of Higher Education,* 52, no. 6 (30 Sep. 2005), <*http://web104.epnet.com/*> (16 May 2006).

40. Jennifer Washburn, *University, Inc.* (New York: Perseus, 2005), 142.

41. American Association of University Professor, "Statement on Corporate Funding of Academic Research," American Association of University Professor's Committee on Academic Freedom and Tenure, 2004, <*www.aaup.org/statements.Redbook/repcorf.htm*> (18 February 2005).

42. AAUP, "Statement."

43. AAUP, "Statement."

44. Lawrence Soley, *Leasing the Ivory Tower: The Corporate Takeover of Academia* (Boston: South End Press, 1995), 5.

45. Soley, *Leasing,* 45.

46. Soley, *Leasing,* 51.

47. Soley, *Leasing,* 69–70.

48. Regina Warwick, "To Spurn a Star," *Chronicle of Higher Education,* 50, no. 19 (14 Jan. 2004), <*http://chronicle.com/jobs/200401/2004011401c.htm*> (19 May 2005).

49. Soley, *Leasing,* 127.

50. Soley, *Leasing,* 130–9.

51. Washburn, "*University, Inc.*," 203.

52. Eyal Press and Jennifer Washburn, "The Kept University," *Atlantic Monthly*, 285, no. 3 (March 2000), *<http://find.galegroup.com/>* (17 August 2006).

53. Press and Washburn, "The Kept University."

54. Clean Water Action Council, "University Credibility Compromised by Polluter Donations," *Fox River Watch,* Green Bay, WI, 2003, *<www.foxriverwatch.com/university_com/university_credibility.html>* (18 February 2005).

55. "University Credibility Compromised."

56. Joan Obra, Stacy Schwandt, and Peter Woodall, "Corporate Donors' Influence Spilling into UC Classroom," *San Francisco Chronicle*, 26 June 2001, *<http://sfgate.com/cgi-bin/article.cgi?f-/c/a/2001/06/s6/MN78493.DTL/>* (18 February 2005).

57. Gerald T. Horton and Kathryn M. Birmingham, "The Working Connections Program: Highlights," *Community College Journal of Research and Practice* 26 (2002): 25–34.

58. Noble, *Digital Diploma,* 3.

59. Quoted. in Noble, *Digital Diploma*, 53.

60. Noble, *Digital Diploma*, 91.

61. Noble, *Digital Diploma*, 94–5.

62. Nancy Knowles and Lina Carro, "McDonald's U: Virtual Technology and Humanities' Futures in the Corporatized University" (paper presented at the 1999 Modern Language Association's Annual Conference, Chicago, IL, 30 December 1999), *<www.eou.edu/~knowles/mcdon.html>* (18 February 2005).

63. Noble, *Digital Diploma,* 90.

64. Michel Foucault, quoted in Knowles and Carro, "McDonald's U."

65. Knowles and Carro, "McDonald's U."

66. Press and Washburn, "The Kept University," 42–5.

67. Jennifer Washburn, *University, Inc.,* Chapter 5.

68. John Borland, "Universities: A Marriage of Convenience," CNET News.com, 11 November 2003, *<http:news.com.com/2009-1023-5103748.html>* (18 February 2005).

69. Press and Washburn, "The Kept University," 42.

70. Press and Washburn, "The Kept University," 40.

71. Press and Washburn, "The Kept University," 50.

BIBLIOGRAPHY

Aliff, John. "Are Students 'Customers' of College Education?" Paper presented at the Annual Meeting of the Georgia Academy of Science, Savannah, GA, 1998. 4, Speech, ERIC, ED 438748.

American Association of University Professors. "Background Facts on Contingent Faculty." 2005. *<www.aaup.org.Issues/Contingent/Ptfacts.htm>* (17 May 2006).

———. "The Devaluing of Higher Education: The Annual Report on the Economic Status of the Profession, 2005–2006." 24 April 2006. *<www.aaup.org/surveys/zrep.htm>* (17 May 2006).

————. "Statement on Corporate Funding of Academic Research." Committee on Academic Freedom and Tenure, 2004. <*www.aaup.org/statements.Redbook/repcorf.htm*> (18 February 2005).

American Federation of Teachers. "Standards of Good Practice in the Employment of Part-time/Adjunct Faculty." 2002. <*http://aft.org/about/resolutions/2002/standards_ptadjunct.htm*> (20 July 2006).

Aronauer, Rebecca. "Princeton's War on Grade Inflation Drops the Number of A's," *Chronicle of Higher Education* 52, no. 6 (30 Sep. 2005), <*http://web104.epnet.com/*> (16 May 2006).

Birk, Lisa. "Grade Inflation: What's Really Behind All Those A's?" *Harvard Education Letter* 16, no. 1 (Jan/Feb 2000). <*www.edletter.org/past/issues/2000-jf/grades.shtml*> (25 July 2006).

Boretz, Elizabeth. "Grade Inflation and the Myth of Student Consumerism," *College Teaching* 52, no. 2 (Spring 2004): 2–3. <*http:findgalegroup.com/*> (20 July 2006).

Borland, John. "Universities: A Marriage of Convenience." CNET News.com, 11 November 2003. <*http:news.com.com/2009-1023-5103748.html*> (18 February 2005).

Clean Water Action Council. "University Credibility Compromised by Polluter Donations." *Fox River Watch,* Green Bay, WI., 2003. <*www.foxriverwatch.com/university_com/university_credibility.html*> (18 February 2005).

Delmonico, Matthew. "Is Treating Students as Customers the Right Move for Community Colleges?" 18 July 2000. 5, Report, ERIC, ED 448838.

Edmunson, Mark. "On the Uses of a Liberal Education: 1. As Lite Entertainment for Bored College Students," *Harper's Magazine* 295, no. 1768, Sep. 1997, 7–10.

Germain, Marie-Line, and Terri A. Scandura. "Grade Inflation and Student Individual Differences as Systematic Bias in Faculty Evaluations." *Journal of Instructional Technology* 32, no. 1 (March 2005): 2. <*http://web104.epnet.com/*> (15 May 2006).

Goldberg, Mark F. *Profiles of Leaders in Education.* Bloomington, IN: Phi Delta Kappa Educational Foundation, 2000.

Hamilton, Lee H. "What We Owe our Children." Speech delivered at the Congressional Conference on Civic Education, Washington, D.C., 25 September 2005. <*http://congress.indiana.edu/speeches/we_owe_our_children1.php*> (9 October 2006).

Horton, Gerald T., and Kathryn M. Birmingham, "The Working Connections Program: Highlights." *Community College Journal of Research and Practice* 26 (2002): 25–34.

"Ivy League Grade Inflation." *USA Today,* 7 February 2002, A14. <*http://web34epnet.com*> (12 November 2004).

Kaplan, Robert B. "Death by Mindlessness: Thoughts on Faculty Governance." A letter to the University of Southern California Academic Senate, The Academic Senate Forum, University of Southern California, December1997/January 1998. <*http://www.usc.edu/academe/ascen/resources/newsletter/9801/news9801Mindlessness.html*> (14 January 2005).

Knowles, Nancy, and Lina Carro, "McDonald's U: Virtual Technology and Humanities' Futures in the Corporatized University." Paper presented at the 1999 Modern

Language Association's Annual Conference, Chicago, IL, December 1999. <*www .eou.edu/~knowles/mcdon.html*> (18 February 2005).

Noble, David. *Digital Diploma Mills: The Automation of Higher Education*. New York: Monthly Review Press, 2001.

Obra, Joan, Schwandt, Stacy, and Peter Woodall. "Corporate Donors' Influence Spilling into UC Classroom." *San Francisco Chronicle*, 26 June 2001. <*http://sfgate .com/cgi-bin/article.cgi?f-/c/a/2001/06/s6/MN78493.DTL/*> (18 February 2005).

Organizational Paradigm Shifts. Washington, D.C.: National Association of College and University Business Officers, 1996. 4, Book, ERIC, ED 402888.

Press, Eyal and Jennifer Washburn. "The Kept University," *Atlantic Monthly* 285, no. 3 (March 2000). <*http://find.galegroup.com/*> (17 August 2006).

Reinventing Undergraduate Education: A Blueprint for America's Research Universities. Stonybrook, NY: Boyer Commission on Educating Undergraduates in the Research University/ State University of New York at Stonybrook, 1998. <*http:// naples.cc.sunysb.edu/Pres/boyer.nsf*> (16 Aug. 2006).

Scarlett, Mel. *The Great Rip-Off In American Education*. Amherst, NY: Prometheus Books, 2004.

Soley, Lawrence. *Leasing the Ivory Tower: The Corporate Takeover of Academia*. Boston, MA: South End Press, 1995.

Warwick, Regina. "To Spurn a Star," *Chronicle of Higher Education,* 50, no. 19 (14 Jan. 2004), <*http://chronicle.com/jobs/200401/2004011401c.htm*> (19 May 2005).

Washburn, Jennifer. *University, Inc*. New York: Perseus, 2005.

Watson, Elwood. "College Grade Inflation Getting Out of Hand," *Headway 9*, no. 5 (May 1997). <*http://web34.epnet.com/*> (12 November 2004).

Weiss, Laura B. "Little Homework, Yet Reaping A's." *School Library Journal 51, no. 6 (June 2005)*. <*http://web104.epnet.com/*> (16 May 2006).

Chapter Four

Commercialization Goes High-Tech: The Online Classroom

Catherine O'Neill

"Even as students become more habituated to virtual learning, many of them are looking for more than online bells and whistles. They want to learn in ways that computers cannot replicate; they want to earn their degrees from real schools, not contrivances. . . ." [1]

David Kirp, *Shakespeare, Einstein, and the Bottom Line: The Marketing of Higher Education* (2003)

Technology and privatized, for-profit online universities are probably the largest threat to traditional universities. States are spending less and less on higher education. To institutions trying to cut costs, going online seems too tempting to pass up, even if the research on how technology impacts student learning is less than clear. The one-on-one interaction called for by the Boyer Commission can be fairly time consuming when faculty are teaching online because it takes time to write an answer to an e-mail or discussion board question, and it takes more time to determine whether or not the answer was understood. Thus, the Boyer Commission model of teaching has, in some cases, already been replaced with generic courseware. Many online courses are taught by part-time faculty, many of whom never come to campus. Some campuses offer no support to part-timers for the development of an online course. These campuses are often totally unaware (and apparently unconcerned) as to how students are faring in these classes, as opposed to students who are attending regular classes taught by campus faculty.

Online campuses and courses are tough to accredit, since they don't physically exist in any one place, and their faculty and students may be spread literally around the globe. Nevertheless, enrollments continue to rise, as do the profits, with prestigious schools offering MBAs that cost up to $85,000 to complete.[2] The University of Phoenix uses the following quotation from a graduate of their M.A. program in Office Management to entice potential applicants:

> Most of my study was done in hotel rooms in Bangkok, Beijing, Lima, Zurich, and London. I investigated other options, but I picked University of Phoenix Online because of my boss's recommendation. I earned my degree in 22 months.[3]

The quotation suggests an after-hours sort of portability; instead of doing needlepoint or watching TV, a person might elect to get a masters' degree. It can be done quickly, as online study will not propose enough of a challenge to interfere with a vigorous full-time job or a packed travel schedule. What happens if a student has a question, or needs to see some modeling, or might benefit from interaction with other students or a professor? That might take longer; it might involve more commitment of time and energy from both student and boss — and the boss may not be interested in David Noble's notions of education as opposed to training. Instead, there is an emphasis on quick progress and on the competition and demands of the business world. True, good communication skills are important "on the job" — but if their implications for individuals as citizens are relevant, too, it seems the University of Phoenix might at some point mention them in informative materials for prospective students. When such goals are not even stated by a university, it seems unlikely they'll be met as a byproduct of the packaged courseware, the "Tang" or instant coffee of the education world. Those who can afford to study at a more leisurely pace might enjoy a deeper, broader learning experience. Those who lack the patience or the resources to embark on a four year course of study can "advance" best by focusing on what the boss expects and forget about more esoteric considerations.

According to Susan Gallick, Research Director of the University of California at Los Angeles Faculty Association, students too can choose from "mass-provider," "brand name," or "prestigious, highly selective, high status" institutions of higher learning, just as shoppers can choose from Wal-Mart, Sears, or Neiman Marcus.[4] The more money a student has, it seems, the better an education, including an impressive transcript, he or she can purchase. However, if the large public universities can't improve the quality of teaching and learning, they can't expect to compete with the convenience schools, not in an environment where "taking a class and ultimately receiving a college degree are going to be added to the list of stay-at-home, electronic activities that people can select if they wish to."[5]

According to a 2000 study done by the Institute for Higher Education Policy, 1.6 million students were already enrolled in distance learning courses almost a decade ago.[6] Since then, the numbers have skyrocketed. Researchers interviewed students, faculty, and administrators for their impressions with respect to twenty-four educational benchmarks in an attempt to determine the relative quality of distance learning. Institutions studied offer more than one complete degree program online, are regionally accredited, and are considered to be leaders in Internet-based distance education, which means that the results of this study would probably represent the best quality of distance learning available in recent years. Although the accommodation of different learning styles was important enough to be listed as a benchmark, when asked about whether or not their courses were suited toward different learning styles, faculty and administrators simply dismissed this benchmark, claiming that the research on the topic wasn't yet sufficient.[7] In fact, there is a wealth of reliable information on how to adapt instruction to different learning styles, and some of it relates directly to the use of various media online. It is not necessary to assess each student's learning style to offer accommodations for a variety of styles. Hence, it seems these faculty and administrators were simply making excuses. They apparently didn't want to devote the time or resources to create the best possible learning opportunities for all students enrolled in their classes. Instead, they registered students, took their money, and didn't worry much about the ones who would drop out because the online learning environment turned out to be inappropriate for them. Students demand online classes, and so campuses are just "moving ahead without all of the answers." Too many campuses have "made a conscious decision to serve students immediately and plan later."[8] But are the students actually being served? It seems obvious that the demand for dollars coupled with the Total Quality Management (TQM) philosophy is causing otherwise principled administrators and legislators to leap before they look, and students may be the eventual losers.

The same study revealed that "benchmarks related to collaboration and modular learning were not endorsed widely" and that "faculty and administrators suggested that collaboration as an end in itself was not a necessity."[9] This is surprising, since much professional work is done in teams. Again, it seems evident that some educators are more than willing to devalue another key benchmark rather than to invest the time and resources necessary to modify course requirements toward this benchmark in this new medium. The Internet does in fact offer rich opportunities for collaboration and the creation of work groups and learning communities—but managing and evaluating this work is not as simple as the computation of the right and wrong answers on an automated multiple choice test. If important educational benchmarks can be so quickly dismissed by the best in online higher education, it's reasonable to assume that students enrolled elsewhere in online classes are getting even less. In fairness, it is worth mentioning that the study also showed that faculty who taught online were well aware that regular, frequent faculty interaction with students was very important, and many of the students who responded to the study were satisfied with the amount of attention they received.[10]

Information revealed on class sizes, however, raised some questions. One school had a two-credit course with over three hundred students enrolled, and the instructor who taught it reported spending twenty hours, or half a work-week, teaching the course every week.[11] Quick calculations show that if this instructor spent twenty hours a week doing nothing teaching-related other than interacting with students in this class (which is unlikely), each student would get about four minutes. While this situation may reflect what often happens on campuses with inordinately large lecture sections of general education courses, the Boyer Commission report clearly calls for the reversal of such a trend. The movement toward online teaching and learning seems to have all too often ignored that call, and is either repeating or worsening what has been confirmed as an ineffective mode of instruction.

To further compound the problem, many campuses have insufficient support staff for instructional technology. While the institution is collecting money from students enrolled in online classes, the support these students are getting may not be anywhere close to what they really need. Gartner Group researchers advised a minimum of "One IT person for every fifty to seventy-five users, whereas colleges and universities report an average of one IT support person for every 150–180 users."[12] This finding again suggests institutional and legislative preoccupation with bringing dollars in and a general unwillingness to spend the money necessary to ensure that students and faculty will have what is needed to maximize learning opportunities in online classes.

The University of Phoenix cites Thomas Russell's catalog of studies entitled *No Significant Difference,* begun in 1928, as solid proof to potential students that their online learning experiences will be just as meaningful as those of students in traditional college classrooms. The University of Phoenix simply ignores the objections of researchers like Richard Clark, who in 1994 claimed that "most if not all of *No Significant Difference* studies were in some way flawed."[13] Some studies used grades as a measure, and others were too old to be relevant. Recently, North Carolina State University studied their online courses and discovered that faculty thought that teaching a new course online was "high stress" and involved "large time investments." These instructors, while they felt that Internet delivery could be quite effective, expressed concern that there might not be enough interaction with students.[14] These concerns seem to speak directly against the overly optimistic claims of *No Significant Difference.* It's almost impossible to accurately study the effectiveness of Internet instruction because it's impossible to control all the variables such as the population of students, the intrinsic nature of courses compared, and so on. Instead of conceding that this is true, "Reviews of the research on both sides of the effectiveness argument tend to lump disparate studies into the same mold in order to serve their own ends."[15]

A study published in 1999 by the Institute for Higher Education Policy for the National Education Association and the American Federation of Teachers concluded, with respect to the effectiveness of distance learning in higher education, that a disturbing number of questions are "left unaddressed or unanswered in the research."[16] The executive summary of the report directly addresses *No Significant Difference,* saying that "a closer look at the evidence suggests a more cautious view of the effectiveness of distance education," reminding us that studies done in the 1990s and after would be most useful in determining the efficacy of online college instruction.[17] This study reiterates the idea that at first glance, all seems well in distance learning land, yet "a closer look at the research, however, reveals that it may not be prudent to accept these findings at face value" and "the overall quality of the original research is questionable and thereby renders many of the findings inconclusive."[18] This study repeats concerns about lack of control of important variables, and questions the "validity and reliability of the instruments used to measure student outcomes and attitudes" in distance learning situations.[19] In addition, studies don't break data down with respect to factors like age, gender, or other important factors. Drop-out rates for distance learners are higher, but the studies don't seem to address this: "The issue of student persistence is troubling because of both the negative consequences associated with dropping out, and the fact that research could be excluding these dropouts—thereby tilting the student outcome findings toward those who are 'successful'."[20] The study further goes on to express concern with respect to how online courses may not be set up to address different learning styles. Finally, these reviewers thought it was quite possible that "the curriculum objectives of some distance learning courses have been altered because of a limited variety of books and journals available from the digital library." This study concludes with a strong assertion: "It seems clear that technology cannot replace the human factor in higher education."[21] Further, the study calls for more focus on pedagogy as opposed to mode of delivery. The key question that needs to be asked is, "What is the best way to teach students?" Unfortunately, this question seems to be all too often silenced in the scramble for fast dollars.

A quick exploration of www.Theonlinedegree.com finds endorsements for at least sixteen online schools offering degrees, some of them making rather curious claims. Westwood College Online, for example, assures us that "Bachelors degrees can be completed in as little as 17 months." DeVry University seems highly interested in a Boyer Commission style of teaching and learning, inviting students to "earn your degree from an accredited university that allows you to interact with faculty and other students as you learn." Likewise, Walden University claims to be "renowned" for "one-on-one relationships with students just like you." The University of Phoenix's (UOP) Official Online FAQ sheet cites the U.S. Department of Commerce: "today, college graduates earn an average of 75% more income than high school graduates."[22] Apparently, all UOP sites aren't cross-referenced, since another cites the U.S. Department of Commerce as having reported that "today, college graduates earn an average of 98% more income than non-college-graduates."[23] Their promises sound reassuring, if perhaps a bit euphemistic: "The more credits you transfer in, the faster you'll complete your degree. . . . Students taking online college classes one class at a time are usually able to complete their bachelors' degree in two or three years."[24] UOP's FAQ sheet explains to prospective students that, while working professionals could only expect to complete around eighteen hours of academic credit a year at a typical university, they could complete 27 credits per year at UOP without any real problems. Taking into account that the traditional university requires a minimum of 120 credit hours for a baccalaureate degree, the promise of a two to three year degree completion has a distinctly false ring. A student who could manage to complete 27 credits a year would still take over four years fulfilling degree requirements. This promise seems to imply an expectation of transfer and CLEP credit, something many students are unlikely to have.

With respect to faculty, UOP assures potential recruits that their faculty are of the highest quality:

> To ensure the value of your education, all of our "8,000" faculty members have masters or doctorate degrees. In addition, they hold high-level positions within the fields they teach. When they are not teaching class, our instructors are successful CEO's, CFO's, CIO's, supervisors, managers, business owners, executives, and professionals. They know what it takes to be successful.[25]

However, UOP does not claim that their faculty are qualified instructors specially trained for the medium of online instruction. To an educated reader, UOP is confessing that the bulk of their faculty are part-timers, adjuncts who work day jobs and therefore have significantly less time for prepping for classes, evaluating student work, and meeting either electronically or in real time with students in need of their attention. According to a 2003 *Business Week* article entitled "Cash Cow Universities," 95 percent of UOP's instructors are part-time.[26] This is over double the already abysmal 45 percent of instruction provided by part-timers on more traditional campuses around the nation. Even more troubling is UOP's FAQ sheet reassurance that "Students are not required to pass an entrance exam to enroll in an undergraduate degree program at University of Phoenix."[27] In answer to the question "Am I required to take the SAT, GMAT, GRE or MAT?" still another UOP FAQ sheet assures students, "No national admission tests are required."[28] Most colleges are accustomed to using placement tests to appropriately place students into courses where the highest level of success is likely; since it has already been established that a growing number of college freshmen require remediation, no respectable institution of higher learning would completely ignore entrance exam scores. Although the customer—the potential student—finds such tests problematic and bothersome, most universities find these scores essential in placing students at both the graduate and the undergraduate levels. It is difficult to imagine a quality graduate program that doesn't at least glance at GMAT, GRE, or MAT scores. Correct student placement is an issue most campuses take seriously, and it seems a distinctly bad sign that UOP has apparently solved its placement problem by having no placement standards at all, other than the equivalent of a high school diploma and student age and employment status (though the latter two requirements can be waived, apparently).

These practices make UOP and several other for-profit universities fundamentally different from traditional institutions of higher learning, whether they are community colleges, large public universities, or Ivy League institutions. Unfortunately, UOP and some other for-profit universities have also distinguished themselves with a record of lawsuits and citations from the U.S. Education Department. Recently, UOP's parent, Apollo Group, was sued by shareholders who were reacting to bad reports from the U.S. Education Department concerning their overly-aggressive recruitment practices. Apollo was accused of violating the Higher Education Act, which doesn't allow institutions to pay recruiters according to the number of students they attract. Apollo was also cited for apparent attempts to cover up these violations. Two other for-profits, ITT Educational Services and Care Education Corporation, have also been sued by their own shareholders.[29] Evidence continues to suggest that the for-profit universities are more interested in making money than they are in serving the unique needs of their target populations. A 2006 article in *The Chronicle of Higher Education* relates the disturbing story of American InterContinental University's (AIU) takeover by Career Education Corporation, which resulted in a preoccupation with making money. Faculty and staff were pressured and offered incentives to enroll themselves and their family members in an attempt to meet enrollment goals set by Career Education Corporation. Faculty on most campuses don't

consider inflating enrollment figures as part of their job description, but at
AIU this expectation was made clear. Not surprisingly, Career Education is
facing class-action lawsuits, the end result of their "aggressive and misleading recruiting and admission tactics" meant to "obtain student financial aid
money from the federal government, and to win favor with investors in order to drive up stock prices."[30] Career Education's chief CEO, Jack Larson,
had already been sued in federal court for securities fraud, but apparently
this didn't keep him from landing the company's top position, nor did the
shut down of Phillips College, Inc., where he had been senior vice president
amidst "allegations that it had defrauded the federal government and consumers."[31] Recent lawsuits and violations have led David Hawkins, director
of public policy at the National Association for College Admission Counseling, to conclude, "The pressure to enroll that Wall Street places on these
companies is almost unbearable and creates incentives to misbehave. Unfortunately, we're seeing plenty of evidence that the 'recruit at any cost' mentality is becoming more rule than the exception."[32]

The Chronicle of Higher Education found the issue important enough to investigate; consequently, they reviewed court and internal documents and interviewed students, faculty, and administrators to determine the extent of the
problem at Career Education. Their investigation confirmed that "hundreds of
dissatisfied students dropped out each year, heavily in debt with student
loans, but without the skills they needed to pursue careers in the fields in
which they sought training."[33] This is in part because the university admitted
students who had no GEDs or high school diplomas, but instead "directed
many of those students to unaccredited high schools where they could obtain
high-school diplomas the very same day."[34] The Southern Association of Colleges and Schools responded by putting the campus on probation for violation
of fifteen rules. This is especially disturbing, since 85 percent of Career Education's revenue in 2004 came from federal student aid and private student
loans. Unfortunately, there have been other serious breaches of student trust.
AIU has also been accused of misleading students into thinking that it has
programs it doesn't actually have. For example, one student who was recruited into a supposed computer animation program discovered that the campus had only one course in the subject. Many leaders in higher education have
serious misgivings that the for-profit wrongdoings are actually much more
widespread than what is currently known. The Director of the For-Profit
Higher Education Research Project, David W. Breneman, expressed dismay
at what Wall Street expectations have done to "even the most established
companies."[35]

Just like AIU, UOP has been accused of enrolling unqualified students for
financial gain. Apparently, rather than reflecting upon their practices as an or-

dinary college would, Apollo pays cash to settle suits and assures shareholders that there is still plenty of money to be made. And there is. UOP's recruiting practices have been described almost like telemarketing scenarios, where seniors whose reputations are based on "productivity" (read a smooth sales pitch) hover over the newer, less schmoozy recruiters who have not yet met their quotas. The response of investors? "Wall Street seems to have taken the matter in stride, with many investors and analysts deciding that aggressive sales practices are to be expected from a growth-oriented institution like Phoenix."[36] David Hawkins, director of public policy at the National Association for College Admission Counseling, called for further restriction of the rules allowing for-profit universities to qualify for federal grants and loans. He has concerns that students are "still being treated in a way that Congress clearly intended to outlaw."[37]

As of the fall of 2004, UOP had enrolled more than 323,000 students at more than 150 campuses, with their federal aid totaling over $869 million dollars. Revenue for the company, which was $69 million dollars in 1991, was a whopping $1.3 billion dollars in 2004.[38] Apollo's CEO earns a salary and bonus of over $4.5 million dollars a year, with stock options "worth at least six times that amount."[39] Where does all this money come from? For-profit institutions of higher learning are under investigation by the U.S. Department of Justice, the U.S. Securities and Exchange Commission, the U.S. Department of Education, the California Attorney General, and various accrediting bodies, some of which have put for-profit schools onto probation for their less-than-standard practices.

The Case of Grand Canyon University illustrates a current option for private colleges close to insolvency. Recently, the school was bailed out by a group of investors hoping to turn a profit in part by "eliminating waste."[40] The investors plan to expand the school's enrollment from 1,600 in 2003 to 30–40,000 students "in a few years," and they're hoping to offer courses to students in locations as remote as the United Arab Emirates. Michael J. Clifford, the university's vice chairman, never went to college himself; instead, he was a drug-abusing musician who toured with popular groups in the 1970s. What qualifies him for the role of vice chair? He has a reputation for raising money. Clifford went shopping and decided that Canyon was a school that he and his group of investors could afford. Interestingly, Canyon U's financial collapse had been caused by the discovery of a real estate pyramid scheme that had resulted in $590 million dollars worth of nonprofit fraud, "what appears to have been the largest nonprofit fraud in history."[41] This is rather startling, from a traditionally Christian university.

In a buyer's market, buyers should beware. Even so, it seems a marked departure from tradition to expect students to be able to unravel the histories and alternative motives of those making glib sales pitches online. A review of on-line programs in *T+D* (short for *Training and Development*) found much awry online: "GetEducated.com has identified more than 20 fake Internet universities that award graduate degrees. These diploma mills specialize in cranking out diplomas without offering instruction. The only admission re-quirement is a valid credit card."[42] For-profit schools online use deceptive practices to fool even bright students into thinking they are legitimate: "How about a degree from an online university that's accredited by the American Council on Educational Quality (ACEQ)? It sounds impressive until you re-alize that ACEQ is a bogus accrediting agency."[43] Historically, students have not had to do in depth research on accrediting bodies to ensure that the schools they attend are at least attempting to offer them a standard education. This trust has now been broken, and the dilemma could become even worse as for-profits pull even more money away from traditional universities. The Boyer Commission's report delivered a somewhat hard verdict on the ethics of traditional schools—could the Commission have dreamed the lengths that for-profits might go to in their attempts to lure unsuspecting students away from the traditional curriculum for a four-year degree? According to a 2004 article in *Business Week,* almost half of for-profit students are minorities. Un-fortunately, those who are often marginalized socioeconomically are being taken advantage of by the slick for-profit promises of fast success for those who enroll. Undoubtedly, students enrolled in Concord Law School online don't realize that their program is not respected by the American Bar Associ-ation, which has decided that "Concord doesn't offer 'a sound program of le-gal education.'" University of Phoenix's business students likewise are prob-ably ignorant of the fact that the Association to Advance Collegiate Schools of Business won't accredit UOP's business school because it depends too much upon "moonlighting amateurs" instead of qualified professors.[44] The Online University Consortium (OUC) screens online universities and has ap-proved "several hundred online degree programs from dozens of top quality providers." The OUC only recommends universities and programs that are accredited regionally and by appropriate, discipline-specific accrediting bod-ies; moreover, admission and graduate standards are reviewed, and faculty must be campus-based. To be listed by OUC, online universities must main-tain a "proper balance between program development and promotion." OUC endorses programs from many large public universities, but the large for-profit universities are conspicuously absent from their list of qualified online degree programs. OUC offers help for both potential students and participat-ing employers who are seeking to determine whether online degree options might suit their needs.[45] Although the consortium has apparently received lit-tle critical or scholarly attention, it appears a step in the right direction, particularly when, as *The Chronicle for Higher Education* reports, for-profit educational corporations are "a politically potent force on Capitol Hill, where Republican Congressional leaders have been pushing to loosen government regulations on proprietary colleges."[46] The implications of this corporate force are profound and far reaching. After all, much of the for-profit growth comes from federal aid—tax dollars—and a large portion of the rest comes from student loans that minority and lower middle class students, many of whom never achieve their educational dreams, will spend decades of their lives paying back. If our nation's legislators aren't influenced in the better interest of our students, many of whom are serving in the military, our nation's future looks bleak indeed.

Some former UOP students are less than enchanted with the quality of service they received and so took the trouble to publicize their complaints online. Lynette of Pacifica, California, complains that her "admissions counselor" turned out to be a UOP grad who strongly pressured her to apply for financial aid. She also complains that advertising with respect to class requirements was false, and that her schedule was without her knowledge or consent changed in a way that didn't accommodate her work schedule. Former students began to tell her their own stories of "lousy counselors, schedule changes at whims," and "increased and 'hidden' and 'extra' fees." Fearing "horror stories" of UOP "messing up people's credit reports," Lynette felt forced to quickly pay whatever amounts were charged her.[47] Heather of Kansas City reports that her first UOP teacher was "awful," that she never cracked a book and still got an A. She calls her classes "worthless" and is angry that UOP "cannot provide anything in writing about repayment or collection procedures." She cautions potential students, "This school is awful and I want everyone to know that UOP is not who they say they are."[48] One other student, self-identified as Stewart of Austin, Texas, reports similar experiences. According to Stewart, "A week into it, I was having doubts—the instructor was scatter-brained and much of the instruction was contradictory." He also claims that he was overcharged, and got contradictory answers on the phone when attempting to discern how and when he would be billed and for how much. He agrees with Heather, saying that UOP's "written tuition policy is well-hidden from students until such time as it suits their purposes. I wasted $700 on this online class."[49] While such anecdotal reports can't be taken as fact, these commentaries do suggest that accusations leveled against Apollo by the U.S. Education Department are in fact true. University of Phoenix has received so much negative attention that the web site www.Universityof PhoenixSucks.com is listed among the top two hundred web sites under the category "What's New in Society" on the Best of The Web, a respected site that self-reports a mission of "providing the Internet community with meaningful guidance that it can trust." In spite of this embarrassing publicity, University of Phoenix continues to make the same exaggerated claims it made before the lawsuits and the pressure from accrediting bodies, students, and traditional universities. When potential students view the official UOP web site, they don't see the links to information standard on traditional university web sites. Instead, they get the same sort of sales pitch they'd get on another dot-com, a quick solicitation of personal information so that an "enrollment counselor" can contact them.

In fairness, it must be said that University of Phoenix has been given some positive reviews that praise the campus for bringing opportunities to under-served populations of students who wouldn't have access to education otherwise. They have been applauded for offering technical skills to working students, yet this still doesn't justify the troubling lawsuits and investigations. It seems quite likely that UOP and other for-profit institutions could make a tidy profit serving their target populations without making fraudulent claims or recruiting too aggressively. But why would they, when Wall Street investors seem to be encouraging them to go to extremes to earn them an extra dollar or two?

Cameron Fincher, from the Institute of Higher Education, offers the following analysis of the situation:

> The horns of our technological dilemma can be identified as remaining competitive through technology without excessive commercialization of educational programs and services—and adapting technological innovations to institutional purposes and responsibilities without depreciating the university's intellectual and cultural capital.[50]

A disappointing lack of ethical reflection from many for-profits would seem to indicate that we're losing this battle.

SUMMARY AND CONCLUSION

While partnerships between universities and corporations can be beneficial to both, an overwhelming body of evidence confirms that financial benefit made possible by legislation in the 1980s has caused too many universities to lose focus on what had mattered most to them in the past: the uninhibited quest for objective truth that would not be silenced in the interest of profit. Too many researchers have sold out, resulting in a loss of public trust. The coming generation of researchers in fields like medicine and environmental science have been given the implicit but clear message that corporate interest, not the quest for truth or the public good, is the highest ideal. Important research is being neglected; some problems aren't being explored simply because companies don't see a potential profit in exploring them; worse yet, some problems aren't being explored because companies already know what truths research will reveal, and do not want to be held accountable for their own unethical behavior.

The TQM mentality has caused many state legislatures as well as the federal government to view our institutions of higher learning as businesses; unfortunately, this model poses some clear threats, not only to the universities and their students, but to the public good, if our democracy is to continue. Disciplines that aren't easily commodified, the very disciplines that might help our society reflect meaningfully on the quick changes brought by mass media and faster and better technology, have been seriously devalued; at the same time, Wall Street investors are hoping to make quick money from for-profit ventures in online education, preying upon those who lack the resources to take advantage of the sort of education that produces citizens who are truly prepared to face the opportunities and challenges of a twenty-first century democracy.

In *Shakespeare, Einstein, and the Bottom Line: The Marketing of Higher Education,* David Kirp speaks of current student attitude toward learning:

> Even as students become more habituated to virtual learning, many of them are looking for more than online bells and whistles. They want to learn in ways that computers cannot replicate; they want to earn their degrees from real schools, not contrivances . . . ; they want to talk with faculty and fellow students, and not just in chat rooms. They want, in other words, to participate in a community.[51]

In short, whether they know it or not, they want what the Boyer Commission on Educating Undergraduates was calling for in *Reinventing Undergraduate Education.* While it is true that meaningful learning can happen online, and that thriving learning communities have been established on the Internet, too many university administrators have jumped too quickly to save a dollar or to increase enrollment, gambling with the minds and futures of their students. Too many online educational ventures aren't adequately funded in terms of technical support or quality instruction; as a result, the educational potential of this new medium often goes unrealized.

The only hope seems to come from student and faculty resistance to and organization against attempts to package college courses and sell them like items in Wal-Mart. Markets are consumer driven—yet consumers do not have to be driven by markets. Moreover, organizations like the AAUP and the Boyer Commission on Higher Education have tremendous potential for shaping the academies of the future and for communicating the value of the core ideals held by visionaries like Senator Claiborne Pell and Ernest Boyer, including the democratic ideal of equal opportunity and access to everyone who is able and willing to take advantage of the rich store of knowledge found on our campuses as well as the essential habits of mind our nation's universities still attempt to inspire.

NOTES

1. David Kirp, *Shakespeare, Einstein, and the Bottom Line: The Marketing of Higher Education* (Cambridge, MA: Harvard University Press, 2003), 184.

2. Susan Gallick, "Technology in Higher Education: Opportunities and Threats," (18 February 1998), Position Paper, ERIC, ED 415929.

3. "Key Advantages of Online Degree Programs." University of Phoenix Online, 2006, <*http:online.phoenix.edu/Online_Advantages.asp/*> (18 July 2006).

4. Gallick, "Opportunities," 10.

5. Gallick, "Opportunities," 10–11.

6. Ronald Phipps and Jamie Merisotis, "Quality on the Line: Benchmarks for Success in Internet Based Distance Education," (Washington, D.C.: Institute for Higher Education Policy, April 2000), 1, ERIC, ED 444407.

7. Phipps and Merisotis, "Quality on the Line," 15.

8. Phipps and Merisotis, "Quality on the Line," 14.

9. Phipps and Merisotis, "Quality on the Line," 16.

10. Phipps and Merisotis, "Quality on the Line," 17.

11. Phipps and Merisotis, "Quality on the Line," 18.

12. "Council for Higher Education Update No. 3," Distance Learning in Education Series (Washington, D.C., 2000), <*www.chea.org/Research/distance-learning/distance-learning-3.cfm/*> (22 November 2004).

13. Quoted in Thomas R. Ramage, "The 'No Significant Difference' Phenomenon: A Literature Review," *e-Journal of Instructional Science and Technology* 5, no. 1 (2002): 1, <*www.usq.edu/au/electpub/e-list/docs/html2002/ramag.html*> (22 November 2004).

14. Ramage, "'No Significant Difference,'" 3.

15. Ramage, "'No Significant Difference,'" 5.

16. Ronald Phipps and Jamie Merisotis, "What's the Difference? A Review of Contemporary Research on the Effectiveness of Distance Learning in Higher Education," (Washington, D.C.: Institute for Higher Education Policy, 1999), Foreword, Information Analysis, ERIC, ED 429524.

17. Phipps and Merisotis, "What's the Difference," 1.

18. Phipps and Merisotis, "What's the Difference," 3.

19. Phipps and Merisotis, "What's the Difference," 4.

20. Phipps and Merisotis, "What's the Difference," 5–6.

21. Phipps and Merisotis, "What's the Difference," 6–8.

22. "Frequently Asked Questions," University of Phoenix Online, 2006, *<www .universityofphoenix-online.com/faq.aspx/>* (26 July 2006).

23. "University of Phoenix Online," *Online College Degrees,* 2006, *<www.online-college-degree.com/university-of-phoenix/cost.htm>* (26 July 2006).

24. "Frequently Asked Questions," University of Phoenix Online, 2006.

25. "Frequently Asked Questions," University of Phoenix Online, 2006.

26. William C. Symonds, "Cash-Cow Universities," *Business Week*, no. 3858, 17 Nov. 2003, *<http://web24.epnet.com/>* (20 July 2006).

27. "Top Ten Questions and Answers," University of Phoenix, 2006, *<www .universityofphoenix.com/campus/questions.aspx#five/>* (26 July 2006).

28. "FAQs," University of Phoenix Online, 2006, *<www.university-of-phoenix .com/faq.php/>* (26 July 2006).

29. Thomas Bartlett, "Shareholders File 3 Suits Against Apollo Group," Give and Take, *Chronicle of Higher Education* 51, no. 9 (22 October 2004), *<http://web24.epnet .com/ >* (27 December 2004).

30. Stephen Burd, "Promises and Profits: A For-Profit College Is Under Investigation for Pumping Up Enrollment while Skimping on Education," *Chronicle of Higher Education,* 52, no. 19 (13 January 2006), *<http://chronicle.com/free/v52/i19/19a02101 .htm>* (18 July 2006).

31. Burd, "Promises and Profits."

32. Burd, "Promises and Profits."

33. Burd, "Promises and Profits."

34. Burd, "Promises and Profits."

35. Burd, "Promises and Profits."

36. Goldie Blumenstyck, "U. of Phoenix Uses Pressure in Recruiting, Report Says," *Chronicle of Higher Education,* 51, no. 7 (7 October 2004), *<http://web24.epnet .com/>* (27 December 2004).

37. Blumenstyck, "U. of Phoenix."

38. Rhea Borja, "Apollo Group Fined," *Education Week,* 24, no. 5 (24 September 2004), *<http://web24.epnet.com/>* (27 December 2004).

39. Blumenstyk, "University of Phoenix Uses."

40. Bollag Burton, "For the Love of God (and Money)," *Chronicle of Higher Education,* 52, no. 2 (Sep. 3, 2004), *<http://web24.epnet.com/>* (12 December 2004).

41. Burton, "For the Love of God."

42. Vicky Phillips, "Distance Degrees," *T+D* 58, no. 3 (March 2004), *<http:// web24.epnet.com/>* (27 December 2004).

43. Phillips, "Distance."

44. Symonds, "Cash-Cow."

45. "About OUC," Online University Consortium, 2003, *<www.onlineuc.net/ about.html>* (26 July 2006).

46. Burd, "Promises and Profits."

47. " Lynette of Pacifica CA," *University of Phoenix—Withdrawal Credit,* 27 June 2003, Consumeraffairs.com, *<www.consumeraffairs.com/education/phoenix_withdraw .html>* (27 July 2006).

48. "Heather of Kansas City," *University of Phoenix—Withdrawal Credit,* 26 June 2003, Consumeraffairs.com, *<www.consumeraffairs.com/education/phoenix_withdraw .html>* (27 July 2006).

49. "Stewart of Austin, Texas," *University of Phoenix—Withdrawal Credit*, 20 July 2001, Consumeraffairs.com, *<www.consumeraffairs.com/education/phoenix_withdraw .html>* (27 July 2006).

50. Cameron Fincher, "Investments in the Future, IHE Perspectives." (Athens, GA: Institute of Higher Education Perspectives, 1999), Opinion Paper, ERIC, ED 430496.

51. David Kirp, *Shakespeare, Einstein, and the Bottom Line*, 184.

BIBLIOGRAPHY

"About OUC." Online University Consortium, 2003. *<www.onlineuc.net/about.html>* (26 July 2006).

Bartlett, Thomas. "Shareholders File 3 Suits Against Apollo Group." Give and Take. *Chronicle of Higher Education* 51, no. 9 (22 October 2004). *<http://web24.epnet .com/>* (27 December 2004).

Blumenstyck, Goldie. "U. of Phoenix Uses Pressure in Recruiting, Report Says." *Chronicle of Higher Education,* 51, no. 7 (8 October 2004). *<http://web24.epnet .com/>* (27 December 2004).

Bollag, Burton. "For the Love of God (and Money)." *Chronicle of Higher Education* 52, no. 2 (3 Sep. 2004). *<http://web24.epnet.com/>* (12 December 2004).

Borja, Rhea. "Apollo Group Fined," *Education Week* 24, no. 5 (24 September 2004). *<http://web24.epnet.com/>* (27 December 2004).

Burd, Stephen. "Promises and Profits: A For-Profit College Is Under Investigation for Pumping Up Enrollment while Skimping on Education." *Chronicle of Higher Education* 52, no. 19 (13 January 2006). *<http://chronicle.com/free/v52/i19/19a02101 .htm>* (18 July 2006).

"Council for Higher Education Update No. 3." Distance Learning in Education Series, Washington, D.C., 2000. *<www.chea.org/Research/distance-learning/ distance-learning-3.cfm/>* (22 November 2004).

"FAQs." University of Phoenix Online, 2006. *<www.university-of-phoenix.com/faq .php/>* (26 July 2006).

Fincher, Cameron. "Investments in the Future, IHE Perspectives." Athens, GA: Institute of Higher Education Perspectives, 1999. Opinion Paper, ERIC, ED 430496.

"Frequently Asked Questions." University of Phoenix Online, 2006. *<www.university ofphoenix-online.com/faq.aspx/>* (26 July 2006).

Gallick, Susan. "Technology in Higher Education: Opportunities and Threats." (18 February 1998). Position Paper, ERIC, ED 415929.

"Heather of Kansas City." *University of Phoenix—Withdrawal Credit.* 26 June 2003. Consumeraffairs.com. *<www.consumeraffairs.com/education/phoenix _withdraw.html>* (27 July 2006).

"Key Advantages of Online Degree Programs." University of Phoenix Online, 2006. *<http:online.phoenix.edu/Online_Advantages.asp/>* (18 July 2006).

Kirp, David. *Shakespeare, Einstein, and the Bottom Line: The Marketing of Higher Education.* Cambridge, MA: Harvard University Press, 2003.

"Lynette of Pacifica CA." *University of Phoenix—Withdrawal Credit,* 27 June 2003. Consumeraffairs.com. *<www.consumeraffairs.com/education/phoenix_withdraw .html>* (27 July 2006).

Phillips, Vicky. "Distance Degrees." *T+D* 58, no. 3 (March 2004). *<http://web24.epnet .com/>* (27 December 2004).

Phipps, Ronald, and Jamie Merisotis. "Quality on the Line: Benchmarks for Success in Internet Based Distance Education." Washington, D.C.: Institute for Higher Education Policy, 2000. 1, ERIC, ED 444407.

———. "What's the Difference? A Review of Contemporary Research on the Effectiveness of Distance Learning in Higher Education." Washington, D.C.: Institute for Higher Education Policy, 1999. Foreword, Information Analysis, ERIC, ED 429524.

Ramage, Thomas R. "The 'No Significant Difference' Phenomenon: A Literature Review." *e-Journal of Instructional Science and Technology* 5, no. 1 (2002): 1. *<www.usq.edu/au/electpub/e-list/docs/html2002/ramag.html>* (22 November 2004).

"Stewart of Austin, Texas." *University of Phoenix—Withdrawal Credit*, 20 July 2001. Consumeraffairs.com. *<www.consumeraffairs.com/education/phoenix_withdraw .html>* (27 July 2006).

Symonds, William C. "Cash-Cow Universities," *Business Week*, no. 3858, 17 November 2003. *<http://web24.epnet.com/>* (20 July 2006).

"Top Ten Questions and Answers." University of Phoenix, 2006. *<www.universityof phoenix.com/campus/questions.aspx#five/>* (26 July 2006).

"University of Phoenix Online." *Online College Degrees*, 2006. *<www.onlinecollege degree.com/university-of-phoenix/cost.htm>* (26 July 2006).

Chapter Five

Education from a Distance

Fredrick Chilson and David Rutledge

"Educators around the world are faced with a new reality of unprecedented parallel. This reality is the cyber-campus. Now, an educator's campus is no more the school buildings and the related physical infrastructure, but the entire world."[1]

George K. Kostopoulos,"Global Delivery
of Education via the Internet" (1998)

While it is hard in certain areas of academia to present a compelling case for overcommercialization, this problem does not surface in the realm of online or distance education. The recent proliferation of online technology and the overflow of information and data on the Internet make this teaching channel especially attractive to commercialization. This up-rise was fueled by the tech and Internet-boom that took place at the end of the twentieth century.

Demographically, anyone born between the years 1946 and 1964 has been considered a baby boomer. Baby boomers grew to be the most influential group of individuals over media, business, and government; that is until the Net Generation (N-Generation) arrived.[2] There are an estimated 88 million children in the United States and Canada who fit into this category.[3] This generation uses digital mastery to learn, play, communicate, work, and perform just about every task thinkable. There has been a change in the way that people gather, accept, and retain information.

HIGHER EDUCATION AND ONLINE LEARNING

The amicable relationship between institutions of higher education and online service providers has flourished for the last decade. However, when this venture began, the commercial aspect was less pronounced and conspicuous and the "pursuit of knowledge" was still at the center of this communication revolution. The line was blurred after World War II when profit-minded corporations and expansion-driven schools sought actively to engage in mutually beneficial partnerships. The dawn of this blunt proclamation of commercialism could be witnessed when the Internet was developed at Stanford University. Back then, this first communication link was undertaken with bulky switchboards that were capable of sending only a few signals at a time. And still, this innovation ensured the opportunity for other schools to climb onto the World Wide Web bandwagon to gain riches in the upcoming years. Driven by an insatiable appetite for globalization, the communication and Internet companies and academic institutions together broke down borders and created a trillion-dollar industry and plenty of research opportunities and monies for universities.

In his book *Shakespeare, Einstein, and the Bottom Line: The Marketing of Higher Education,* David Kirp reports about an instance in which an online venture was financially beneficial. Kirp showcases Columbia University, which teamed up with U.next Corporation. "In return for the right to adapt the school's [Columbia Business School] courses, U.next promised the university $20 million as well as a 5 percent stake in the company."[4] In a related matter, in his work *Universities in the Marketplace: The Commercialization of Higher Education,* Derek Bok reports that, "fortified by Columbia's example, such Institutions as the University of Chicago, Carnegie Mellon, and the London School of Economics quickly signed on with U.next under terms similar to those" agreed by Columbia University.[5] Another reason why this new technology receives such a warm welcome from educators is that it seems to "liberate academic [faculty] superstars, because they [will] no longer have to be the tethered to an institution. Those luminaries [have] no need for the lecture hall stage: now they [can] be sages on virtual stages."[6] A convenient side effect for these superstars is that the (physical) student-faculty interaction would be cut to a minimum. However, it is too early to know about the long-lasting impacts of online education on students, faculty, and the academic community in general and whether the frontrunners in this e-learning revolution, in later years, will not find themselves at the end of the distance education procession.

Another online development that evolved next to mainstream Internet education and that has come of age in recent years, are educational intranet systems or electronic classroom platforms (i.e., Integrated Distributed Learning Environments or Learning Management Systems). These platforms can be thought of as intranet-like systems that allow only a limited number of people access to a virtual classroom. In the case of a particular course only the students enrolled in this course, together with their instructor, would have access and could communicate within a specifically designated web space (e.g. BlackBoard or WebCT). These platforms possess, next to the basic functions of sending e-mails and documents, various other advanced capabilities such as multi-user chatrooms, video-screening, and scheduling features. These systems are marketed under the premise that users enter a secure and, for them, exclusively reserved work and web space. However, companies that sell these systems conveniently neglect to mention that they come with a very hefty operational and maintenance price tag that runs in the tens of thousands of dollars and gives a handful of companies—such as WebCT, BlackBoard, and e-College—a chance to oligopolize the market. Outgrowths of these intranet-like systems are web-enhanced classes that provide faculty with the opportunity to teach 50 percent of a course physically in the classroom whereas the other 50 percent are taught online through the intranet platform.

The following chapter will reflect on the recent developments in online (distance) learning and, then, branch out to discuss its hybrid developments of intranets and web-enhanced classes and how their teaching quality can be assessed.

Electronic Classroom Platforms

The electronic classroom platforms or intranet spaces provided by companies such as WebCT, BlackBoard, and e-College can be compared to university Internet portals that are still prevalent with many campuses. They are exclusive communication spaces that allow only subscribers, in this case students, to access them and exchange or look-up information. From the outset these systems might look appealing and help the school and its faculty to more easily manage students and their data and work. However, once an institution subscribes to a certain system, it is hard to switch to another system or extrapolate certain data to other media. In addition, very often universities forget that such intranet systems need to be maintained and updated within certain frequencies to be able to cope with the enormous developments and speedy advancements in the world of data-transmission. For small schools, these maintenance fees can run in the tens of thousands of dollars, whereas for bigger institutions hundreds of thousands of dollars have to be set aside for system upkeep. It is sad to say that, nowadays, aspiring administrators and faculty members have to literally put on their resumes that they are "BlackBoard or WebCT-literate" in order to be employable in an increasingly competitive academic market.

Let us compare what products such as BlackBoard, WebCT, and e-College have to offer by examining their service descriptions and their commercial nature that could be potentially harmful to a learning-focused setting:

The Blackboard Learning System™
    The goal of many forward-thinking institutions is to establish a Networked Learning Environment™ (NLE), in which any student or teacher can view instructional content, collaborate with educators, evaluate academic performance and access any learning resource at any time in order to achieve their educational objectives. . . . The Blackboard Learning System is designed for institutions dedicated to teaching and learning. Blackboard® technology and resources power the online, Web–enhanced, and hybrid education programs at more than 2,000 academic institutions. Whether a research university, community college, high school, or virtual MBA program, the Blackboard Learning System offers a proven solution to meet an institution's needs.[7]

WebCT Campus Edition—Course Management System
    WebCT Campus Edition is a market-leading course management system used by institutions around the world [in more than 70 countries], in all stages of e-learning deployment. Built on a strong technical foundation, WebCT Campus Edition includes a Virtual Course Environment with a complete set of tools for course preparation, delivery, and management, resulting in an e-learning system that is easy to use, innovative, and reliable.[8]

eCollege—Comprehensive Solution
    By providing products, services and technology as an integrated solution, eCollege uniquely delivers all of the critical success factors for online program success and growth. Only eCollege can provide single-point assurance that the program will be up and running and one-call accountability to meet any support need. The eCollege Outsource Solution includes the following key components: Teaching Solutions . . . Program Administration System... Technology Infrastructure . . . Support Services. . . .[9]

These are clear endorsements for and, literally, invitations to improve the market presence of BlackBoard, WebCT, and e-College and these products' positions as the leading e-learning platforms on the market. Unfortunately, in practice for many of these products ease-of-use and flexibility are still major issues that need to be worked out before these applications can be efficiently utilized by different kinds of learners.

From the outset, the idea of having a service that provides secure access for students to communicate and share information with each other is a useful one. However, in the spirit of a competitive market, it might not be in the best interest of higher education to have only a few market leaders, such as the aforementioned companies. This creates a condition, which is oligopoly-like in nature and can stifle future advancements in this particular area. Furthermore, the current situation might, and will, disadvantage colleges and universities that do not have the means to put effort into such systems. Moreover, often financially disadvantaged schools are forced to implement such a system, with money that is badly needed in other areas of their operation. Finally, being able to choose only from a small number of electronic classroom platforms provides these companies with certain level of control of what and how the information is presented to students. The inventors of these intranets did not mean to have schools create classes for students and faculty that teach them how to operate and navigate through these applications; there could be a better use of resources than supporting a service that supposed to make academic life easier and more transparent and not harder and more complex.

Alternative E-Learning Platforms

An outcrop of the intranet platforms are web-enhanced classes. As an alternative to the secure BlackBoard, WebCT, and e-College spaces this teaching approach employs conventional web pages that are furnished with the information needed by students. Very often, faculty members use their own websites to create such information hubs. The big advantages are, compared to intranet systems, that this approach allows access from almost anywhere where a computer with an Internet-connection is located and positing of an abundance of information without worrying about security protocols or information-blocking applications. However, the downsides of these freely accessible web spaces are that, very often, users have to battle information clutter and insecure communications.

Blogs or personal web logs are, like Podcasting, one of the more recent fads that emerged in the tech-space. However sophisticated and informative blogs can be, their primary purpose is to convey personal information presented in a diary-like fashion and manner; the emphasis is on "personal information" and its form of presentation. Good teaching prides itself by being presented in an objective manner that allows all sides and opinions to become part of the knowledge-conversation. Blogs, for this matter, seem to be a little bit too personal. In addition, the way information is prepared for teaching is somewhat contrary to the way Blogs are designed to be used and function.

Even though the enterprising spirit and technological drive of today's institutions has to be admired, this electronic proliferation of higher education and its commercialization and commoditification also harbors some dangers.

Education attained over the Internet can never replace the real thing—the physical element of lectures—and contributes to the notion that the priorities of digital diploma mills are to mass-produce and vocationalize education and seek to maximize profit. At the same time, such an online approach brings with it the dangers of reducing general academic qualifications (e.g., math, English, and science skills) to a bare minimum and eliminating the human element and first-hand experience of students. Online producers create dumbed-downed specialists rather than well-educated generalists while charging hefty prices for their educational services. BlackBoard, WebCT, and eCollege bear witness to this development, a development that is said to replace the traditional university.

Furthermore, students are naturally exposed to and drilled to use only one particular setting to take online classes and administer their online work; so much so that company names such as WebCT and BlackBoard have become generic and synonymous with certain functions such as the participation in an online class. This is no different from using the company name Xerox as a verb when duplicating material rather than describing this activity with its proper verb of "photocopying." In this context, even though the World Wide Web is such a diverse and rich place with so many opportunities for e-scholars, limiting the possibilities to teach and learn to just one way—the WebCT-way, BlackBoard-way, etc.—confines and stifles the entire enterprise of knowledge exchange.

When looking at electronic platforms, many issues arise for a learning environment that still need to be researched before this setting can conscientiously be deemed appropriate for course delivery. And even if it is deemed to be appropriate and effective, there still remain doubts over what is to become of faculty, what role instructors will play in this environment, and how to cope with the human element that is often needed for successful learning? Over the last few years there has been a tremendous push to expand web course development and put tools in place that create and manage courses online. However, with the quality, accessibility, and reliability of this medium still in question, the world of higher education has to make sure that the push to expand web education does not push an already damaged system of higher learning over the edge.

ASSESSING ONLINE EDUCATION: DO ONLINE STUDENTS GET THEIR MONEY'S WORTH?

Sutherland and Tham & Werner suggest that learning is developing from the traditional classroom to distance learning and that more and more students are learning in invisible classrooms.[10, 11, 12] "In the past decade, there has been tremendous growth in the availability of college and university courses taught entirely on-line."[13]

Allen and Seaman add that the online enrollments at colleges and universities continue to grow at a faster rate than the overall student population growth. In the fall of 2003, over 1.9 million students were recorded as enrolled in online courses with that number projected to be 2.6 million by the fall of 2004. These researchers also state that "schools believe that on-line learning is critical to their long term strategy . . . the majority of all schools (53.6%) agree that on-line education is critical to their long-term strategy."[14]

"Educators around the world are faced with a new reality of unprecedented parallel. This reality is the cyber-campus. Now, an educator's campus is no more the school buildings and the related physical infrastructure, but the entire world."[15] To educators, the rise of technologically-enhanced and computer-supported education means being able to integrate technology into the classroom or create virtual classrooms infused with technology. In response to the classroom tech revolution, the number of colleges and universities that are integrating online classes continues to surge. However, many faculty members are not completely sold on the use of online instruction. "Most professors simply don't believe the learning experience of a face-to-face classroom can be reproduced on-line."[16] Then again, Schulman and Sims have found that the "learning of the on-line students is equal to the learning of in class students,"[17] when comparing pre- and post-tests of knowledge for both groups of participants. This comparison begins to indicate that the online learning environment and the traditional lecture environment may be equally as effective.

Many institutions have adopted the criteria already in place for traditional courses to be used for their on-line courses. This raises a question posed by Ryan: "Can on-line classes be judged by the same quality standards as traditional lecture classes?"[18]

Moving from "Dumping" to "Building"

We, the authors have been in-class and online educators for several years. I, Fredrick Chilson, have made the following observations, based on a biographical overview, about the professional and institutional shifts that occur during on-line teaching experiences.

I am currently an Assistant Professor at Adams State College (ASC) in Alamosa, Colorado. Prior to coming to Adams State, I was an instructor of an entire online program at Eastern New Mexico University (ENMU), where I remained on faculty during the transition period in order to assist in teaching in the program and transitioning between faculties. While developing and teaching in this program, I found that the evaluation process used for online courses at ENMU did not ask the questions that faculty members thought were necessary to improve course content and instruction.

At Eastern New Mexico University (ENMU) I developed and taught Professional/Technical Education courses in the Bachelor of Occupational Education Program. This position required teaching courses entirely online, which at the time, I felt would be an easy task. The idea of an online course was to develop course materials, everything from syllabi to assessment, as if the course was going to be in a traditional classroom setting and then put all that information (PowerPoint slides, class notes, discussion boards, etc.) on BlackBoard (content teaching platform used at ENMU). Naively, I did not know that this method of "dumping" a traditional face-to-face format onto the online medium would prove to be ineffective. The portions of the course that would illicit discussion amongst the students turned out to be mere regurgitations of the material, and it became apparent that the students did not achieve a higher level of knowledge. Students had not been asked to apply new knowledge to anything that they do on a daily basis. Furthermore, the students were not asked to construct any new knowledge or build upon any previous knowledge.

The next semester, I considered a more constructivist learning approach, which allowed the "building" of a learning environment that accommodates the teaching to a variety of learning styles in order to be effective for a wider range of students. I had students take a learning style inventory at the beginning of the course and used the results from that inventory to create experiences that would be most beneficial to each individual learner. I also developed an online chat forum within the course that would allow students to share experiences and thoughts with other members of the course. This allowed students to use their previous experiences as building blocks to construct new knowledge or add to previous knowledge.

One of the most beneficial aspects to the construction of knowledge among the students was this addition of the on-line chat forum. This aspect of the course allowed students to interact with each other to share experiences and build connections with each other. Students commented to me, through informal feedback, that this forum created a supportive learning environment; a learning environment unlike any other they had ever experienced in a traditional classroom setting.

I found that by allowing students to relate the knowledge received through the course to a 'real life' application, they were better able to take the concepts taught in the course and develop effective strategies, critical thinking skills, analysis, and synthesis skills to complete the assignment.

Since many learning environments continue to develop from the traditional classroom to distance learning, there are more and more students learning through the medium of technology. As the number of college and university programs that are integrating online classes continues to increase, a system needs to be developed that focuses on the pedagogy practices that occur in the online environment. By doing so, instructors and course developers of on-line content will be better able to effectively design their course(s) in order to allow for more student learning within the online courses; and ultimately more student success.

Program Design Description—In Consideration of Learners' Needs

As a way to further present the shift in the integration of online classes, faculty in the Department of Curriculum and Instruction at New Mexico State University have been in the process of providing an online doctorate (Ph.D.) program that attempts to take advantage of the technological advances. To begin, the need for working professionals to continue their educational aspirations became quickly apparent in a large, mostly rural state like New Mexico. Unlike traditional doctoral students these professionals are unable to quit their jobs and leave their family structures in order to pursue a doctoral degree. Finally, the program design, university status (Carnegie Research recognized), and financial accessibility made the opportunity for continuing education much more viable. Any one of these three major components would have been favorable to the prospective doctoral candidate but it has become apparent that the combination of a hybrid program, scholastic recognition, and fiscal plausibility has created a trifecta for recruiting and retaining committed doctoral students.

The hybrid nature of the Ph.D. in Curriculum and Instruction program comprises two main components. First, the doctoral candidates are required to attend classes for two weeks during the first summer session on the main campus in Las Cruces, New Mexico. These face-to-face sessions have been utilized to create a space for the candidates to become personally acquainted with each other, to faculty in the department, and to complete the core requirements in philosophy and research. These two weeks of on campus experience have been embedded within a five-week session that includes online interactions to prepare the candidates before arrival and debrief them after their departure. In previous attempts at this type of doctoral program at NMSU the candidates were very familiar with each other and created very strong personal and academic bonds, but most of the candidates remained unknown to a majority of the departmental faculty. Therefore, in subsequent cohorts, the campus faculty members have been encouraged to participate in the program as a way to develop a more robust relationship between all the members of the cohort and faculty. Additionally, during the two weeks of face-to-face interaction the faculty members that have an expertise in the philosophical and research components of the required courses have two weeks to develop their own interactions with the candidates. This first component of the program has remained essential to the success of the candidates.

As for the recognition of New Mexico State University (NMSU) as a research institution, it had been a bit of a surprise to find that this fact was as relevant as it has become. Upon posting the program of study for the doctoral program on the NMSU College of Extended Learning web site inquiries abounded about the status of NMSU research and how it compared to other online doctoral granting institutions (University of Phoenix, Cappella, Pepperdine University etc.). First and foremost, the NMSU doctorate in Curriculum and Instruction could depend on the goals and objectives of the university to pursue research while maintaining an emphasis on teaching for student success. Clearly any other online program could claim similar goals and objectives; however the unique focus of a Ph.D. in Curriculum and Instruction distinguished the NMSU program from other online institutions. Therefore, secondarily, the types of doctoral candidates that were attracted to the program were particularly focused on teaching and learning in a myriad of settings, and the value research brings to understanding education remains important. This second component has become even more relevant as prospective candidates search out other online programs to continue their education.

The fiscal feasibility of pursuing any doctoral program is important for candidates to consider regardless of the institution (face-to-face or online). Fortunately, for the potential online doctoral candidates interested in a Ph.D. from NMSU, the tuition structure at the institution is in their favor. When the administration decided to commit time and energy to developing the online programs at NMSU they recognized that charging exorbitant fees to participants in such programs would reduce the likelihood of successful program development. Distance education students at NMSU pay the same in-state tuition costs as those attending on-campus plus a $15 dollar per credit administrative fee. For the Ph.D. candidates in the Curriculum and Instruction program this additional cost calculates to only $90 dollar per semester based on the six credits per semester that the candidates are registered. For candidates this additional fee is nominal when compared to minimal opportunity of attending a more traditional program with its additional roadblocks of high tuition, parking fees, and gasoline costs. For less than $1,000 dollars a semester the doctoral candidates are able to further their education while partici- pating in technologically based course delivery. With this third component explained the trifecta is complete. An advanced degree is more likely possi- ble when the program meets students' needs with components such as face- to-face sessions, scholastic recognition, and a tuition structure that encour- ages student involvement.

The unique nature of an online doctoral program has opened up some op- portunities to allow the creation of learning situations that might have been perceived as impossible until only recently; in particular, having the online doctoral students feel as if they are able to participate in a class setting that engages them. As mentioned above, the most common packaged learning management systems (WebCT, BlackBoard, e-College) and even open source products (i.e., Moodle) are particularly very text-based and asynchronous. Al- though the chat function allows for immediate feedback and interaction, many times students comment that the time to response is minimal and op- portunity to engage brief. However, in an attempt to bring the online doctoral students to a more active learning environment some newer technological re- sources have become available. What follows is an example of a personal and professional shift that occurred with one of the authors.

I had been teaching online doctoral students for over two years and felt that there were many instances when I was disconnected from the candidates. De- spite face-to-face summer sessions on the main campus and all the asynchro- nous discussions in a Learning Management System (LMS) the personal en- gagement seemed reduced (at least from the instructors' perspective). In a first attempt to bridge this gap, I began to record five minute "lecturettes" onto dig- ital video in order to produce a learning object that could be uploaded to the LMS for doctoral candidates to view. Although this seemed to be a plausible so- lution to a personal contact problem, many of the candidates did not have suffi- cient Internet speed to efficiently download and view the video's content.

At the same time, homework feedback was becoming an issue of continued concern. Sometimes it seemed that printing homework, providing feedback, and returning the work via snail mail would be the most convenient way. But it became clear that it was a bit too traditional for the class environment. The first attempt to provide feedback using the reviewing tools within a word pro- cessing program became too tedious. Next, a tablet style PC laptop was used to write comments directly onto the candidate's work and, then, return the file (in the form of a .gif files), which became feasible and mildly effective. However, the solution that appeared to be the most valued by candidates and least time consuming (see Problems Confronting Distance Education below) to the in- structor was a combination of highlighted text with verbal feedback. The process brings together the benefits of commentary on the written work while providing guidance to improvement. While reading the text the first time, I highlight sections of text that are well written or make strong arguments in one highlight color and indicate areas of improvement in another color. The second time through the paper I create a digital audio recording (mp3) of my comments, in conjunction with the highlighted segments, and provide additional suggestions. Both of these files are resent to the candidates and a grade is assigned. This method has worked well for feedback and faculty engagement with the students but it has been mostly a one-way street that demanded more personal interaction with the candidates.

As a way to bring the distance education doctoral candidates to the campus environment, I planned to develop a distance education course that coincided with a face-to-face course during the same semester. The course that has been the focus of this "experiment" was Educational Learning Technology 610 (EDLT 610)—Technology, Society, and Education. Through the use of a more varied Learning Management System, Centra, the doctoral candidates in the online program have been able to "sit-in" the concurrent face-to-face course offered on the main campus. Centra allows the instructor to connect a web cam (in this case a digital video camera using WebDV® software attached to a laptop), open a text chat feature, and record the audio portion of the class session for later review. Clearly, this arrangement was not the original design but developed as differing needs became apparent to me. Furthermore, the classroom environment endured many difficult sessions before my candidates were comfortable with the arrangement of the class. This current "experiment" has yet to be declared a success (some may say it has not been successful). However, it has definitely created a class environment that produces a more diverse and challenging classroom setting.

These examples of creating communities of learners in a challenging doctoral course load shows that as technology advances and learning environments shift, keeping abreast of students' needs, along with recognizing instructors' constraints (time, technological, and personal) must remain issues of concern for all parties involved. In particular, if the goal is student success, then understanding their needs is paramount.

PROBLEMS CONFRONTING DISTANCE EDUCATION

Another issue that concerns most faculty members is the time and energy needed to develop and effectively deliver online courses. According to many researchers, online courses are time intensive:

Contrary to intuition, current web-based online college courses are not an alienating, mass-produced product. They are labor intensive, highly text-based, intellectually challenging forum which elicits deeper thinking on the part of the students, and which presents, for better or worse, more equality between instructor and student.[19]

Although many in academia would suggest that teaching should be as rigorous as learning, requiring faculty with little or no training to develop such courses could be equivalent to requiring students to take their final exam without presenting them with the training necessary to be successful in such endeavors.

In addition, these resources could include the development of an orientation course that instructs students, among other important distance learning skills, on how to navigate through the various components of the course and how to develop a closer relationship with the IT services at their institution. Also, by letting students know up front that some types of computers and Internet speeds may have an impact on what they are able to access within the course, or how fast additional resources can be loaded, students may be less inclined to become frustrated when participating in the course.

The more instructors receive information that is pertinent to the online environment and the dynamics that take place within such an environment, the more effective they will be able to make their online courses. The more research that is done regarding the online learning environment, the better the courses become, as they tend to focus more on correct pedagogical practices.

Course Evaluation Problems

Despite the potential similarities between traditional classrooms and online classrooms, the question remains as to whether or not online courses should be evaluated the same way as traditional lecture classes.

> A convenient means of gathering online class assessment would be to use criteria already in place for lecture classes. Success can be evaluated by comparing lecture and online class assessments and final outcomes. However, this raises a primary question. Can online classes be judged by the same quality standards as traditional lecture classes?[20]

Researchers suggest that the main purpose of student evaluations of teaching (learning) is to provide formative feedback to instructors to enhance their teaching effectiveness. [21, 22, 23, 24, 25] However, John Centra suggests that in order for student evaluations of teaching to be formative in nature, four criteria need to be met. These criteria are as follows: "First, teachers must learn something new from them. Second, they must value the new information. Third, they must understand how to make improvements. And, finally, teachers must be motivated to make the improvements, either intrinsically or extrinsically."[26]

Trout indicates that student course evaluations are used by approximately 80 percent of institutions of higher learning. Other researchers suggest that although forms may differ from institution to institution, and often times within the various colleges of an institution, there are some similarities.[27, 28] Many of these student evaluations of teaching ask students to rate the instructor on such things as mastery of subject matter, organization of course, clarity of presentation, stimulation of interest, and availability for assistance. Sproule states that the Student Evaluation of Teaching (SET) forms may be analyzed and characterized according the following six components:

1. The SET survey instrument is comprised of a series of questions about course content and teaching effectiveness. Some questions are open-ended, while others are closed-ended.
2. Those which are closed-ended, often employ a scale to record a response. The range of possible values, for example, may run from a low of 1 for 'poor', to a high of 5 for 'outstanding'.
3. In the closed-ended section of the SET survey instrument, one question is of central importance to the 'summative' function. It asks the student: "Overall, how would you rate this instructor as a teacher in this course?"
4. In the open-ended section of the SET survey instrument, students are invited to offer short critiques of the course content and the teaching effectiveness of the instructor.
5. The completion of the SET survey instrument comes with a guarantee to students; that is, the anonymity of individual respondents.
6. The SET survey instrument is administered: (i) by a representative of the university administration to those students of a given class who are present on the data-collection day, (ii) in the latter part of the semester, and (iii) in the absence of the instructor.[29]

Typical course evaluation instruments focus on the qualities of the instructor; administration of the content; objectives of the course; assignments, tests, projects, etc. relating to the course objectives; timely feedback; and accessibility and responsiveness of the instructor. Research indicates that many of the evaluation questions typically used for course evaluations are not applicable to the online environment.[30, 31, 32, 33]

I, Fred Chilson, found that there is widespread inconsistency in the type of student course evaluation tools that are used for online courses. These inconsistencies are oftentimes seen even within an individual institution, but across the different departments. The most common perception of ineffectiveness of these tools is the fact that many schools use the same tool in their face-to-face courses as they do in the online environment. There is also some concern that the student course evaluation tools are not representative of the issues that arise in an online venue.

The possible use of course evaluations mid-semester, may enable instructors to receive formative feedback from their students, thus allowing them to make any necessary changes to benefit current students. The way that course evaluations are administered now, at the end of the semester, only give instructors summative feedback. While this feedback is necessary, it does not allow the instructors to make changes to instructional issues until the next semester.

There is much research regarding the purpose of student evaluations, the validity and reliability of student evaluation, student perceptions of teacher evaluations, and faculty perceptions of student evaluations of teaching. Henderson stated "as more college and university courses are offered via asynchronous learning networks, such institutions face an important question: How can classroom assessment techniques be implemented for distance students, especially students communicating asynchronously?"[34]

CONCLUSION

It may be necessary to develop a way to have more formative feedback throughout the year, rather than just the summative feedback that is typically received at the end of the semester or the beginning of the next semester. Formative evaluation is an important factor in teaching, no matter what the venue. By developing a process that could provide formative feedback to the instructors throughout the course, instructors may be able to make the necessary changes to enhance their courses to affect the students that are currently enrolled. As it is, with most evaluation methods, there is just the summative evaluation, which only allows the instructor to make changes for the next group of students; this does not allow for total student success within the current course.

There should also be some opportunity to customize the student course evaluation tool to address the actual issues that occur within their particular course. For instance, if not all faculty members use all of the functions within the course; those who do not may receive lower scores if they are not allowed to customize their evaluations to reflect that. Many faculty members also indicated that an effective student course evaluation tool for the online environment would discuss issues such as discussion boards, student to student interactions, navigation, aesthetics, and instructor responsiveness.

Since a major portion of many online courses is the chat aspect, or the threaded discussion, it proves effective for the student course evaluation tool to address such issues. It is important for the instructor to know how often the students participated in such venues, as well as how beneficial the student felt such venues were to their overall learning and understanding of the course content. The organization of the course is key to student success, especially since the instructor is not actually physically present to explain how the course will be run. Students need to know how to navigate through the course, and access the information in a timely manner, in order to be successful in the course.

Since some institutions link the results of student course evaluations directly to the promotion and tenure decisions of the faculty, the information received from such evaluation tools should be of importance to the instructors and aid them in making any necessary changes that might be needed to make their particular course(s) more effective, thus allowing for more student success. Whatever forms are used, most instructors feel that the student course evaluations should only be considered as part of the total faculty evaluation process.

The more instructors receive information that is pertinent to the online environment and the dynamics that take place within such an environment, the more effective they will be able to make their online courses. The more research that is done regarding the online learning environment, the better the courses become, as they tend to focus more on correct pedagogical practices. And, the more institutions of higher education increase their number of online courses offered, the more will the need and demand for these institutions to develop effective online environments increase.

NOTES

1. George K. Kostopoulos, "Global Delivery of Education via the Internet," *Internet Research* 8, no. 3 (1998): 257.

2. Don Tapscott, *Growing Up Digital: The Rise of the Net Generation* (Boston: McGraw-Hill, 1998).

3. Tapscott, *Growing Up Digital.*

4. David L. Kirp, *Shakespeare, Einstein, and the Bottom Line* (Cambridge, MA: Harvard University Press, 2003), 172.

5. Derek Bok, *Universities in the Marketplace: The Commercialization of Higher Education* (Princeton, N.J.: Princeton University Press, 2004), 80.

6. David L. Kirp, *Shakespeare, Einstein, and the Bottom Line* (Cambridge, MA: Harvard University Press, 2003), 166.

7. "Advancing Learning and Teaching with Technology," BlackBoard Learning System, 2004, *<http://library.blackboard.com/docs/AS/Bb_Learning_System _Brochure.pdf>* (25 August 2006).

8. "WebCT Campus Edition-Course Management System," *<www.webct.com/ software/viewpage?name=software_campus_edition>* (25 August 2006).

9. "Comprehensive Solution," e-College, 2005, *<www.ecollege.com/products/Total .learn>* (25 August 2006).

10. L. Sutherland, "A Review of the Issues in Distance Education" (Information Bulletin, Australian Catholic University School of Education, 1999), 40.

11. Chee Meng Tham and Jon M. Werner, "Designing and Evaluating E-Learning in Higher Education: A Review and Recommendations," *Journal of Leadership and Organizational Studies* 11, no. 2 (2005): 15–26.

12. Tham and Werner, "Designing and Evaluating," 15–26.

13. I. Elaine Allen and Christopher A. Seaman, "Entering the Mainstream: The Quality and Extent of Online Education in the United States, 2003 and 2004," (Needhamm MA: Sloan-C Foundation, 2004).

14. Kostopoulos, *Global Delivery*, 257.

15. Andrew Feenberg, "No Frills in the Virtual Classroom," *Academe* 85, no. 5 (1999): 26–31.

16. Allan H. Schulman and Randi L. Sims, "Learning in an Online Format versus an In-Class Format: An Experimental Study," *T.H.E. Journal* 27, no. 6 (1999): 26.

17. Richard Ryan, "Student Assessment Comparison of Lecture and Online Construction Equipment and Method Classes," *T.H.E. Journal* 26, no. 11 (1999): 54–56.

18. Glenn Gordon Smith, David Ferguson, and Mieke Caris, "Teaching Over the Web Versus in the Classroom: Difference in Instructor Experience," *International Journal of Instructional Media* 29, no. 1 (2002): 61.

19. Ryan, *Student Assessment*, 78–83.

20. William J. Campion, Diann V. Mason, and Howard Erdman, "How Faculty Evaluations are Used in Texas Community Colleges," *Community College Journal of Research and Practice* 24 (2000): 169–79.

21. Narendra K. Rustagi, "A Study of the Retention of Basic Quantitative Skills," *Journal of Education for Business* 73, no. 2 (1997): 72–76.

22. H. Richard Smock and Terence J. Crooks, "A Plan for the Comprehensive Evaluation of College Teaching," *The Journal of Higher Education* 44, no. 8 (1973): 577–586.

23. Robert J. Thompson and Matt Serra, "Use of Course Evaluations to Assess the Contributions of Curricular and Pedagogical initiatives to Undergraduate General Education Learning Objectives," *Education* 125, no. 4 (2005): 693–701.

24. James J. Wallace and Wanda A. Wallace, "Why the Costs of Student Evaluations Have Long Since Exceeded Their Value," *Issues in Accounting Education* 13, no. 2 (May 1998): 443–48.

25. John A. Centra, *Reflective Faculty Evaluation: Enhancing Teaching and Determining Faculty Effectiveness,* (San Francisco: Jossey-Bass, 1993).

26. Paul A. Trout, "What the Numbers Mean," *Change* 29, no. 5 (1997): 24–30.

27. Robert Sproule, "Student Evaluation of Teaching: A Methodological Critique of Conventional Practices," *Education Policy Analysis Archives* 8, no. 50 (2000).

28. Trout, "What the Numbers Mean," 24–30.

29. Sproule, "Student Evaluation of Teaching," 1.

30. Lawrence A. Beard and Cynthia Harper, "Student Perceptions of Online versus Campus Instruction," *Education* 122, no. 4 (2002): 658–63.

31. Samuel K. Riffell and Duncan H. Sibley, "Learning Online: Student Perceptions of a Hybrid Learning Format," *Journal of College Science Teaching* 32, no. 6 (2003): 394–99.

32. Ryan, "Student Assessment," 78–83.

33. Schulman, "Learning in an Online," 54–56.

34. T. Henderson, "Classroom Assessment Techniques in Asynchronous Learning Networks," *Technology Source* (September/October 2001).

BIBLIOGRAPHY

"Advancing Learning and Teaching with Technology." BlackBoard Learning System, 2004. <*http://library.blackboard.com/docs/AS/Bb_Learning_System_Brochure.pdf*> (25 August 2006).

Allen, I. Elaine and Christopher A. Seaman. "Entering the Mainstream: The Quality and Extent of Online Education in the United States, 2003 and 2004." Needham, MA: Sloan-C Foundation, 2004.

Beard, Lawrance A. and Cynthia Harper. "Student Perceptions of Online versus Campus Instruction." *Education* 122, no. 4 (2002): 658–63.

Bok, Derek. *Universities in the Marketplace: The Commercialization of Higher Education*. Princeton, N.J.: Princeton University Press, 2004.

Campion, William J., Diann V. Mason, and Howard Erdman, "How Faculty Evaluations are used in Texas Community Colleges," *Community College Journal of Research and Practice* 24, (2000): 169–79.

Centra, John A. *Reflective Faculty Evaluation: Enhancing Teaching and Determining Faculty Effectiveness*. San Francisco: Jossey-Bass, 1993.

Feenberg, Andrew. "No Frills in the Virtual Classroom." *Academe* 85, no. 5 (1999): 26–31.

"Comprehensive Solution." e-College, 2005. <*www.ecollege.com/products/Total.learn*> (25 August 2006).

Henderson, T. "Classroom Assessment Techniques in Asynchronous Learning Networks." *Technology Source* (September/October 2001).

Kirp, David L. *Shakespeare, Einstein, and the Bottom Line*. Cambridge, MA: Harvard University Press, 2003.

Kostopoulos, George K. "Global Delivery of Education via the Internet," *Internet Research* 8, no. 3 (1998): 257.

Riffell, Samuel K. and Duncan H. Sibley. "Learning Online: Student Perceptions of a Hybrid Learning Format." *Journal of College Science Teaching* 32, no. 6 (2003): 394–99.

Rustagi, Narendra K. "A Study of the Retention of Basic Quantitative Skills." *Journal of Education for Business* 73, no. 2 (1997): 72–76.

Ryan, Richard. "Student Assessment Comparison of Lecture and Online Construction Equipment and Method Classes." *T.H.E. Journal* 26, no. 11 (1999): 54–56.

Schulman, Allan H. and Randi L.Sims. "Learning in an Online Format versus an In-Class Format: An Experimental Study." *T.H.E. Journal* 27, no. 6 (1999): 26–31.

Smith, Glenn Gordon, David Ferguson, and Mieke Caris. "Teaching Over the Web Versus in the Classroom: Difference in Instructor Experience." *International Journal of Instructional Media* 29, no. 1 (2002): 61.

Smock, H. Richard and Terence J. Crooks. "A Plan for the Comprehensive Evaluation of College Teaching." *The Journal of Higher Education* 44, no. 8 (1973): 577–86.

Sproule, Robert. "Student Evaluation of Teaching: A Methodological Critique of Conventional Practices." *Education Policy Analysis Archives* 8, no. 50 (2000).

Sutherland, L. "A Review of the Issues in Distance Education." Information Bulletin, Australian Catholic University School of Education, 1999.

Tapscott, Don. *Growing Up Digital: The Rise of the Net Generation.* Boston: Mc-Graw-Hill, 1998.

Tham, Chee Meng and Jon M. Werner. "Designing and Evaluating E-Learning in Higher Education: A Review and Recommendations." *Journal of Leadership and Organizational Studies* 11, no. 2 (2005): 15–26.

Thompson, Robert J. and Matt Serra. "Use of Course Evaluations to Assess the Contributions of Curricular and Pedagogical initiatives to Undergraduate General Education Learning Objectives." *Education* 125, no. 4 (2005): 693–701.

Trout, Paul A., "What the Numbers Mean," *Change* 29, no. 5 (1997): 24–30.

Wallace, James J. and Wanda A.Wallace. "Why the costs of Student Evaluations have Long Since Exceeded their Value," *Issues in Accounting Education* 13, no. 2 (May 1998): 443–48.

"WebCT Campus Edition-Course Management System." <*www.webct.com/software/viewpage?name=software_campus_edition*> (25 August 2006).

Chapter Six

College Sports

Michael Malec

"Over the last decade, the commercialization of college sports has bur-
geoned. Vastly larger television deals and shoe contracts have been signed,
and more and more space in stadiums and arenas has been sold to advertisers. In too many respects, big-time college sports today more closely re-
semble the commercialized model appropriate to professional sports than
they do the academic model. The NCAA's [former President Cedric]
Dempsey warned the NCAA membership recently that 'the level of cyni-
cism over the commercialization of our most visible athletics programs has
reached epidemic proportions.'"[1]

> The Knight Commission: *A Call to Action: Reconnecting*
> *College Sports and Higher Education* (2001)

"The critics are wrong. In fact, I want to argue that college sports needs
more commercial dollars, not fewer."[2]

> Myles Brand, President of the NCAA (2005)

The quotes above indicate a clear divide in the perception of big-time college
sport. On the one hand, the members of the Knight Commission, a body that
includes several former university presidents, see the commercialization of
sport as a serious problem and have issued a call for reform. On the other
hand, Myles Brand, who in his previous position as president of Indiana University was perhaps best known among sports fans for firing basketball coach
Bobby Knight, says that college sports needs to become more commercial.
Can these perspectives be reconciled?

In his text on the sociology of sport, Jay Coakley lists several conditions
necessary for the historical development of commercialized sport. These include market economies "where material rewards are highly valued"; a highly

urbanized society; a standard of living "high enough that people have time and resources they can use to play and watch events that have no tangible products"; large amounts of capital; and lifestyles that "involve high rates of consumption and emphasize material status symbols."[3] Commercialized sport is thus a modern phenomenon; until very recently, it has also been largely a phenomenon of Western industrialized societies.

THE COMMERCIALIZATION OF COLLEGE SPORT

When we think of commercialized college sport, we think mainly of football and men's basketball played at the Division One level of the NCAA. These are the only sports that generate sufficient revenue to enable them to be considered commercial. Although others may raise modest amounts of income, none comes close to these two economic giants on our campuses. How did these two sports become commercialized, while others did not?

The development of collegiate commercial sport is intimately tied to the revenues generated by television. *The Fifty-Year Seduction* details the relationship between the television networks and college football.[4] Although those who controlled football in the 1950s initially feared television as a source of "free" access to the game, they soon came to see that this medium could and would create new fans, and heighten the interest of old fans, for a game that was, since the 1920s, perhaps the most popular college sport.

Looking at the modern college sports scene, Allen Guttmann has argued that modern sport, in part because of its emphasis on commercialism, has become a phenomenon far removed from the notion of "play" and from our conception of amateur sport as a somewhat pristine environment in which athletes challenge each other and themselves. "The tendency to transform human behavior into transactions of the marketplace has made sports into a matter of profit and loss."[5] Is his criticism valid? Has sport changed over the last thirty or three thousand years in the extent to which business considerations affect modern sport? Let us consider a few illustrations.

Example 1: When you watch a "big time" college basketball game, the chances are that you are actually watching two contests. The obvious contest is the one between the two teams. Consciously, this is the one to which we pay most of our attention. However, when "big time" teams meet, there is almost always a second contest. The players in this second contest are giant corporations, such as Adidas and Reebok, and their advertising agencies. (In an interesting side game, in 2005 these two companies announced plans to merge and then, later on, merged; one reason for this move was to enable both to compete more successfully against a third player, Nike.) The "game" that they are playing has as its prize a share of the lucrative market in sports clothing, especially sneakers. The sneaker and apparel companies are a multi-*billion* dollar industry.

According to a Nike press release, for the fiscal year ended May 31, 2005, Nike revenues rose to $13.7 billion dollars, a 12 percent increase from 2004.[6] A year earlier, its net income had increased to $945.6 million. Nike, the largest of the shoe and apparel companies, spends hundreds of million dollars a year on advertising. Even more money, $1.4 billion in fiscal year 2003, is spent on its endorsement deals with athletes such as Tiger Woods ($20 million a year) and Venus Williams ($8 million a year). In recent years, a portion of Nike's advertising budget went to about sixty of the nation's college coaches, whose players tended to wear the sneakers "endorsed" by their coaches. Coaches earned as much as two hundred thousand dollars per year from their contracts with sneaker companies. The practice even filtered down to the high school level.

Example 2: I have seen the "Bud Lite Daredevils" entertain a crowd during half-time of a basketball game. The entertainment was provided not because Anheuser-Busch feels especially philanthropic toward higher education but because the brewery's advertising agency knows that a sports audience is composed of many people who are likely to buy beer, and it's profitable to remind these people that beer and basketball and good times go together. Alcohol producers spent $991 million on television advertising in 2002; of this sum, 60 percent—more than a half-billion dollars—was spent on sports programming.[7] In 2002, the alcohol industry spent more than $27 million dollars on NCAA basketball games and more than $5 million on football bowl games.

Looking at these examples from a slightly different perspective, a key question to ask when studying the relationship between sports and the economy is: Who is selling What to Whom? Very often, *what* is being sold is the audience at a sporting event, whether that audience is in the stadium or at home in front of the TV. That audience is being sold to a television network or to a news magazine or to some other vendor who, in turn, sells the audience to an advertiser. Advertising exists, in part, to sell an audience to a client; sport is often the means used to capture that audience.

The "rights" to a sporting event are sold to a TV network for a price that is determined by the size of the audience. The television network sells viewing time to an advertiser who, in one sense, is buying ten or thirty or sixty seconds of air time, but, in another sense, is buying an audience of several million 18–34-year-old-males, who just happen to constitute a demographic profile of people who are highly likely to buy a pair of athletic shoes or a six-pack of beer. A member of the audience later buys some sneakers or beer, in part because he (or with increasing frequency, she) has associated the product with the sporting event, thus providing income to the corporation who hired the ad agency who purchased the air time from the network that successfully bid for the TV rights. Is it any wonder that in 1998 the TV networks and cable companies began an eight-year, $17.6 billion deal with the National Football League? The NFL's television contracts for 2006–13 include:[8]

ESPN Monday night football
• 8 years, 2006–13
• $1.1 billion per year

NBC Sunday night game
• 6 years, 2006–11
• $600 million per year
• Super Bowls in 2009 and 2012

Fox Sunday afternoon NFC
• 6 years, 2006–11
• $712.5 million per year
• Super Bowls in 2008 and one other year during deal

CBS Sunday afternoon AFC
• 6 years, 2006–11
• $622.5 million per year
• Super Bowls in 2007 and one other year during deal

DirecTV Sunday Ticket satellite
• 5 years, 2006–10
• $700 million per year

SPORT AS A BUSINESS: WHY AND HOW?

It seems almost self-evident that modern sport has become, at least in part, a business enterprise. Indeed, one cannot conceive of the modern Olympics, college football or basketball, auto racing, beach volleyball, or virtually *any* sport without considering the financial implications. Was it always this way?

Three thousand years ago when what we now call sport began to emerge in ancient Greece and a few other places, it was certainly less commercial than it is today. Indeed, in its beginnings, sport was associated with religious festivals or with military or hunting practices. No one viewed these activities as having any significant economic, commercial or business function. No one viewed sport in terms of profit-and-loss statements, except insofar as one might think it "profitable" to propitiate the gods or to secure food or a military victory.

The games played by the ancient Greeks initially bore no relationship whatsoever to any sort of economic reward. These games were primarily religious celebrations, and the athletic contests that were part of these religious festivals were conducted as a means of honoring a god or gods. A victorious athlete at one of the four most prestigious competitions in the eighth century B.C. received as his prize not a million-dollar purse or an endorsement contact with a sneaker company, but a simple crown made of the leaves of a local tree or bush.

As Greek sport developed, its emphasis became more secular, its prizes more substantial, and its nature somewhat more commercial. Victorious athletes quickly began to receive recognition and accolades from their fellow citizens and began to develop a certain degree of fame based on their athletic accomplishments. As the games evolved from essentially religious festivals into essentially athletic festivals, the nature of the prizes also evolved. A leafy crown was soon augmented by rewards which were more material: a bronze tripod, a warm oxhide cloak, silver cups, and even more valuable rewards were heaped upon the victors. By the time of Plato (c. 400 B.C.), the winner of the two hundred-meter dash at Olympia won as a prize one hundred jars of olive oil which was worth the equivalent of the wages earned by a skilled craftsmen in three years.[9] Calculated in a different fashion, this prize can be estimated as being worth at least $100,000 in current tax-free dollars.

As the fame and honor associated with athletic skill increased, the prestige of the athlete became associated with the city and state from which he came. Soon, the contest between individual athletes was slightly transformed so that it also became a contest among Athens, Sparta, Corinth, and other cities. And as these intercity rivalries developed, cities began to seek out (recruit) promising athletes and provide them with training facilities, professional coaches, and the necessary financial support to compete at the highest levels. Of great importance was the fact that cities quickly began to add to the prizes reaped by an Olympic victor. In the sixth century B.C., Athens awarded an Olympic champion five hundred drachmas which, in today's currency, would be the equivalent of over $350,000.[10] Indeed, it was not uncommon by this time for cities to "raid" other cities for athletic talent. For example, the sprinter Astylos was a double Olympic champion in both 488 and 484, when he competed for the city of Croton, which was a political and athletic powerhouse at that time. In 480, when Astylos again repeated his victories he competed not for Croton, but for the city of Syracuse, which probably purchased his services for a larger gift than the citizens of Croton offered.

The points to be noted here are that modern athletics is not inherently corrupt because it has become commercialized and ancient athletics were not "pure" because they were "amateur." Amateurism, as a concept in sport, is more properly a phenomenon of the nineteenth century British aristocracy and the founders of the modern Olympic games.

AMATEURISM AND PROFESSIONALISM

The Amateur

When Pierre de Coubertin founded the modern Olympics in 1896, one of his basic tenets was that participants should be amateurs. Ultimately, the definition of an amateur was provided by Rule 26 of the International Olympic Committee. An amateur was "one who participates and always has participated solely for pleasure and for the physical, mental or social benefits he [sic] derives there from, and to whom participation in sport is nothing more than recreation without material gain of any kind, direct or indirect."[11] This definition accords with what most people think defined the athlete in ancient Greece as well as the modern amateur athlete. However, even as early as the first modern Olympics, 1896, it was recognized that such a definition would be problematic for some athletes, especially in England and the United States. As the years went by, the line between amateur and non-amateur (or professional) became increasingly blurred. In the 1980s, socialist countries argued that many American collegiate athletes were "professional" because they received "material gain," i.e., a college scholarship, from their athletic participation. In reply, Americans noted that Soviet athletes often were fully subsidized by the state and that this, too, constituted professionalism.

The "classic" concept of amateurism, however, is not simply a matter of whether one receives material gain from sport. "The term embraces ideas of fair play, good sportsmanship, honesty, adherence to the technical rules of the sport, a lack of commercialization, a certain ambivalence in relation to victory or defeat, and the acceptance of a code of moral behavior. In short, purity of intent and conduct are of paramount importance. . . . "[12] This particular notion of amateurism can be traced to the mid-nineteenth century British upper classes. Springing from aristocratic sources, the intent of this definition was, by today's standards, elitist, hardly noble, and quite undemocratic. Indeed, when one looks beneath the surface, the function of the British definition of amateurism was to exclude from participation in sport the members of the "lower" classes, i.e., those who were not aristocrats.

The nineteenth century British concept of sport developed in the "public" (i.e., private) schools. Attended by the sons of the aristocracy, schoolboy sports became a cornerstone of the British educational system. The enthusiasm for sport that was nurtured in boys at schools such as Rugby, Harrow, and Eton carried over into university life at Oxford and Cambridge and then into their adulthood. It was these people who codified this notion of amateurism into the rules of the governing bodies of sport that emerged toward the end of the century. At this time, the development of both British soccer and rugby football was as much a struggle between the working and upper classes as it was a contest of athletic skill.[13] As another example, the rules of the famous Henley Regatta explicitly prohibited from participation anyone who worked as a mechanic, artisan, or laborer. In 1920, an American named John B. Kelley was disqualified from the regatta for this reason; ironically, a generation later the daughter of this "unaristocratic" Kelley became Princess Grace of Monaco.

The narrow concept of amateurism, as espoused by the International Olympic Committee, had been under attack for several decades and was radically altered by the time of the 1984 Los Angeles games. In that year, the definition of amateur was left up to the governing body of each individual sport. Thus, in ice hockey, an amateur was anyone who had played in fewer than ten games in the National Hockey League; if one played for pay in a high minor league, one was still an amateur. In tennis, the concept of amateur was defined by age: anyone over age 20 was, by definition, a professional and players aged 20 and younger were amateurs, even if they had earned a million dollars the year before. In track and field, two world-class hurdlers were defined as professionals because they had signed contracts with football teams, while other runners who had earned over a half-million dollars in "appearance fees" were deemed amateurs because their prizes were paid to them through a trust fund.

The implications of these changes in the concept of amateurism are now clear: by its centennial year, 1996, the Olympics became, in effect, an "open" Olympics, open to all athletes regardless of the amount or manner of financial compensation. Coubertin's aristocratic notion of the amateur athlete is now only a memory. In the United States, amateur athletics, as envisioned by Coubertin, is almost unknown once one goes beyond the high school level.

Semi-Pros and Shamateurs: Big Time College Sports

The economic impact of the mass media on sport can be seen very clearly in the case of the coverage of college football and basketball. Consider men's basketball. The paramount event of college basketball is the season-ending NCAA national championship tournament. In 1963, when Loyola of Chicago won the tournament, there was no live TV coverage of the game in the Windy City; it was shown on a tape-delay basis. However, as the size of the national television audience grew during the 1960s, so too did interest in televised sport. The NCAA eventually put together a basketball package that was sold to the highest bidder. In 1979, the TV rights to the tournament cost $5 million dollars. When the contact was negotiated for the years 1982–84, the high bid was $15 million per year. The 1988–90 price rose to $55 million; from 1991–97 the rights belonged to CBS for an average cost of $143 million per year.[14] Currently, the CBS network has an eleven year, $6 billion dollar contract that runs

Figure 6.1.   Television Revenues for Selected College Athletic Events

Network	Property	Length	Total Value	Final Season
ABC	NCAA football	4 years	$400 million	2005–06
CBS	NCAA men's basketball	11 years	$6 billion	2012–13
NBC	Notre Dame football	7 years	$45 million	2005
ESPN	NCAA championship	11 years	$200 million	2012–13

through the 2012–13 season; this averages to more than $540 million per year. Figure 6.1 presents the magnitude selected university-commercial engages in college sports have.

From the point of view of the universities, these dollar figures belie the notion of an "amateur" sporting event. If we hesitate to consider the NCAA tournament as a *professional* event, we must nonetheless concede that, for the NCAA member institutions, it has become an exceedingly *commercial* event. But what about the players? In the modern era of highly commercialized collegiate sport (i.e., football and men's basketball), are the college players amateurs or professionals? Perhaps it is appropriate to consider them as semi-professional athletes. On the one hand, very few college players could live on what they "earn" from their participation in college sport. But on the other hand, these athletes do receive a good deal of "in kind" compensation: tuition, room, board, and some minor expenses at many public universities can easily total $15,000 per year, while the same items at some private universities can easily exceed $40,000. Over a five-year period (which is not uncommon for many football players), that's a "salary" of $200,000.

BROADER ISSUES

Corporate Takeover

Athletic departments conduct themselves like corporations. In addition to their amateur or collegiate goals, they pursue the bottom line and operate almost independently from general university operations. Perhaps a classic representation of this, for almost every major university, is the separation between the Internet domains of its academic and athletic realms. My own university has as a general domain name the expected www.bc.edu. However, if one links to the athletic department, one is automatically transferred to a new domain, www.bceagles.com. This separation of .edu and .com web domains reflects the separation between the educational and commercial domains of American universities. This is because a "main purpose of college sports is commercial entertainment. Within most universities with big-time intercollegiate programs, the athletic department operates as a separate business and has almost no connection to educational departments and functions of the school."[15]

The athletic departments and the infrastructures they create have all the makings of a typical corporation. A corporation can be defined as "a legal entity with assets and liabilities separate from those of its owner(s)."[16] Collegiate sports entities are not very different. In this context, perhaps the most prevalent feature of a corporation is its ability to buy or sell property and products. For college sports, some other convenient features are limited legal liability and fundraising. When laying the corporate blueprint over a college sports department and its operations, striking similarities emerge between a corporation and a collegiate athletics department.

A corporation can buy and sell property and products. A sports department or its host institution can purchase training equipment and facilities and build stadia that can hold more than 110,000 spectators. For instance, the University of Michigan's college football stadium, the largest in the country, is undergoing a $200 million dollar renovation to add luxury boxes and upgrade the facilities to increase revenues. In this context, Zimbalist reports that "a sample of 25 major college athletic programs found that [from 1996 to 1999] these schools had spent or committed over $1.2 billion on sports facilities."[17]

In addition to the merchandise and entertainment offered, college athletes can also be treated as goods that can be sold or traded like baseball collectors' cards. Examples are the annual football and basketball drafts that decide which professional franchises get which college athletes.

The limited legal liability of corporate personhood that comes with corporate life has become a part of college sports. Often, no one is held accountable for the escalation of costs that result from participation in the athletic arms race. This term refers to the often lavish expenses that are incurred when recruiting athletes, paying coaches, or maintaining facilities. Furthermore, only limited liability is assigned when teams do not provide a top performance or sports programs do not break even.

Another feature not to be overlooked in the collegiate realm is raising money by selling a stake in the corporate sports program. Whether this is done through soliciting alumni contributions, selling syndication rights to TV networks, or offering advertising space in university-owned sports venues, depends on the institution. Examples of these promotional gambits include alumni fundraising flyers, watching a college football game on TV and hearing a commercial every few minutes, and watching the sponsored events during the half-time show while attending a college game. However, very often universities neglect to consider that tied to the selling of a major stake in their sport properties is the loss of control and identity over their operations.

Richard Lapchick has stated that even the NCAA, the body charged with overseeing collegiate sport activities and protecting the integrity of this enterprise, is, as a matter of fact, a "business organization which is part of the entertainment industry whose product is competitive intercollegiate sports events."[18] Therefore, if even the agency that is entrusted with safeguarding sports behaves like a commercial enterprise, it is no wonder that schools might favor economic prowess over athletic prowess.

In 1976, sixty-one schools with major football teams formed the College Football Association. This was done in order to escape the authoritarian control of the NCAA and take their commercial fortunes—especially the lucrative TV contracts—into their own hands. Soon the CFA began to negotiate its own broadcasting deal, independent of the NCAA. In 1984 some member-schools of the CFA sued the NCAA, claiming that the NCAA is a monopoly and, thus, in violation of the Sherman Antitrust Act. The Supreme Court ruled against the NCAA in March of 1984. Justice John Paul Stevens wrote for the majority of the Court that "There can be no doubt that the challenged practices of the NCAA constitute a restraint of trade in the sense that they limit members' freedom to negotiate and enter into their own television contracts."[19]

This ruling opened the floodgates for big media enterprises to enter and claim a commanding stake in the collegiate sports venture at a cheaper rate than before the NCAA monopoly was challenged. When the football TV contracts were signed subsequent to the Supreme Court decision, the new total for the 1984 football season was $30.8 million instead of the expected $74 million under the old NCAA monopoly deal.[20] However, it did not take long before schools were able to recapture their revenue momentum. This development was supported by the fact that, in 1989, CBS signed a deal with the NCAA and its schools for "$1 billion over seven years"[21] and then renewed the contract in 1999 for "$6 billion over eleven years"[22] to broadcast the NCAA basketball tournament. One can only imagine the stakeholder power and control these television and syndication contracts create. Multinational companies and media outlets utilize the commercial potential of college sport to reach their customers. The danger in merging the academic and commercial sphere lies in the fact that "it is not to sponsor the culture, but to be the culture."[23] In other words, corporations such as Nike and Adidas are aiming to not simply sponsor the university but to *be* the university.

Increased Collegiate Professionalism

Another sport sociological issue that presents itself in this context is the loss of the Olympic spirit *of citius, altius, fortius* (faster, higher, stronger) that supports amateur achievements and condemns professional monetarism. The Lombardi Program on Measuring University Performance argues that "college sports work closely with television networks and their corporate sponsors to bring the games, especially football but also basketball [to their audiences]. The spectacle of today's top-level college sports contests equals professional sports [in all aspects]."[24]

When looking at this increased professionalism, and the commercialization that comes with it, the following fundamental question has to be asked: What is the purpose of athletics in the realm of higher education? Is it to uphold the amateur spirit that was asked for by our academic forefathers; or is it to perpetuate commercialism? Given the previous evidence and all of the signs pointing towards the corporatization of college sports, Sperber concludes that "intercollegiate athletics has become a College Sports Inc., a huge commercial entertainment conglomerate, operating from and mainly opposed to, the educational aims of the schools that house its franchises."[25]

When looking at the collegiate sports enterprise after the formation of the NCAA in 1905, it is clear that many things in the academic arena had been or were about to become professionalized (commercialized); one of these was the role of the coach. Whether in football, basketball, or baseball, the college coach and some of his staff members began to benefit from the commercial agreements and power arrangements. This is underscored by the fact that a coach may make more than his university president or prize winning faculty colleague.

Another disturbing professional development has recently emerged. Colleges are looking for ways to manage their growing sports enterprises in a more organized and sophisticated manner. For example, Boston College recently set its sights on the marketing company that handles the promotional fortunes of the Boston Red Sox. Fenway Sports Group has become a willing partner in this academic-commercial venture, giving the Eagles a more professional look and image.[26]

UNDERMINING ACADEMIC INTEGRITY AND IDENTITY

"Since their inception, colleges and universities have tried to protect the integrity of the academy from outside encroachment and blandishments. . . . However, athletic departments, as commercial entertainment ventures, see nothing wrong . . . in corporate or any kind of sponsors."[27] Sperber and others argue that schools should make do without outside commercial help, relying solely on alumni support, tuition revenues, and government contributions. Others argue that colleges and universities have to open up a little bit in order to thrive and survive in an educational environment, which is increasingly plagued by competitiveness and cuts in governmental spending. In the latter case, institutions of higher education have to ask themselves whether everything in a university is up for sale. "Making money in the world of commerce often comes with a Faustian bargain in which universities have to compromise their basic values—and thereby risk their very souls—in order to enjoy the rewards of the marketplace."[28] It is this Faustian bargain that NCAA President Brand dismisses in his quote at the beginning of this chapter. Brand notes that "[t]he level of advertising at professional basketball games, for example, would cause complaints at many college venues," and "extensive signage and loud in-venue ads may be acceptable for professional sporting events that are not accepted by fans—even the same fans—in collegiate venues," but dismisses these concerns, in part, because "college sports depend on commercial revenues to present and broadcast their games and, especially, to support their operations and missions."[29] What Brand does not do is place limits on the extent to which the commercialization of sport may occur. We already know that commercial sponsors have altered the terrain of college sports; we need only to look at mid-week televised football games, at "TV time-outs" that disrupt the flow of basketball games, and other instances where commercial television has changed the games we play. He suggests that the multiple logos on a NASCAR driver would not be acceptable on a college jersey. But multiple commercial logos are no more unlikely than the presence of commercial ads that can be now found in the lavatories of many college arenas.

Much of the existing literature points out one particular shortcoming within the college sports enterprise: the degradation of academic standards for the sake of college sport success. Today more than ever, students and their coaches are faced with a dilemma that requires them to yield to the commercial pressures without hesitation in order to survive and thrive. Education and future job security assume second place to winning and profits and stand no chance against the endeavor of corporations to take a stake and the willingness of institutions to sell out.

Many students who are athletes, especially in sports such as college football, basketball, and baseball, hope to make the professional leagues after they have graduated from a university. But the reality is that college athletes have a better chance of becoming a manager, lawyer, or engineer than signing a million-dollar contract with a professional team.

The rise in commercialization of revenue-producing sports, primarily due to the surge in commercial sponsorship and television revenues, has caused low graduation rates.[30] According to the 2004 NCAA Division I Graduation Rates Report, the graduation rate for football players is 53 percent and male basketball players is 43 percent. These rates are lower than the average graduation rates in other college sports, which are around 60 percent, or the overall college graduation rate which averages 58 percent.[31]

Not restricted to college anymore, young aspiring athletes even drop out of high school to join the professional circus. Professional sports teams and corporate sponsors contribute, in no small part, to this early high school and college drop out phenomenon. However, both sides neglect to think about an unsuccessful transition from student to professional. What if the athlete fails to perform, his career gets cut short due to injury, or he gets in trouble with the law? Contingency plans for these kinds of situations are often not in place.

It is an open secret that coaches are reluctant to be monitored based on anything other than athletic performance. One can only guess why. If, along with athletic performance, the academic performance of the student athletes should enter a coach's evaluation, the coach often would not make the grade. This lack of accountability is compounded by a laxity and blind-sightedness of academic officials when it comes to improving the academics of student athletes. Coaches and academic official have to realize that these shortcomings need to be addressed in a commercialized college sport system.

President Brand asserts that what is most important is not the source of the money, but what one does with it. What he ignores, however, is the fact that commercial sponsors can and do dictate a great deal of what happens in the realm of college sport. He minimizes the dangers that result from the pursuit of more dollars (to feed the athletic arms race), bigger stadiums, more lavish facilities, increased hype, and other concomitants of commercialization.

TAKING ACTION

It is easy to criticize the status quo without suggesting appropriate actions to improve or solve the existing problem. It has to be mentioned though that attempts to improve the current situation have been undertaken before. However, these attempts have at times been stifled or nullified by university administrators and sports managers who are eager and willing to support the commercial. Especially at the Division I level, university officials introduced business-like routines to the academic setting and commercialized many university operations in an attempt to emulate successful professional sports enterprises.

Following are ten suggestions to reduce the commercial penetration of the college sports realm:

- Big-time athletic departments are run like for-profit corporations in many respects. In order to decorporatize these operations, coaches' salaries need to be capped, sponsorship contracts need to be strictly regulated, and the fierce competition for every commercial dollar needs to be disengaged.[32] As I write these words, the NCAA is preparing a report on the "Future of Division I Intercollegiate Athletics." This report will detail certain suggestions for the reform of the financial state of big-time intercollegiate athletics.

- NCAA-endorsed professionalism becomes particularly vivid when taking a closer look at the recruitment packages for student athletes. These recruitment agreements look like professional sports contracts for academic stakeholders that should not be considered as professionals.

- Zimbalist has proposed several useful reforms that could help overcome the commercial hurdle. He suggests changes such as improving the relationship between collegiate and professional sports, allowing a certain number of nonmatriculated athletes on teams, and abolishing freshmen eligibility.[33] His suggestions should be revisited.

- A vocabulary needs to be introduced to college athletics that does not evolve around marketing exposure, operational efficiency, and financial viability, but focuses on pride, achievement, and honor.[34] The people that were "once called fans" and are "nowadays called customers" need to be fans again.[35] The officials in charge have to make sure that at the center of the college experience is learning and not college sports.

- The graduation rates for football players and male basketball players are poor when compared to the overall graduation rate.[36] These rates tell a sad story. School administrators have to make sure that the graduation guidelines and regulations are more strictly enforced. NCAA graduation regulations need to be amended to reflect higher academic quality standards and be more geared toward the academic well-being of the student athletes rather than the financial well-being of the schools.

- There are only so many hours in a day, and the student in the highly commercialized college sports arena has an almost impossible challenge. Students who are athletes have to be given greater opportunity to be students rather than athletes. The curriculum of athletes has to be more adequately structured to reflect the academic needs of these students and provide them with a chance to be more involved in their own lives.

- The athletic performance and other pressures put student athletes and their coaches in an awkward position: too often they have to choose between performing well athletically or academically. In addition, institutions have to reduce the influence of outside businesses over the college sports enterprise and reclaim the reins of power. In an environment primarily geared towards learning, the choice is clear: academics come first.

- The dream of university athletes, especially in sports such as football and basketball, to become professional after they have graduated from school is in the overwhelming proportion of cases just a dream. It is an open secret that only a miniscule proportion of those students playing college sports will make it to the professional level.[37] Faculty and staff have to communicate this to athletes and inform them that they have a much better chance of becoming a manager, doctor, or engineer. Schools have to put in place infrastructures that allow these students to embark on normal job careers after their athletic lives in college are over.

- Too many aspiring athletes drop out of high school and college, lured by the huge sums of money professional teams promise. But what if their sports careers do not take off? This can be due to a host of reasons ranging from an unsuccessful college-to-professional transition to career-ending injuries. Officials have to put contingency plans in place that allow an appropriate management of these kinds of situations. Furthermore, we need to educate the athletes about the dangers of early leaving.

- More often than not coaches want their only benchmark of assessment to be their athletic performance. However, since academics should be and are the primary focus in a university setting, academic performance has to enter the equation when evaluating coaches. Besides coaches, regulatory bodies such as the NCAA should be held more accountable for the academic quality of student athletes.

We can build an idealized version of a university, but it would be nice if, for a change, we could move toward an athletic program that was much like other extracurricular activities, one that more closely guards scholastic integrity and independence and eschews the commercial influences on the college sports environment.

NOTES

1. Knight Commission on Intercollegiate Athletics, *A Call to Action: Reconnecting College Sports and Higher Education,* 2001 (Report), *<www.knightcommission.org/about/reports/category/A%20Call%20to%20Action/>* (5 June 2006).

2. Myles Brand, "Money Not Corruptive if Actions Uphold Collegiate Mission." *NCAA News Online* 2004, *<www2.ncaa.org/media_and_events/association_news/ncaa_news_online/2005/04_25_05/editorial/4209n04.html>* (5 June 2006).

3. Jay Coakley, *Sports in Society: Issues and Controversies,* 9th ed. (Boston: McGraw-Hill, 2007), 360–61.

4. Keith Dunnavant. *The Fifty-Year Seduction* (New York: St. Martin's Press, 2004).

5. Allen Guttmann. *From Ritual to Record* (New York: Columbia University Press, 1978), 62.

6. Nike, "Company Overview," 2006, <*www.nike.com/nikebiz/nikebiz.jhtml ;bsessionid=T1NY1UFGWVXT0CQFTARSF5AKAWMEOIZB?page=3&item=facts*> (14 June 2006).

7. The Center on Alcohol Marketing and Youth, "Alcohol Advertising on Sports, Television 2001 and 2002," Georgetown University, 2006, <*http://camy.org/factsheets /index.php?FactsheetID=20*> (14 June, 2006).

8. Mark Maske, "TV Deals Show League's Might," *Washington Post*, 19 April 2005, <*www.washingtonpost.com/wp-dyn/articles/A825-2005Apr19.html*> (14 June, 2006).

9. David C. Young. "Professionalism in Archaic and Classical Greek Athletics," in *The Olympic Games in Transition*, ed. Jeffrey O. Segrave and Donald Chu. (Champaign, IL: Human Kinetics Books, 1988), 27.

10. Young, "Professionalism," 30.

11. Charles W. Thayer, "A Question of Soul," *Sports Illustrated,* 15 August 1960, 74.

12. Andrew Strenk. "Amateurism: The Myth and the Reality," in *The Olympic Games in Transition*, ed. Jeffrey O. Segrave and Donald Chu. (Champaign, IL: Human Kinetics Books, 1988), 306.

13. William J. Baker, *Sports in the Western World* (Lanham, MD: Rowman & Littlefield, 1982), Chapter 9.

14. William C. Symonds, "'March Madness' is Getting Even Crazier," *Business Week*, 2 April 1990, 102.

15. Murray Sperber, *College Sports, Inc.: The Athletic Department vs. The University* (New York: Henry Holt, 1990), 1.

16. Louis E. Boone and David L. Kurtz, *Contemporary Business 2006,* 11 ed. (South-Western College Publisher, 2005), Chapter 5, <*http://websites.swlearning.com/ cgi-wadsworth/course_products_wp.pl?fid=M20b&product_isbn_issn=0324320892 &discipline_number=407&audience_code=030*> (27 June 2006).

17. Andrew Zimbalist, *Unpaid Professionals* (Princeton: Princeton University Press, 1991), 133.

18. Richard Lapchick, *Fractured Focus* (Boston: Heath & Co, 1986), 46.

19. Justice John Paul Stevens, cited in Sperber, *College Sports Inc.,* 51.

20. Sperber, *College Sports Inc.*, 53.

21. Zimbalist, *Unpaid*, 112.

22. James J. Duderstadt, *Intercollegiate Intercollegiate Athletics and the American University* (Ann Arbor: University of Michigan Press, 2000) 75.

23. Sheila Slaughter and Gary Rhoades, *Academic Capitalism in the New Economy* (Baltimore, MD: The Johns Hopkins University Press, 2004), 258.

24. The Lombardi Program on Measuring University Performance, "The Sports Imperative in America's Research Universities," *Annual Report: The Top American Research Universities* (November 2003), 15.

25. Sperber, *College Sports Inc.*, xi.

26. Scott Voorhis, "Touter of Sox to Add Teams at BC," *Boston Herald,* 15 February 2005, 29.

27. Sperber, *College Sports Inc.,* 65.

28. Derek Bok, *Universities in the Market Place: The Commercialization of Higher Education* (Princeton, N.J.: Princeton University Press, 2003), 200.

29. Brand, "Money Not Corruptive."

30. Arthur Padilla and David Baumer, "Big-Time College Sports: Management and Economic Issues," *Journal of Sport and Social Issues*, 18, 2 (May 1994).

31. Coakley, *Sports in Society*, 9th ed., 499.

32. Knight Commission on Intercollegiate Athletics, "New Study Debunks Link Between Winning Teams and Financial Benefits," *News*, 7 September 2004, *<www.knightcommission.org/students/item/frank_2004/>* (27 October 2006).

33. Zimbalist, *Unpaid*, 197–202.

34. Dunnavant, *The Fifty-Year Seduction,* 189.

35. Dunnavant, *The Fifty-Year Seduction,* 189.

36. Jay Coakley, *Sports in Society: Issues and Controversies,* 8th ed. (Boston: McGraw-Hill, 2004), 500.

37. Coakley, *Sports in Society*, 9th ed., 344.

BIBLIOGRAPHY

Baker, William J. *Sports in the Western World*. Lanham, Md.: Rowman & Littlefield, 1982.

Bok, Derek. *Universities in the Market Place: The Commercialization of Higher Education*. Princeton, N.J.: Princeton University Press, 2003.

Boone, Louis E., and David L. Kurtz. *Contemporary Business 2006,* 11 ed. Southwestern College Publishers, 2005. Chapter 5. *<http://websites.swlearning.com/ cgi-wadsworth/course_products_wp.pl?fid=M20b&product_isbn_issn =0324320892&discipline_number=407&audience_code=030>* (27 June 2006).

Brand, Myles. "Money Not Corruptive if Actions Uphold Collegiate Mission." *NCAA News Online.* 2004. *<www2.ncaa.org/media_and_events/association_news/ncaa _news_online/2005/04_25_05/editorial/4209n04.html>* (25 April 2005).

The Center on Alcohol Marketing and Youth, "Alcohol Advertising on Sports, Television 2001 and 2002," Georgetown University, 2006, *<http://camy.org/factsheets/ index.php?FactsheetID=20>* (14 June 2006).

Coakley, Jay. *Sports in Society: Issues and Controversies.* 8th ed. Boston: McGraw-Hill, 2004.

———. *Sports in Society: Issues and Controversies,* 9th ed. Boston: McGraw-Hill, 2007.

Duderstadt, James J. *Intercollegiate Intercollegiate Athletics and the American University.* Ann Arbor: University of Michigan Press, 2000.

Dunnavant. Keith. *The Fifty-Year Seduction*. New York: St. Martin's Press, 2004.

Guttmann, Allen. *From Ritual to Record*. New York: Columbia University Press, 1978.

Knight Commission on Intercollegiate Athletics. *A Call to Action: Reconnecting College Sports and Higher Education.* 2001 (Report). *<www.knightcommission.org/ about/reports/category/A%20Call%20to%20Action/>* (5 June 2006).

————. "New Study Debunks Link Between Winning Teams and Financial Benefits." *News.* 7 September 2004. *<www.knightcommission.org/students/item/frank _2004/>* (27 October 2006).

Lapchick, Richard. *Fractured Focus*. Boston: Heath & Co, 1986.

The Lombardi Program on Measuring University Performance. "The Sports Imperative in America's Research Universities." *Annual Report: The Top American Research Universities*, November 2003.

Maske, Mark. "TV Deals Show League's Might." *Washington Post*, 19 April 2005. *<www.washingtonpost.com/wp-dyn/articles/A825-2005Apr19.html>* (14 June, 2006).

Nike. "Company Overview." 2006. *<www.nike.com/nikebiz/nikebiz.jhtml;bsessionid =T1NY1UFGWVXT0CQFTARSF5AKAWMEOIZB?page=3&item=fact>* (14 June 2006).

Padilla, Arthur and David Baumer. "Big-Time College Sports: Management and Economic Issues." *Journal of Sport and Social Issues*, 18, 2 (May 1994), 123–43.

Slaughter, Sheila, and Gary Rhoades. *Academic Capitalism in the New Economy*. Baltimore, MD: The Johns Hopkins University Press, 2004.

Sperber, Murray. *College Sports, Inc.: The Athletic Department vs. The University*. New York: Henry Holt, 1990.

Strenk, Andrew. "Amateurism: The Myth and the Reality." in *The Olympic Games in Transition*, edited by Jeffrey O. Segrave and Donald Chu. Champaign, IL: Human Kinetics Books, 1988.

Symonds, William C. "'March Madness' is Getting Even Crazier." *Business Week,* 2 April 1990, 102.

Thayer, Charles W. "A Question of Soul." *Sports Illustrated*, 15 August 1960, 74.

Voorhis, Scott. "Touter of Sox to Add Teams at BC." *Boston Herald,* 15 February 2005, 29.

Young, David C. "Professionalism in Archaic and Classical Greek Athletics." Pp. 27–35, in *The Olympic Games in Transition*, edited by Jeffrey O. Segrave and Donald Chu. Champaign, IL: Human Kinetics Books, 1988.

Zimbalist, Andrew. *Unpaid Professionals*. Princeton, N.J.: Princeton University Press, 1991.

Chapter Seven

The Spending Nation: Liberal Education and the Privileged Place of Consumption

Juliet B. Schor

"Can the ethical and moral responsibilities demanded by a liberal education be maintained when the society around us is more and more like a mega shopping mall and the production system is based on the repression of basic liberal values?"[1]

Juliet B. Schor, *Spending Nation: Liberal Education and the Privileged Place of Consumption* (2007)

INTRODUCTION: THE UNITED STATES AS MEGAMALL

America has become the world's most prominent consumer nation. Our corporations have expanded throughout the globe, first selling Coca-Cola, KFC, jeans and hip-hop, now adding toothpaste, Windows operating systems, hotel rooms at Hilton, and SUVs. They are bringing U.S.-style marketing, advertising and retailing to countries around the world, setting up big box stores, and making their way into existing retail outlets, with appealing new products hitherto unavailable. The United States has also become a kind of global consumer Mecca itself. Foreigners come in droves for weekend shopping jaunts at our outlet malls. They shop online at retail sites. The great consumer bazaar that is our retail sector has expanded spatially, temporally, and culturally. If the United States stands for anything globally, it is the consumer paradise, with its megamalls, great selection and prices, ubiquitous consumer credit, and carefree attitude to spending.

Of course, the United States is not merely a consumer paradise for others. In recent years the domestic population has accelerated its consumer spending and acquisition, while retaining considerable consumer passion. A wide variety of indicators suggest that consumerism, as an ideology and way of life has intensified in recent years. Last year the fraction of their income that Americans spent surpassed the 100 percent threshold and went into negative numbers, as our national personal savings rate registered at negative .5 percent.[2] The ratio of consumer spending to disposable personal income began rising in the 1980s, when it hovered in the 90 percent area, and has been increasing relentlessly, now exceeding 100 percent.[3]

Other indicators suggest a strong consumer orientation. There are more than 46,000 shopping centers in the country, a nearly two-thirds increase since 1986.[4] Despite fewer people per household, the size of new houses continues to expand rapidly, with new construction featuring walk-in closets and three- and four-car garages, to store record quantities of stuff. According to my estimates, the average adult now acquires more than one new piece of apparel every week. (She's also been discarding clothes at record rates, in comparison to historical precedents.) Americans own more television sets than inhabitants of any other country, nearly one set per person. Observers blame TV for plummeting levels of civic engagement, the dearth of community, and the decline of everyday socializing.[5] Some research has tied television viewing to longer working hours— the United States now leads the industrialized world in average hours worked, another indicator of a lifestyle of getting and spending.

Heavy viewing has also resulted in historically high levels of ad exposure. Ads are now present before, after, and during programming and have moved beyond the television screen, as well, to virtually every social institution and type of public space, from museums and zoos, to elementary school classrooms, restaurant bathrooms and menus, at the airport, even in the sky. (The virtual suggests at least one major exception—religious institutions. Interestingly, however, in the last year, Disney inaugurated the practice of promoting a children's movie, The Chronicles of Narnia, through Christian churches.)

Now what does this have to do with liberal education? A great deal, I believe, and will hope to convince you. The "consumer stance" is in many ways counter-posed to the most deeply held values of the liberalism, and it stands in contrast to cherished ideals and practices in liberal education. I do not offer a full definition of the liberal arts education, but I suspect its outlines are familiar to you. It is centrally about learning how to think, and in particular to think critically, rather than accepting superficial appearances or meanings. It involves a holistic approach to knowledge, across the humanities and sciences. It is a values-driven education, based on liberal ideals of tolerance and diversity, equality of persons, the importance of reasoned argument and discourse, and the duties of citizenry and community in a free and open society. It requires the independence of the university and a climate of openness, engagement, and commitment among faculty and students.

I pose the question of whether the expansion of consumerism, as a way of life, constitutes a threat to liberal education. On the face of this, this may seem an odd question. After all, isn't consumerism merely the logical extension of the liberal paradigm that elevates individual rationality, choice, and freedom? Perhaps. But even on those terms one might wonder if the essence of the contemporary (or in some people's view, postmodern) consumer stance is at odds with the context in which liberal discourse and action must take place, such as full information, deliberate and planning activity, and a community of equals.

As I will argue, there are other aspects of the expansion of consumerism that are troubling for those of us in the sphere of liberal arts. What is the effect of the commercialization of the campus itself? Does our passionate affair with getting and spending jeopardize the nation's urgent need for active and informed citizens? Can the ethical and moral responsibilities demanded by a liberal education be maintained when the society around us is more and more like a mega shopping mall and the production system is based on the repression of basic liberal values? To answer these questions, I turn first to an analysis of trends in contemporary consumer society.

THE PRIVILEGED ROLE OF CONSUMPTION

One of the central features of our economy, society, and culture is what some scholars of consumer society have called the privileged role of consumption in the constitution of individual sovereignty, or to put it in plainer terms, the "I am what I buy" phenomenon. Social analysts are fond of making grand distinctions between different types of societies, and while those distinctions can sometimes be too simplistic, there are important ways in which the West has shifted from a so-called traditional society, in which identity was comprised mostly from statuses tied to birth, religious affiliation, kinship, and various ascriptive characteristics, to a far more open structure in which individuals make of their lives what they will, relatively unconstrained by the accident of birth. While the Uuited States has always been more fluid in this sense than Europe, a transition of this sort has nevertheless occurred here as well. That socio-economic mobility has actually declined in recent decades is not a refutation of this argument, it is merely one of the many paradoxes that abound in consumer society. The individual has more freedom to be who he or she chooses in a cultural sense, at the same time that for many, perhaps the majority, there is less ability to achieve the economic status that will be at his or her disposal to carry out those choices. That is, economic opportunity is declining while cultural opportunity is expanding.

This enhanced freedom to choose one's identity puts far more burden on the individual to define him or herself. As Anthony Giddens has argued, one consequence of this has been a social pressure to live a "reflexive" life, in which the individual is constantly making choices and reflecting on his or her biography, identity, and place in the world. We are not simply who we were born to be, slotted into roles we acquired by the accident of birth.

So how does that reflexive life unfold? For many Americans its organizing principle has become consumption. The market choices we make define the kind of person we are, hope to be, or couldn't be caught dead as; whether it's the type of vehicle we choose to drive, the style of house we live in, the clothes we wear, the brand of the wristwatch, or the size of the diamond. We fret about the material we use for kitchen countertops, the name on the handbag, and of course, the brand of athletic shoe we align with. These decisions matter a lot to us, because each of them is integral to our sense of who we are. This process is far beyond the characters so wittily described by Thorstein Veblen one hundred years ago, whose counterparts today are those slaves of fashion devoted to Marc Jacobs handbags or Jimmy Choo shoes. Old-fashioned status seeking is still with us, as the booming market in luxury products makes clear. But the point I am making is that this process goes far beyond conspicuous consumption as it has been understood. It is much more comprehensive, encompassing a wide range of consumer styles. Whoever we are, our consumer choices have become central to the constitution of self. The super-rationalist consumer toting a copy of *Consumer Reports* in order to maximize the value to price ratio on whatever he buys and the soccer mom in a stylish sweatsuit and a minivan drinking that smoothie Dunkin Donuts is trying so hard to sell her are both constituted as selves through their consumer practices. Even those of us who are staunch critics of consumer society have a set of product choices which define us—I suppose this is the point at which I need to reveal that I'm in the Patagonia (organic cotton, no advertising, profits to environmental groups), Toyota Prius, Adbusters magazine, no sweat clothes, groceries from Whole Foods market niche. We tend to think of these descriptors as "clichés" or "stereotypes," precisely because they are real substantive constellations—consistent brands and product choices that reflect particular values, symbolic constructions, and social communications.

The process of constituting identity through products and brands now begins almost at birth. As I detailed in my last book, *Born to Buy*, children have become highly profitable targets for marketers and advertisers, one of the fastest growing consumer segments in the marketplace. They are exposed to unprecedented amounts of advertising, and ads have moved far beyond the television screen, into their schools, playgrounds, even friends' homes, in a technique called peer-to-peer marketing, which is one of the hottest trends in the industry. As a result of newfound spending power, and attention from marketers, children interact with and define themselves with brands earlier, more powerfully, and more consistently than ever before. A recent article in the *New York Times* on the growth of fashion consciousness among pretweens detailed the extent to which these changes have insinuated themselves in childhood, with its profile of third grader Maisy Gellert ("I'm very particular. Sevens are the only jeans I actually wear.")

One consequence of the commercialization of childhood is that even early elementary schoolers are exquisitely attuned to what is cool, the relation between social acceptance and consumer possessions or style, and the market's definition of acceptable and unacceptable practices. By the time they arrive at the college gates, they have more than a decade and a half in consumer training. And as we are more and more painfully aware, the college admissions process has become the biggest of all consumer decisions.

More generally, the importance of consumption in the construction of identity is reflected in the growing power of brands. Despite the availability of enormous amounts of free information about products, as well as consumers' ability to avoid ads through technologies such as TIVO, actual spending patterns reveal an almost astounding willingness to pay hefty price premia for otherwise indistinguishable products in many categories. Indeed, industry estimates of "brand value" continue to rise. So, too, do outlays for advertising and marketing, activities that attach symbolic meaning to goods, as well as the number of products that are branded. The rise of luxury markets, which are characterized by extremely high status or brand premia, and the parallel growth of markets for counterfeit items are also indicators of high and growing symbolic content. Interestingly, arguments which see consumption primarily in utilitarian or practical terms, would have predicted just the opposite, as the internet dramatically reduced informational costs, made price comparisons widely available with almost no costs to the consumer, delivering near-textbook conditions of free information and retail competition. The staying power of brands, while it may seem paradoxical from a pragmatic orientation, is testament to the fact that consumption is deeply symbolic and tied to people's sense of meaning, identity, and place in a social order. Brands are essential because without them one's identity and place in the system is not adequately represented.

But perhaps you are wondering why individuals aren't more defined by other factors, such as personality traits? Or the set of values they believe in? Or their political preferences? Of course, each of these do play a role in identity formation—and they can be connected to consumer choices. In the last presidential election, one of the innovations of the Republican National Committee was to use a major market research database to identify likely

Republican voters by their brand and product choices. But I argue that consumption has become the core of these identities.

First, consumption has assumed a privileged status in our society. As the twentieth century progressed, spending came to be linked with nationalism, the health of the economy, our notions of a well-functioning democracy, and other aspects of society in both an ideological embrace and in practical, structural connections. After 1980, a celebratory rhetoric of spending, and especially luxury spending, became even more common, and the nation's faith in itself grew more closely connected to an abundance of products. In the 1990s, optimism about new technologies was closely connected to their uses for consumers, and cheap imports began to flood the country. As American lifestyles grew ever more dependent on imported oil, our leaders asserted that the American way of life is not up for negotiation and foreign policy grew increasingly tied to ensuring access to a steady supply of imported fossil fuels. In the days after September 11, 2001, George W. Bush's now-famous dictate to show patriotism by getting back to the malls and shopping was troublesome to many, but was perhaps most notable for how little "official" complaint it drew.

Second, the privileging of the status of consumer became a pillar of state and corporate policy, as the model of the consumer came to dominate in a wide range of institutions outside the retail sphere. Margaret Thatcher is best known for turning citizens into "consumers," but right-wing critics of the state pushed the model in the United States as well. Under the rhetoric of bringing much-needed accountability and responsiveness to state bureaucracies, governments began calling their citizens consumers. Similar rhetorical and conceptual changes swept over health care, education, and other social services. Whether the linguistic change led to changes in the real sovereignty of citizens, is another question. This has also been a period in which corporate and private elites enriched themselves at the expense of ordinary citizens as well as the state bureaucracy.

Now what have been the consequences of this privileging of consumption? In the macro sense, one effect has been a kind of spending imperative. The economy came more and more to depend on steady increases in consumer spending, not merely for particular periods, but as a permanent feature. Investment spending by firms, expenditures of government, and exports (the three alternative options as "drivers" of economic activity) took on less importance, as the "heroic" consumer, time and time again seemed to step up to the plate when the economy looked like it might be slowing down, or slumping. Steady expansion in consumer credit, whether on plastic, or through home equity financing, enabled the spending to continue, even if income wasn't keeping pace. The possibility of an economy driven by principles other than an almost slavish devotion to more and better, came to be seen as impractical, idealistic, or dangerous, even as many felt uneasy about rising debt, the disappearance of frugality, and the "buy now pay later" mentality. The simultaneous appearance of structural deficits in the government account, the trade balance (exports versus imports), and household finances have led, not to pressure for reform, but to the sense that even more consumer spending is required to keep the system afloat, and to avert the catastrophe which would result if consumers pulled in their purse strings. There's a sense in which consuming, at least in aggregate terms, has shifted from the realm of choice and freedom to that of imperative. Structurally, at least, the possibility of choosing "not to consume" has become less feasible, at least without major structural change.

And what of the micro? Earlier in this chapter, I argued that everyone has gotten caught up in the practice of constituting identity through consumption, whether they like it or not. That even consumer critics, who prefer a stance of "anti" are neatly bundled and packaged into a trendy, no logo brand. For the wholesome do-gooder types, the choices are fair trade coffee and Guatemalan handicraft purses, the more rebellious may go for Che Guevara beer and anarchistically fashionable black. But whatever the particulars, the conceptual point is the inability of any of us to opt out of the consumption matrix. It is comprehensive, in that no product choices or lifestyles, are beyond the grid. Even those that begin there are quickly, and amazingly quickly these days, brought into it, repackaged and "sold" back. Adbusters has become a "brand." Voluntary simplicity is a brand, with "Real Simple" magazine, catalogs like Harmony, market research about the so-called LOHAS demographic — LOHAS meaning Lifestyles of Health and Sustainability. Even the Compact, which started as a group of friends on the west coast who decided to distance themselves from the consumer culture by not buying anything but food and basics for a year, has become a phenomenon with articles about them and their own yahoo group and web site.

This insight is in some ways radically different from the critiques of corporate influence on consumer desire that were so popular in the 1950s and 1960s, such as those of Ken Galbraith, David Potter, Vance Packard, Betty Friedan, and Herbert Marcuse. Those critics, influenced by the Frankfort School and Marxism, objected to the ability of advertisers and marketers to *make* people want things they would not otherwise, or at the very least to want the particular brands of things that advertisers were selling. Whatever the merits of the argument at that time, and I believe it was a view with a fair amount of validity, the situation today is dramatically different. Advertising is no longer necessary to ensure consumer demand. Need as a concept has become isomorphic with want, or desire. The idea, common fifty years ago, that consumer wants were limited, now appears quaint. We seem to have no trouble constantly coming up with new things we want or even must have. The neoclassical assumption of infinite consumer wants seems almost eerily true. In recent years, the canonical consumer story was more likely to be the woman trampled to death by a horde of Wal-Mart consumers rushing in to buy bargain-priced DVD players when the big box opened on Black Friday than the earlier twentieth century fear of goods sitting unsold in the stores.

In an important sense, this (by which I mean insatiable desire, not the unfortunate trampling incident) is what we would expect in a culture where consuming constructs identity. To stop buying is to stop creating oneself—it implies a condition of personal stagnation, a kind of cultural or social death. Ours is a dynamic culture in which consuming yields meaning and status, and spending is the system's answer to problems. This is true even of problems of overconsumption—eaten too much? Buy a diet pill or an exercise bike or weight loss club membership. Bought too many clothes? Order a closet organizer system, or a book on simplifying to teach you how to throw them out. House too full of things you don't use? Purchase a pod for the back yard to put them in.

This is also why consumption has become so naturalized—why consumer desire seems innate, taken-for-granted, and inevitable. Human needs for identity, meaning, and status *are* deeply ingrained in us, perhaps "natural," and consumption has become the way we meet those needs.

LIBERAL EDUCATION AND CONSUMPTION

So far I have argued that we have become a thoroughly consumer-oriented culture and society, in which consuming is the structurally privileged form of behavior and being. What are the consequences of these developments for the viability of liberal arts education? The most direct, and perhaps obvious is the commercialization of higher education itself, from student life to the classroom.

One major dimension of this change is the rise of a consumer choice model of course selection, complete with a "shopping period" in which students sample, accept and reject the "product" on offer. The earlier paternalistic model in which faculty decided what was best for students to study has been eclipsed by a system in which required courses are far less common, and students are more or less free to choose to study what they want. Given what I have argued above, we should not be surprised at this development. America's youth have been given product choice about virtually all aspects of their daily lives. As early as pre-school they are taught to "choose." Summer camps offer a menu of activities. High schools have wide curricular options.

This shift to a market model has virtues and vices—it ferrets out faculty who do not keep up with developments in their fields, or who are poor teachers, but it can also create a race to the bottom in terms of workload and expectations.

The commercialization of the campus has other dimensions. One is the growth of corporate influence in the setting of research agendas, outcomes and curricula. While the former is most pronounced in the sciences, the process has infiltrated colleges and universities more generally. At my former university, Harvard, many of my colleagues in the department of economics sat on corporate boards as directors. They take significant sums from corporations, as the roster of academics who accepted big payouts from Enron revealed. Outside of Harvard, they sit in corporate chairs, such as the KMart Corporate Chair of Marketing at Wayne State University or the Mitsubishi Professor of Economics at MIT. The impact of these developments on the content of curricula is a topic that has not yet been explored by researchers. However, the corrupting influence of money is a well known problem. Are reading lists less likely to present anti-corporate views when faculty salaries come from corporate coffers? Will students be wary of expressing criticism of the company when they're sitting in a classroom paid for by it?

Another development is the growth of on-campus shopping. In earlier decades, campuses, particularly liberal arts institutions, or campuses located in suburban or small town settings, tended to be isolated from retail shops and commercial enterprises. Meals were paid for with a lump sum and there was little retailing beyond the college bookstore. Today, campuses are much more likely to provide a variety of shopping opportunities, fast food outlets, and other dining options. Commercial advertising is now much more common on campuses. Credit card companies solicit customers in the student union.

Commercial isolation was not only an accidental feature of college life in earlier years. It was also part of an educational vision that held that separation or isolation from ordinary life conditions was beneficial for cultivating a contemplative space and a community of scholars. The campus as a haven idea incorporated the idea of a respite from commercialism. But in contemporary consumer culture, the willingness and/or ability to go for extended periods of time without shopping or purchasing is becoming rarer. And in any case, with the rise of Internet shopping, college administrators can't isolate students from retail opportunities even if they want to—except perhaps by keeping UPS trucks outside the campus gates.

These developments have been joined by widespread upscaling in facilities and dorm rooms, on the grounds that students demand more elaborate and luxurious sleeping quarters, athletic facilities and the like. While a certain amount of facilities upgrading is obviously necessary, it has yielded an intercollegiate arms race that drains scarce resources, creates the conditions for more pursuit of corporate monies and undermines institutional independence. It also heightens pressure to raise tuitions, which in turn undermines socioeconomic diversity, forces students to spend more hours working, and leaves them deeper in debt.

The mallification of the campus also means that we are missing out on an enormous opportunity to teach a vital life lesson. As a now very large literature in social psychology on the relationship between human well-being and material values suggests, individuals who are more concerned with money, things, appearances, and status, are less well-off. They are more inclined to depression and anxiety, less able to live vital and fulfilling lives, have more psychosomatic ailments, and have poorer social relations. My own research on children found that those who became more involved with consumer culture were much more likely to develop depression and anxiety, low self-esteem, boredom, and psychosomatic complaints such as headaches and stomachaches. Although all the causes are not yet well understood, it seems that they include the tendency of consumer culture to perpetuate dissatisfaction, the substitution of highly satisfying activities for less satisfying ones (e.g., television watching supplants outdoor socializing), and the precariousness of constructing identities based on money and goods.

And yet, despite this growing body of evidence that high involvement in consumer culture is not conducive to human well-being, the population, and young people especially are growing ever more enmeshed in the culture of getting and spending. Perhaps colleges and universities could combat this trend, and provide an antidote to the saturated consumer world students have grown up in, rather than assimilating to it. College occurs at an important transitional period in students' lives. And as institutions, they remain relatively independent and self-determining. Indeed, if liberal arts institutions took up this challenge seriously, they could become real leaders in a vital social transformation. In the end, the lasting contributions and satisfactions of college life come from social connections made, with peers and faculty, and the power of the ideas encountered, rather than the opulence of the gymnasium or the selection of merchandise in the bookstore.

DENIAL AND THE CONSUMER CULTURE

Let me turn now to the indirect effects of consumerism on university life. There are core aspects of the operation of our consumer economy and culture that I believe are antithetical to the basic values of a liberal arts education. I will confine my argument to the way in which the consumer culture promotes denial. However, I do want to signal one other effect, however, which is the impact of consumerism on the political process—as elections get more like a choice between similar brands, a Coke vs. Pepsi process, and as young people are heavily disaffected from politics, we must ask whether the commercialization of society is part of why this is happening.

The now-substantial literature that attempts to analyze modern and postmodern consumption has failed to produce a consensus model of the consumer. Is she an informed, rational, deliberate and conscientious actor, which is the model of economics and political science? Does she know her interests and act on them? Or is she impulsive, unconcerned about consequences? Status oriented? Practical and utilitarian? Does she maximize value relative to price? Does she even care about price? Do the answers to these questions vary based on the particular good or service being purchased? Stage of life? Time of day?

Of course, every conceivable type of consumer is represented in the marketplace, and the attempt to produce general models can do no more than identify the dominant model or models. But I would argue that the rational, fully-informed maximizer of neoclassical economic and liberal political theory is no longer the dominant consumer type, if it ever was. The evidence for such a model is stronger in the nineteenth century, when those theories were being developed, and poor consumer decisions might mean life or death for a family. The emergence of a mass consumer culture in the twentieth century occurred in part because consumers became less deliberate and "rational," and were more likely to approach the marketplace with passion, impulse, fantasy, and abandon. In this regard, the consumer researcher would do better to read Sigmund Freud, than Adam Smith, a point well understood by marketers themselves (if not by economists).

As an example, consider impulse buying. Researcher Dennis Rook has found that impulse purchasing, which comprises a significant, although hard to quantify, portion of total consumer spending, often occurs because of an almost magnetic feeling between the buyer and the object, of coming under the sway of an item, and feeling powerless to resist it. Similarly, many of the most successful consumer goods and experiences are about suspending belief, entering a fantasy world, or becoming enchanted, as a now growing literature explores. A trip to Vegas, or Disneyworld, or even a themed mall or restaurant is as much about not thinking about what's behind the curtain as it is experiencing the show. In my studies of status consumption I found a related dynamic. Individuals were reluctant to admit, indeed they were almost adamantly unwilling to acknowledge the extent to which their purchasing is driven by the desire to keep up with the Joneses, or better them. And yet some of their brand buying behavior, and the statistical models I developed, show that keeping up and purchasing valued brands is widespread. It's far easier to believe that one wants the big house in the fancy suburb because the "schools are good," than because of its social meaning. Or that the purchase of the SUV is to keep the kids "safe" rather than because everyone else is upgrading. Similarly, research on consumer debt finds that Americans are unable to come to terms with how much in debt they actually are—surveys which ask people how much debt they have find that consumers underestimate it by half. Throughout these examples, the less one knows, or admits, the better, as exposure, calculation and true information only serve to dampen consumer desire.

The widespread stance of "consumer's denial" has even more serious repercussions. One is the generally passive acceptance by consumers of an ongoing shift to exploitative labor conditions in offshore factories. As factories moved abroad, and companies distanced themselves from production conditions through subcontracting relationships, consumer goods have increasingly been produced in sweatshops, with repressive working conditions and below subsistence wages. The rise of sweated labor is most extreme in apparel, but has also been documented in footwear, toys, and a variety of other products. This global separation of production and consumption, is itself a kind of spatial denial, because consumers are so disconnected from the conditions of production. Companies have gone to great lengths to conceal the locations of their factories and what is going on inside them. Indeed, there are powerful forces that benefit from the system, and which operate to keep consumers ignorant, whether it's the corporate contributions to affect government policies on labeling, product safety, and labor unions, or the neoliberal discourse which insists that there is no alternative to the current global economy.

And for the most part consumers have acquiesced, averting their eyes and snapping up the extraordinarily cheap products made possible by this widespread abuse. Apparel is again the canonical case. Consumers don't like the idea that their clothes are made in sweatshops. They wish the companies would improve their policies, raise wages, and guarantee a decent working environment. Survey data shows this, and indeed indicates they'd be willing to pay more to ensure the workers are paid reasonably. But it's easy to do nothing, shrug one's shoulders, and keep on shopping. Indeed, the continuing decline in the price of apparel has led, not to a rejection of the low wages that make possible the low prices, but to record rates of apparel purchasing—the fifty-three garments per year I noted at the beginning of this chapter. It has also led to record rates of garment discard, which unpublished research I've done with Kristen Drummey shows is predicted by cheap imports. The enthusiastic consumer embrace of cheap manufactures that has characterized the last ten years is notable for the pervasive denial of the economic injustice that has made it possible.

My point about liberal education is of course obvious, and I need not belabor it. At the core of a liberal education is the imperative to be critical and to unmask superficial, but deceptive appearances. The posture of consumer denial is thus its antithesis. It allows the individual to yield to impulses without questioning their origins, meanings or consequences. It accepts the public relations spin of a Nike or a Wal-Mart, that their factories are in compliance with a labor code when they're not. It lets the consumer go on buying, without coming to terms with the how, why, when, what, and where of the consumer system. It's not a posture we are comfortable with in the classroom. But when the consumer model is the privileged one, how can we keep it out?

Denial is also central to the biggest consumer challenge of our time—the contribution of our consumption to global warming. If, as I argue, we are unwilling to confront the consequences of our lifestyles, this failure is most profound when it comes to environmental impacts. While consumers evince a concerned attitude about the natural environment, and happily recycle in order to do their part, they remain generally ignorant and incurious about the gross unsustainability of American lifestyles. Six or seven years ago, my organization, the Center for a New American Dream, gathered sympathetic individuals (subscribers to *Utne Reader*, and other generally progressive publications) to talk about our mission and message. We gave the participants a picture of the many shopping bags of natural resources that comprise the 123 pounds that every day go into producing the U.S. standard of living to gauge how a straightforward environmental impacts message would go over.[5] The participants reacted strongly—this can't be right they said. Absolutely not. They responded with skepticism about our organization. Is it a cult? Why would you produce this disinformation?

The release of Al Gore's movie, *Hurricane Katrina*, and the hot summer seem to have had a significant impact on the public's willingness to accept the reality of global warming, and the connection to the way we live. Perhaps we've reaching what is faddishly referred to as a "tipping point." I certainly hope so. But even if we have, the larger task of transforming the way we consume to make it sustainable with respect not only to climate change, but also biodiversity, water sufficiency, ocean and forest ecosystems, toxic substances, and human well-being requires a profound alteration in our attitude to consumption and lifestyle. Not only will we have to give up on denial, but we'll also have to let go of core tenets of consumer society, such as new and improved, more is always better, you can never have enough, and finally, you are who you buy. If we could teach our students that, perhaps we would have fulfilled the lofty goals of liberal education.

NOTES

1. Juliet B. Schor, "Spending Nation: Liberal Education and the Privileged Place of Consumption," in *Higher Education: Open for Business*, ed. Christian Gilde (Lanham, MD: Lexington Books, 2007).

2. *Economic Report of the President* (Washington, D.C.: GPO, 2006), 318, Table B-30.

3. *Economic Report*, Ch 3.

4. Data on Shopping Centers from 2002 NRB Shopping Center Census. *The National Research Bureau Shopping Center Database and Statistical Model*, 2002, Table 1, 17 Year Trends, <*www.nrbonline.com*> (28 September 2006).

5. Robert Putman, *Bowling Alone: The Collapse and Revival of American Community* (New York: Simon & Schuster, 2000). (On the decline of community and its connection to television viewing.)

"The Information Age," *Data from World Bank*, 2000, Table 5.10, <*www.worldbank.org/data/databytopic/itc.html#ti*> (28 September 2006). ("Television ownership in the United States stood at 854 per 1,000 people in 2002.")

6. Iddo K.Wernick, "Consuming Materials: The American Way," in *Environmentally Significant Consumption,* ed. Paul Stern et al, (Washington, D.C.: National Academy Press, 1997), 29–39.

BIBLIOGRAPHY

Economic Report of the President. Washington, D.C.: GPO, 2006.

"The Information Age." *Data from World Bank*, 2000. Table 5.10. <*www.world bank.org/data/databytopic/itc.html#ti*> (28 September 2006).

NRB Shopping Center Census. The National Research Bureau Shopping Center Database and Statistical Model, 2002. <*www.nrbonline.com*> (28 September 2006).

Putman, Robert. *Bowling Alone: The Collapse and Revival of American Community.* New York: Simon & Schuster, 2000.

Schor, Juliet B. "Spending Nation: Liberal Education and the Privileged Place of Consumption." in *Higher Education: Open for Business*, ed. Christian Gilde. Lanham, MD: Lexington Books, 2007.

Wernick, Iddo K. "Consuming Materials: The American Way." Pp. 29–39 in *Environmentally Significant Consumption,* edited Paul Stern et al. Washington, D.C.: National Academy Press, 1997.

Chapter Eight

Profits, Politics, and Social Justice in the Contemporary American University

Eve Spangler

". . . the word 'education' has an evil sound in politics; there is a pretense of education, when the real purpose is coercion without the use of force."[1]

Hannah Arendt, *Between Past and Future* (1961)

INTRODUCTION

For purposes of this book, overcommercialization is defined as the processes through which, and the state in which, commercial interests supercede intellectual ones in ordering the affairs of the university. There can be many components to overcommercialization. Some are more distasteful than disastrous—for example, the intrusive billboards full of corporate logos now lining university stadia, visible in the background of every athletic play by university teams. Others come closer to changing the university as a whole for the worse, compromising its core research and teaching functions. Examples of this latter, more catastrophic, form of overcommercialization include the refusal to hire faculty unacceptable to corporate sponsors or the dismissal of faculty whose research has led them into conflict with donors or sponsors; the development of curriculum blindly supportive of market forces or reflexively hostile to social justice challenges to "business as usual;" the privileging of programs that promise short-term product development or other market boon over equally intellectually challenging programs with less immediate commercial potential. In short, the most egregious forms of commercialization threaten to change the conditions under which new knowledge is produced.[2]

In the chapter that follows, I argue that not only commercial but also political pressures threaten the relative autonomy of the university. Although conceptually distinct, the forces that historian Beshara Doumani calls "anti-liberal coercions and neoliberal privatization" are always and everywhere intertwined in shaping the integrity (or lack thereof) of the academic process.[3] I will review examples from recent years of such entwined economic and political pressures, with an emphasis on cases that range from well-known fields like Middle Eastern studies to the less well known areas of environmental and occupational health.

On the other hand, however, I will argue that, despite forces pushing for political and economic conformity, a host of new initiatives are available to American universities; initiatives which, if they do not definitively rebuff the forces clamoring for marketization, nevertheless present new directions for responsible university behavior and potential alliances with grassroots communities and projects around the world. I will frequently refer to my own Jesuit and Catholic university as an example of an institution which is experimenting with the new forms of socially responsible behavior—in part, perhaps, because their religious affiliation inspires them to maintain doctrinally-based commitments to religious discernment and social justice. Nevertheless, and in spite of some successes, new projects embodying the commitment to social justice often are met with caution and even trepidation.

Certainly, most up-and-coming private universities face many of the same dilemmas. Tuition (including room and board) is expensive at any of "the new ivies" (upwards of $40,000 per year at this writing). At the same time, however, such institutions are committed to raising their positions in the competitive rankings of American colleges and universities, meaning that they also strive to be ever more selective in admitting undergraduate and graduate students—thus limiting themselves to a small percentage (roughly the top 10 percent) of the applicant pool. The convergence of bottomless financial need with a highly selective admissions policy raises the economic pressure on such universities and this pressure, in turn, has expressed itself in ways both subtle and obvious. Among the obvious is the commercialization of sport discussed elsewhere in this volume. Increasingly common, too, is the demand that auxiliary support services around the university be run on a revenue-generating basis: these demands are now being placed on university parking facilities, university dining halls, the university bookstore and copying services.

More subtle examples include the development of research institutes—new academic units within the university that exist only on a "soft" money basis. Unlike academic departments, institutes do not have regular line item status in the university budget and exist only by raising enough money to cover their own operating costs (i.e., by being "revenue neutral" within the university) and even generating financial as well as reputational returns to the university. In short, the research institute is only as good as its most recent grants, and can be phased out when the topic, which is its particular focus, no longer attracts extramural support. Many people regard the proliferation of "soft money" institutes, projects, and centers as examples of flexible, adaptable and responsive programming. But, in certain instances, more dubious forces may also be at work: as when even the most successful researchers are kept in this irregular relationship to the university in part because of the potential of even highly regarded (and rewarded) research to challenge the behavior of corporations. So, for example, human genome research—worthy in its own right on intellectual grounds—may be systematically preferred to environmental research, even when the latter is also highly successful in attracting grants and favorable peer review, but is nevertheless shadowed by the image of green politics as the enemy of corporate prerogative.

HISTORIC CONTEXT

The current pressures for overcommercializaton in the university need to be understood not only in their immediacy, but also in historic context. It would be a mistake to suppose that there was ever a "golden age" in the American academy when people were wholly, or even largely, dedicated to learning for the sake of learning, without regard to pragmatic outcomes. There was no such golden age. Americans have always been intensely pragmatic and have expected schools at every level to produce economically useful outcomes by fairly direct and discernible pathways. Debates about the role of schooling, while numerous, do not differ on this point. Indeed, they limit themselves to claims and counterclaims about relative economic efficacy. Thus, for example, the debate about classroom, theory-driven pedagogies (often called liberal arts) vs. "learning by doing"(often called vocational education) is largely a debate about which system produces people better prepared for real-world tasks.

In the realm of higher education, the marriage of educational growth to vocational outcomes dates to the earliest moments of American educational history. Colleges founded in the colonial era, such as Harvard and Yale, were designed, among other purposes, to produce ministers for the community. In the public sector, utilitarianism is even more pronounced. The Morrill Land Grant Act of 1862 provided the original impetus for the founding of state colleges and universities. Calculations of economic efficacy were entirely predominant, and most of today's state institutions of higher education began life as agricultural or engineering colleges (for men), sometimes with additional military training, and as "normal schools" or teacher-training institutions for women. Thus from their earliest inception, American institutions of higher learning were handmaidens to the American marketplace.

However, it was worth noting that the Morrill Land Grant Act, passed during the Civil War, also had political purposes: penalizing states attempting to secede from the union by withholding the benefits of the Act from them, and incentivizing undecided states to stay within the Union. An 1890 amendment to this Act subsequently required the states of the former confederacy to eschew racial criteria in admissions to their public universities or to dedicate part of their resources to creating land grant institutions for persons of color—the point of origin of many of today's "historically black universities."[4]

If one is to seek a historic buffer between institutions of higher education and market forces, the history of higher education points in another direction entirely—namely that the presumed universal importance of education for all economic and social aspirations is a fairly new phenomenon. Only recently has education come to be seen as a solution to all social ills—low productivity, joblessness, drug addiction, out-of-wedlock pregnancy, low voter turnout, etc. From the vantage point of the early twenty-first century, it is hard to recall that only one hundred years ago, few people in America were literate. As recently as 1940, only about one sixth of the college-aged population typically went to college and those enrollments were heavily skewed toward wealthier families.[5] College attendance, begun as the preserve of younger sons destined for jobs in the clergy and for those embarking on careers in education, became a vocational necessity for many people only in the years following World War II. If corporations maintained a relatively "hands off" attitude toward institutions of higher education, it was because they did not think universities were a strategic high ground they needed to control. Until the last fifty years, most people went directly from secondary school, which they attended only briefly, to work, and most research relevant to corporate interests was done directly in-house.

Over the course of the twentieth century, however, and especially in the latter half of the century following World War II, college enrollments grew both in number and in the inclusiveness of the experience: ethnic and racial minorities began enrolling in large numbers, as did women. Poor people were still underrepresented on college campuses but they, too, enrolled in ever-increasing numbers. As before, the increased enrollments immediately following World War II were driven as much by labor market dynamics shaped, in turn, by political calculations, as by a disinterested and highminded hunger for learning for its own sake. A key source of increased college enrollments following World War II was the GI Bill of Rights that financed college attendance for war veterans with a mix of low interest loans and outright grants. This landmark bill was itself the product of mixed intentions—partly a reward for service to the nation during a time of war, and partly an anti-inflationary device that staggered labor market reentry for masses of recently demobilized troops.

As an ever-increasing percentage of the labor force—and the best-educated percentage—flowed through universities, the corporate sector developed a greater stake in the university. The corporate interest in American higher education is multi-faceted and includes at least the following objectives: securing a highly educated labor force without shouldering the expense of training, promoting product development (and the basic science undergirding product development) in university laboratories, and ensuring political legitimacy for the notion of equal opportunity and the prevailing capitalist order—again, a mix of economic and political agendas.

If it is true that corporate America seeks to use the university for its own purposes and federal and state governments for theirs, it is also true that American universities have made strenuous attempts to protect their autonomy. While always seeking corporate and state support, universities also seek to establish fiscal autonomy and self-sufficiency, soliciting unencumbered alumni contributions, foundation support for educationally innovative programs, pushing tuition fees as high as market forces allow, and pressing auxiliary university functions to become revenue-generating.

Equally important, however, universities have taken steps to insure the academic integrity of their professors' work—insisting that hiring and promotion include an external peer-review component, and providing the considerable (but not absolute) protection of tenure that allows professors to speak truth to corporate and state power. From it's inception, tenure was the most powerful institutional mechanism dedicated to the protection of academic freedom, buffering faculty not only from the demands of the market but also from the demands of the state. In fact, tenure as a means for securing academic freedom was, in its origins, far more concerned with shielding professors from political than from market pressures, and for good reasons, as we shall see below. But, as a matter of historical perspective, it is worth noting here, that tenure has antecedents that go all the way back to guild privileges in the middle ages, when the guilds' ambition was to set terms of employment, definitions of duties and obligations, for their members vis-à-vis employers and sponsors. In short, tenure within the guild system was to provide protection from economic as well as political pressures.[6]

CURRENT ISSUES

The recitation of historical trends is of more than antiquarian interest. The struggle for university autonomy in the face of economic and political pressure continues to be an active struggle—so much so, that perhaps the title of this volume ought to refer to both the overcommercialization and the overpoliticization of the university. Consider the following examples, currently in play as this chapter is being written, bringing pressure on social scientists and the university that employ them, to inhibit the expression of unpopular views:

- In the realm of pressure brought to bear on universities by private, politically motivated groups to alter or suppress research efforts, consider the vitriolic reaction visited on public policy experts John J. Mearsheimer and Stephen M. Walt, for their literature review/think piece calling attention to the Israel lobby's impact on American foreign policy. Also under attack was the Harvard University Kennedy School of Government, which initially posted the Mearsheimer and Walt piece in the "working paper" series of the school. Following heavy lobbying pressure, the Kennedy School of Government created an unprecedented opportunity for the rebuttal of a working paper. Professor Alan Dershowitz contributed a lengthy denunciation of Mearsheimer and Walt.[7] The mobilization of the American Jewish community to suppress scholarship critical of Israel indeed appears to have been reanimated by the Mearsheimer and Walt controversy, so that the Polish Embassy in New York has cancelled a talk by New York University historian Professor Tony Judt (a member of the Jewish community) about the impact of AIPAC on American foreign policy discourse,[8] and, similarly, the French Embassy cancelled a talk by British author Carmen Callil, who, in a postscript to a book on French collaborators in Vichy, also criticized contemporary Israeli policies in the Occupied Territories.[9]
- Similarly, the University of California Press was pressured to withdraw the publication of a controversial book by Professor Norman Finkelstein: *Beyond Chutzpah: On the Misuse of Anti-Semitism and the Abuse of History.* Threats of a lawsuit from the ubiquitous Professor Dershowitz in fact caused delays during which the University of California Press safeguarded their interests by moving the most controversial issues in the book to an appendix.[10]
- In a most unsettling anthology of studies, Beshara Domani documents a number of incidents of political pressure against scholars and their universities, primarily in the field of Middle Eastern Studies since September 11, 2001. Even more ominously, however, he also shows how many right wing groups are making a concerted effort to challenge the broad standard of academic freedom itself, often under the utterly disingenuous rhetoric of introducing "balance" into the curriculum.[11]

Nor is politically motivated pressure limited to the social science and policy fields. The sciences are also subjected to political pressure and the manipulation of funding. Perhaps the most prominent recent controversies have concerned the Bush administrations dismissal of research on global warming and their reluctance to fund medical research using stem cells.[12]

In a similarly egregious, though perhaps less well-known manner, environmental and occupational health sciences have been fighting an exhausting battle against "junk science." A 2005 special issue of the *International Journal of Occupational and Environmental Health* has documented numerous instances of corporate corruption of science:

- Peter F. Infante reviews the evidence and finds that the chemical industry and its hired scientists have been influential in persuading the International Agency for Research on Cancer, the Scientific Advisory Board of the Environmental Protection Agency and the Occupational Safety and Health Administration in downgrading their evaluation of 1,3-butadiene from the more restrictive finding that this chemical is a human carcinogen to the more permissive finding that it is a probable human carcinogen.[13] Jennifer Sass concurs that industry has succeeded in "negotiating away science" in the government regulatory process in the case of 1,3-butadiene.[14]
- Phyllis J. Mullenix documents a consistent industry pattern in minimizing injury and illness reports among workers exposed to gaseous and particulate fluorides and fluorine. "Selective editing and data omissions allowed bias," she reports, citing also the suppression of industry funded laboratory studies that revealed the harmful impact of these chemical on human lungs.[15]
- William Kovarik reviews the controversy about leaded gasoline. He traces a fifty-year history by the automobile and gasoline industries of financing industry-controlled junk science to counter the growing evidence of the adverse health effects of leaded gasoline.[16]

Nor is the damage documented in studies like those cited above the full extent of the difficulty. In fact, tampering with specific data in single studies is just the tip of the iceberg. Of more systemic import is industry support for inherently flawed epidemiological studies, "designed" to show that various suspicious substances have no adverse health effects on workers and consumers.[17] A key predictor of corrupt science is industry funding for the research which purports to evaluate health hazards.[18] Moreover, industry funds shape not only research studies, but also can create advocacy organizations, influence professional organizations, and fund health charities who parrot the industry line.[19] The pattern of suppressing evidence extends also to attempts at intimidating university presses—for example, the seemingly luckless University of California Press faced the combined legal efforts of

Dow Chemicals, Monsanto, Goodrich, Goodyear, and Union Carbide to intimidate the reviewers who had recommended the publication of Gerald Markowitz and David Rosner's *Deceit and Denial: The Deadly Politics of Industrial Pollution.*[20]

Perhaps the best-known, most media-genic case of industry interference with scientific research in occupational health is the case of Dr. David Kern, an occupational medicine specialist, formerly on the faculty of Brown University's School of Medicine. At stake in this well-known case is the completion of the whole cycle of research from discovery to the dissemination of knowledge about hazards to the general public. In 1997, Dr. Kern, an occupational medicine specialist, was called in by a local manufacturer to investigate the appearance of a rare lung disease among its workers. He subsequently found nine cases of "flock lung disease" directly attributable to substances in the workplace. In 1998, OSHA concurred with his findings, faulting the manufacturer on workplace safety. When Kern reported his findings at a public presentation, he was fired by the Brown University-affiliated Memorial Hospital of Pawtucket, which also closed down the only occupational medicine clinic in the state of Rhode Island. Brown University failed to support its professor and concurred with the decision of the affiliated hospital to terminate his contract. Widespread adverse publicity failed to reverse this decision.[21] Incidents such as these make it very difficult for professors to function as public intellectuals—to move from enjoying academic freedom to using it for public purposes.[22]

Taken together, the foregoing vignettes suggest that threats to the university's autonomy exist on a number of fronts, with economic and political demands combining, and ensuring that university autonomy is likely to remain precarious at least for the duration of the "war on terror" if not longer.

In addition to external threats, bureaucratic considerations internal to the life of the university, also contribute to making academic institutions particularly vulnerable to economic and political pressure in the present moment. For example, rising energy costs impinge on all institutions and challenge the financial well-being of private universities who rely on tuition and auxiliary revenues for nearly half of their budgets, and on public universities, who rely on state and local governments (and the sale of services) for a similar percentage of their income.[23] Both sources of revenue—private propensity to spend discretionary income on children's education and state government ability to spend tax dollars on higher education—are adversely affected by rising energy costs.

More specific to the university is yet another factor that makes academic institutions vulnerable to economic and political manipulation. Universities expanded most recently in American history to accommodate the baby boom generation's educational aspirations. Universities that hired many new faculty members from the late 1960s into the early 1980s are now faced with an aging professoriate. Whereas in 1992, only one quarter of faculty were aged 55 or over,[24] by the year 2000, nearly 30 percent were in that age range.[25] The day when one third or more of the faculty are over 55 is not far away, and explains the sudden popularity of conversations about "post-tenure faculty productivity" which can now be heard on so many campuses.

COUNTERVAILING INITIATIVES

In the face of long entrenched demands for political conformity or economic collaboration, and in the face of rising costs and an aging workforce, there are few movements within the university that directly safeguard academia from overcommercialization in all its forms. On the contrary, many of the experiments being tried in the private sector have also spread to universities: outsourcing of tasks not intrinsic to the mission of the institutions (for example, maintenance or food/catering services), or shifting employment patterns to favor part-time, short term nontenurable faculty slots over full-time, long term, tenure-stream positions, etc. However, the most noxious of these practices—the dilution of the tenure system in favor of stocking the university with part-time professors on short-term contracts—is a limited option, since the ranking systems by which university prestige is assessed and publicized favor universities with a high proportion of long-term, tenured or tenure-stream faculty.

There is also one new frontier, which, if it does not protect the integrity of environmental research, or Middle East policy studies, or the exploration of sexuality in humanistic texts, does nevertheless represent a new horizon for resistance to overcommercialization. In the past few years a number of initiatives have become visible on campuses around the country that have in common the recognition that universities themselves are economic players of significant proportions and that their purchasing power can be harnessed to social justice objectives. A social justice agenda, whether it emphasizes sustainable economics (i.e., abjures sweatshop manufacturing) or sustainable environment (e.g., green buildings, recycling, etc.) is useful and significant in its own right and may serve to offset some of the other capitulations to state and private funders. Most importantly, however, a university social justice agenda, expressed in purchasing practices, has the potential to seed a renewed university-community alliance that is resistive to neoliberalism in both its political and economic forms.

Universities are economic actors in their community. They pay wages to maintenance workers or chose to outsource these jobs to domestic service companies that generally pay lower wages and give poorer benefit packages. They contribute to neighborhood projects with financial contributions and student volunteers. Their students become customers of local businesses. And universities themselves purchase prodigious amounts of paper, computer and laboratory equipment, building supplies, food, catering, and housekeeping services.

Many of these areas of university economic activity have become the site of new social justice initiatives. The four principal ones at this time include:

1. The campaign to make all university insignia merchandise "sweatshop free";
2. The campaign to move the university's enormous paper consumption into "sustainable forestry" products;
3. The campaign to align all new building and major building renovations with "green building" standards that emphasize environmental sustainability;[26]
4. The campaign to stock the university larder with "fair trade" coffee, chocolate, and other foods.

All of these efforts have in common the desire to use the university's purchasing power to acquire goods and services and, simultaneously, to serve larger social justice agendas.

University bookstores, for example, do an estimated $75 million of sales online every year—referred to by one wag as replacing "bricks and mortar" with "bricks and clicks."[27] These revenues, in turn, can be tied to the purchase of "sweat-free" products, particularly the insignia merchandise (clothes, dormitory room furnishings, calendars, notebooks, jewelry) that carry the university's seal or other insignia. Such merchandise is sold not only at the campus bookstore, and on-line at university web sites, but also via catalogues mailed to alumni, donors, and other interested parties. Interestingly, however, the web site of the National Association of College Stores does nothing to promote the acquisition of sweatshop free merchandise sources, while individual college bookstores (e.g. the Seattle University, Colby College) do emphasize the sweat-free character of their merchandise.

Attempts to direct the university's paper consumption to help create and maintain a market for sustainable forest products appear not to be centrally organized as of this writing, and to remain the prerogative of individual schools, especially those which include a forestry program. It is worth recalling, however, that nearly all state universities are rooted in the Morrill Land grant colleges and that virtually all of them in states where logging and paper production are economically significant have the potential to capitalize on this emerging area of socially responsible buying. Purchasing agents could play a leading role here in shifting consumption patterns past the tipping point that would give "sustainable forestry" paper products a wider audience.

"Green building" efforts are better organized, and already represented by U.S. Green Building Council with their own (LEED) certification standard for evaluating building programs around issues of sustainability and mitigating environmental impacts. While colleges do not seem to be rushing to undertake green building projects, the rise in energy costs serves as a purely economic incentive to begin movement in this direction. In certain select areas the public sector is also insisting on green construction, especially in school buildings. Thus, for example, new school construction and major building renovations in Massachusetts' primary and secondary schools must meet the standards of the newly formed Massachusetts School Building Authority, which is empowered to reimburse to localities as much as 90 percent of the construction/renovation costs of school building programs that comply with green building guidelines.[28]

Finally, the market for fair trade coffees and chocolates is growing daily, with even mainstream supermarkets now clearly labeling fair trade merchandise. Campuses are teetering between retaining control over their own food production and outsourcing food services to catering companies. But, in either case, the demand for fair trade food items (as well as locally grown produce, organic food free of genetic modification, and other healthier foods) can be readily accommodated. Indeed, the history of United Students for Fair Trade, founded in 2003 and enrolling over one hundred U.S. campuses only one year later in the exclusive use of fair trade coffees provides a bright spot in the search for buffers against commercialization.[29]

A CASE STUDY FROM A JESUIT UNIVERSITY

My home university has a new holiday-related shopping opportunity for students, faculty, and staff: The Fair Trade Holiday Sale. The first such event, featuring craft goods from around the world manufactured under sweat-free conditions, was held in 2005 and was a huge success, judged by several criteria: it enlisted support in its planning and development from a number of groups around the campus, including the women's resource center and the service learning program which oversees community internship placements; it was heavily patronized by students, faculty and staff—having to restock before the end of the first afternoon of its two day run; and it succeeded in raising substantial amounts of money to be donated as scholarship funds to Jesuit schools in Nicaragua and El Salvador.

The person who took the lead in creating the Fair Trade Holiday Sale had a long history of commitment to social justice and, in fact, was employed in a position of leadership in one of the university's efforts at service and outreach to the highly diverse immigrant community surrounding the university campus.

This individual was motivated to develop the Fair Trade Holiday Sale on a faculty and staff immersion trip to Nicaragua, where participants spent a considerable amount of time at the local Jesuit University in Managua, the Universidad de Centro America (UCA), which is distinguished by its very strong outreach programs to the community and its equally strong commitment to active learning in the community on the part of their students. The faculty/ staff immersion trip, in turn, was supported by funds from a Lilly Endowment grant whose purpose is to promote religious values and practices in church affiliated universities.

In order to create the space in her worklife for organizing the Fair Trade Holiday Sale, the organizer took advantage of the university's employee benefit package that allows staff to enroll in two courses per semester within the university at no cost. The courses she chose brought her to a leadership development program established by a highly unusual, interdisciplinary team of faculty in the business school, the Sociology Department and the School of Education, along with community "business partners," largely business consultants with doctorates.

As attractive as the Fair Trade Holiday Sale is, it enjoys more word-of-mouth recognition than official university sponsorship. In fact, the organizer was cautioned to proceed conservatively, to make modest claims for the project and not to expect it to receive a lot of university publicity. It is unclear exactly why the need for caution felt so compelling, except for the fact that one of the more vociferous student groups to support the project, was treated with great suspicion and caution by the university administration because of their propensity to raise divestment questions about the university's stock portfolio, and to oppose the presence of military recruiters at the university-sponsored job fair (the students typically knelt in prayer in front of the offending booths and were planning to stage pantomime "die-ins" when their permit to demonstrate was rescinded).

The Fair Trade Holiday Sale, still embryonic in its second year, has the potential to cement a number of university-community alliances: to sweat-free craft producers in the region and abroad, to "socially responsible" consumer groups, and to social justice oriented alumni. It also has the opportunity to contribute to consumer education about social-justice driven consumption of a more positive sort than the exhortation not to buy certain goods or brands.

Much of the more ambitious potential of the Fair Trade Holiday Sale remains to be realized. The university bookstore's commitment to sweat free insignia merchandise is a more mature project, albeit one with an equally long and circuitous history whose parallels to the Fair Trade Holiday Sale are, nonetheless, striking. The work of taking the bookstore out of sweatshop merchandise was conceived by a manager who, like the founder of the Fair Trade Holiday Sale, had a long history of community involvement in social justice issues—in his case, around removing landmines in war-ravaged countries. Like the Fair Trade innovator, the bookstore manager visited Nicaragua and was inspired by his exposure to the programs at UCA to undertake his own community outreach project. Also like his Fair Trade Holiday Sale colleague, he used the employee benefits package to enroll in a leadership development program, which, in turn, created a dedicated space within his working life to change "business as usual" in his domain.

Like his counterpart, he was cautioned against trumpeting his social justice agenda, but unlike his counterpart, he was able to move his project forward without university-spanning alliances. On the contrary, he proceeded almost by stealth, introducing sweat free vendors as the most efficient purveyors of reliable, high quality merchandise at the most competitive prices. In short, he did not challenge the cost-minimizing, revenue-maximizing metric prevalent in bookstore acquisitions. Rather, he was able to demonstrate that sweatshop-free merchandise performed well by conventional economic measures. Sadly, it was an absolute necessity that his project do so, despite the fact that, when political motives more acceptable to the established order come into play, the economic metric can be abandoned for political ends: as when local and state police departments buy not the best made and most reliable cars, but American-built sedans, for their fleets.

The real growth edge of his project was to discover the various structural barriers to sweatshop-free purchasing. So, for example, the container ships on which merchandise is sent from third world countries to United States are organized to do business with large volume shippers. Thus, container space is normally made available only on a scale too large for most indigenous cooperatives to utilize. Similarly, the process of being certified as sweatshop free is an expensive and time-consuming one, often beyond the means of small artisanal cooperatives in third world countries.

To overcome some of these obstacles, the bookstore manager used a portion of his acquisition funds to prepay orders for insignia T-shirts, thus, in fact, making loans to cooperatives in Nicaragua who were already tied to the UCA outreach programs. This pattern of financing, while involving a small amount of money, represents an innovative approach to university-community ties in purchasing. Moreover, this project now stands poised for possible expansion in several directions: toward the bookstores in other Jesuit, or Catholic universities, and toward the acquisition of other goods within the university purchasing system.

Central to both of these innovative projects was the creation of a dedicated space within the innovators' worklife to build a new project. The institutional home for such efforts was a leadership development program dedicated to creating a curriculum for socially responsible change, change for the common good, within the business community. A group of some twelve faculty and business partners, led by an interdisciplinary graduate student, met for nearly two years to develop the in-service academic-year certificate program. This original group worked out all the details of university positioning—largely in the School of Management but with cross-school and interdisciplinary ties to the College of Liberal Arts and Sciences and the School of Education. Budgets, timetables, staffing and recruitment of participants were accomplished, although the program had to redefine its client base over time. Originally designed to enroll top level executives, the founding group soon discovered that a ten-month, for-credit program that required extensive reading and writing commitments was, in the normal course of events, simply nonsellable to large numbers of high level executives. However, early career and mid-career manages seemed happy to enroll, especially when employed by corporations who had generous tuition reimbursement policies.

The most powerful part of the leadership program is its "nested" curriculum. In the first semester of the program, participants are offered a series of two-day modules, equipping them through tools for . . .

1. individual self-assessment and deeper insights into their own work- and learning styles;
2. productive team development and group effort, with the potential to establish supportive, cooperative work environments and secure organizational resources for their teams;
3. achieving organizational impact and transformation, driven by the recognition of multiple stakeholders beyond the shareholder—for example, other organizations in the supply chain, neighboring communities, workers and consumers;
4. assessing and connecting to the environment beyond the organization— the "global" environment in the search for allies, leverage points, best case benchmarks and a vision of transforming the whole system of production in a more transparent and accountable direction.

In the second semester, participants are asked to complete a project in "real time" demonstrating the feasibility within their place of employment of doing well by conventional financial criteria at the same time as they do good by social justice standards. The key to the Leadership for Change project is not corporate philanthropy—doing business the same old way and then returning some portion of profits to the community. Rather, participants are asked to build a project that entwines "doing well and doing good" in routine business operations.

The Fair Trade Holiday Sale and the sweat-free bookshop are both fruits of this leadership development project, as well as the creativity, patience, and persistence of their founders. At this writing, these two projects continue to flourish. The leadership training program itself also is continuing to develop new products, including the recruitment of an increasingly diverse set of participants from community groups and labor, and the creation of dedicated consulting within single for-profit and public organizations, a roundtable for CEOs, and, on the drawing boards—a summer institute for higher level executives.

CONCLUSIONS

In the face of the formidable political and economic forces arrayed against university autonomy, how much importance can an internal leadership development program with a social justice agenda hope to have? How much difference does it make that some of the university's purchasing power is being redirected to socially just forms of production? What do we learn from these efforts at one school that might change the whole system in which university autonomy is determined?

By themselves, the university projects I have described probably have little historic importance. But they do have great potential to exemplify a process of building university ties to grassroots and community constituencies, alliances that could fuel community economic development based on more democratic principles and tie this development to a powerful social institution seeking to preserve its autonomy in the face of even-more powerful state and corporate actors. In short, if the pressures on the university are simultaneously economic and political in character, then the response must be too, mobilizing not only new and creative economic behaviors but linking those to new forms of university-community alliance. What have we learned so far from these small seedling projects?

It takes a village. Projects which fundamentally change the university's economic behavior and its presence in the community are not the work of one lone hero—though individual imagination, passion, and courage are certainly required. Many people around the university, in all its various functions—faculty, students, staff, administrators, developers, alumni—will have to be involved in designing, implementing, and institutionalizing changed university processes that move in the direction of greater social responsibility and community connection. And every one of those people, as individuals and as representatives of constituencies, are going to ask "if this is such a good idea, why isn't it already being done?" They will have to consider the idea not only on its merits, but also in comparison to the costs of time and discomfort associated with making even clearly positive changes. They will have to evaluate new projects in the context of other commitments and older alliances that might have to be renegotiated. Thus. . . .

It takes a village a long time. The work of developing new ideas, researching best practices elsewhere so as not to re-invent the wheel, of designing culturally competent programs in a specific organizational context, of implementing programs and monitoring their success, revising as necessary—these tasks are each time consuming and, cumulatively, are the work of years rather than months. The leadership program took two years to develop before the first participant crossed the threshold. It was made possible by the fact that many of its principle architects enjoyed the benefits of tenure and so were free to pursue intellectually and ethically interesting challenges without being told to "stop daydreaming and get back to work." The university bookstore and Fair Trade Holiday Sale initiatives, in turn, were developed over the period of a year and, importantly, drew on networks and the established reputations of their champions as people of probity and efficacy within the university.

It takes a village a long time and lots of resources, especially safe places to incubate new ideas. Time, imagination, and will are, perhaps, the most important resources. All of these qualities are easily swamped by the busyness of ordinary work life, even when they do not attract politically motivated suspicion or opposition. Key to the projects described above were two "incubator" spaces within the university: the Lilly Endowment supported program which brings faculty and staff together to study the university's Jesuit mission and to find ways of bringing it alive in the contemporary setting. This project has the capacity to support immersion trips for faculty and staff. Fortunately, it also possesses the wisdom to trust participants to find ways, in their ongoing work, to integrate their learnings, and to build worthwhile initiatives on the basis of their immersion experiences. The leadership development program also has the capacity to nurture new projects, not only with curriculum materials, but also with a wide-ranging network of alumni and business partners, an interactive and empowering pedagogy, and an invitation to spend a year designing a workplace that is changed to better recognize and honor the common good. Absent these two incubator spaces, it is unlikely that the projects discussed here would have come to fruition.

Even a village with time and resources needs to have a strategic sense of possibilities, a larger vision of how to advance its own agenda in connection with others. It is often easier to identify the sources of constraint than to imagine the new initiatives that might protect the university's autonomy and strengthen its ties to the community. In the case cited here, one particular Jesuit university benefited from ties with brother institutions around the world. Most colleges do not have a network like that of the Jesuit schools—

a series of allies with whom strong ties and interlinked networks already exist. Nevertheless, most institutions have had some practice in reaching out to new constituencies and adapting to new challenges—for example, the online environment. From these connections and challenges come many small and piecemeal projects, which, absent any kind of visionary leadership, remain no more than small and piecemeal projects of varying efficacy. But, grassroots efforts within the university—projects such as the Fair Trade Holiday Sale, or the sweat-free bookshop, or the fair trade coffee concession—can also build alliances with enduring projects that protect creativity within the university, with tenured faculty representatives and interested alumni. And these, in turn, can be insightful about the ways in which university-community alliances can use consumer activities to reshape the market and perhaps even the state. It will take a concerted economic and political program to respond to the pressures that confront the contemporary university. There are certainly a lot of "ifs" in the preceding sentences which outline the possibilities for a new university-community alliance built on socially just and environmentally sustainable purchasing practices. Yet the beginnings of such a program can be found in many universities, giving hope that the wisdom of "thinking globally, acting locally" may yet be realized, allowing the university to fulfill its mission to create new knowledge for a better the world.

NOTES

1. Hannah Arendt, *Between Past and Future* (London: Faber and Faber, 1961), 177.

2. David Shenk, "Money Science = Ethics Problems on Campus," *The Nation*, 22 March 1999, <*www.thenation.com/doc/19990322/shenk*> (22 October 2006) provides a chilling account of the suppression of medical evidence by the manufacturer or a pharmaceutical widely used by patients suffering from hypothyroidism.

3. Beshara Doumani, *Academic Freedom after September 11* (New York: Zone Books, 2006), 11.

4. U.S. Statutes at Large 12 (1862): 503.

5. Christopher Jencks and David Riesman, *The Academic Revolution* (Garden City, N.Y.: Doubleday Publishers, 1969), 94.

6. W.P. Metzger, "Academic Tenure in America: A Historical Essay," in *Faculty Tenure,* ed. W.R. Keast and J.W. Macy, Jr. (San Francisco: Jossey-Bass, 1973), <*www.uh.edu/fs/TITF/history.html*> (24 September 2006).

7. Michael Massing, "The Storm over the Israel Lobby," *New York Review of Books,* LIII (10), 8 June 2006: 63–73. (Provides a thorough review of this controversy.)

8. Michael Powell, "In N.Y., Sparks Fly Over Israel Criticism," *The Washington Post,* 9 October 2006, sec. A, A3.

9. Ed Pilkington, "US Free Speech Row Grows as Author Says Jewish Complaints Stopped Launch Party," *Guardian Unlimited*, 11 October 2006, <*www.guardian.co.uk/usa/story/0,,1892431,00.html*> (30 September 2006).

10. John Weiner, "Giving Chutzpah New Meaning," *The Nation*, 11 July 2005.

11. Doumani, *Academic Freedom*, 11–57.

12. Daniel Smith, "Political Science," *New York Times Magazine*, 4 September 2005, sec. 6, 37 (column 1).

13. Peter F. Infante, "Safeguarding Scientific Evaluations by Governmental Agencies: Case Study of OHA and the 1,3-Butadiene Classification," *International Journal of Occupational and Environmental Health* 11 (2005): 372–77.

14. Jennifer Beth Sass, "Industry Efforts to Weaken the EPA's Classification of the Carcenogenicity of 1,3-Butadiene," *International Journal of Occupational and Environmental Health* 11 (2005): 378.

15. Phyllis Mullenix, "Fouride Poisoning: A Puzzle with Hidden Pieces," *International Journal of Occupational and Environmental Health* 11 (2005): 404–14.

16. William Kovarik, "Ethyl-leaded Gasoline: How a Classic Occupational Disease Became an International Public Health Disaster," *International Journal of Occupational and Environmental Health* 11 (2005): 384–97.

17. Valerio Gennaro and Lorenzo Tomatic, "The Epidemiologic Studies May Underestimate or Fail to Detect Increased Risks of Cancer and Other Diseases," *International Journal of Occupational and Environmental Health* 11 (2005): 356–59.

18. David Egilman and Marion Billings, "Abuse of Epidemiology: Automobile Manufactureres Manufacture a Defense to Asbestos Liability," *International Journal of Occupational and Environmental Health* 11 (2005): 360–71.

19. Michael Jacobson, "Lifting the Veil of Secrecy from Industry Funding of Nonprofit Health Organizations," *International Journal of Occupational and Environmental Health* 11 (2005): 349–55.

20. Jon Wiener, "Cancer, Chemicals and History," *The Nation*, 7 February 2005, 19–22.

21. Richard Knox, "Disclosure Fight May Push Doctor Out of Occupational Health Field," *Boston Globe*, 22 May 1999, B5.

22. Doumani, *Academic Freedom*, 9. (Paraphrasing Edward Said).

23. U.S. Department of Education, *Integrated Postsecondary Education Data System [IPEDS], Spring 2002 Survey* (Washington, D.C.: National Center for Education Statistics).

24. U.S. Department of Education, *1993 National Study of Postsecondary Faculty* (Washington, D.C.: National Center for Education Statistics). (Faculty Survey).

25. U.S. Department of Education, National Center for Education Statistics, *1999 National Study of Postsecondary Faculty* (Washington, D.C.: National Center for Education Statistics). (Faculty Survey).

26. "At Colleges, the Environmental is Hot," *Inside Higher Education*, 24 October 2006, <*www.insidehighered.cm/news/2006/10/24/environment*> (25 October 2006). (A review of environmental efforts in university construction).

27. "Demise of Pure Play Online College Bookseller," *About: Retail Industry*, 14 February 2002, <*http://retailindustry.about.com/library/bl/02q1/bl_ch021402.htm*> (25 October 2006).

28. Charles Levenstein and Eve Spangler (ed.), *The Point of Consumption*, (New York: Bayview Press, forthcoming).
29. Lisa Capone, "There's a New Cause Brewing on Campuses," *Boston Globe*, 2 Feb. 2004, Living/Arts section.

BIBLIOGRAPHY

Arendt, Hannah. *Between Past and Future*. London: Faber and Faber, 1961.

Capone, Lisa. "There's a New Cause Brewing on Campuses." *Boston Globe*, 2 February 2004, Living/Arts section.

"At Colleges, the Environmental is Hot." *Inside Higher Education*. 24 October 2006. <*www.insidehighered.cm/news/2006/10/24/environment*> (25 October 2006).

"Demise of Pure Play Online College Bookseller." *About: Retail Industry*. 14 February 2002. <*retailindustry.about.com/library/bl/02q1/bl_ch021402.htm*> (25 October 2006).

Doumani, Beshara. *Academic Freedom After September 11*. New York: Zone Books, 2006.

Egilman, David, and Marion Billings. "Abuse of Epidemiology: Automobile Manufactureres Manufacture a Defense to Asbestos Liability." *International Journal of Occupational and Environmental Health* 11 (2005): 360–71.

Gennaro, Valerio, and Lorenzo Tomatic. "The Epidemiologic Studies May Underestimate or Fail to Detect Increased Risks of Cancer and Other Diseases." *International Journal of Occupational and Environmental Health* 11 (2005): 356–59.

Infante, Peter F. "Safeguarding Scientific Evaluations by Governmental Agencies: Case Study of OHA and the 1,3-Butadiene Classification." *International Journal of Occupational and Environmental Health* 11 (2005): 372–77.

Jacobson, Michael. "Lifting the Veil of Secrecy from Industry Funding of Nonprofit Health Organizations," *International Journal of Occupational and Environmental Health* 11 (2005): 349–55.

Jencks, Christopher, and David Reisman. *The Academic Revolution*. Garden City, N.Y.: Doubleday Publishers, 1969.

Knox, Richard. "Disclosure Fight May Push Doctor Out of Occupational Health Field." *Boston Globe*, 22 May 1999, B5.

Kovarik, William. "Ethyl-leaded Gasoline: How a Classic Occupational Disease Became an International Public Health Disaster." *International Journal of Occupational and Environmental Health* 11 (2005): 384–97.

Levenstein, Charles, and Eve Spangler (ed.). *The Point of Consumption*. New York: Bayview Press, forthcoming.

Massing, Michael. "The Storm over the Israel Lobby." *New York Review of Books*, LIII (10) (8 June 2006): 63–73.

Metzger, W.P. "Academic Tenure in America: A Historical Essay." in *Faculty Tenure*, edited W.R. Keast and J.W. Macy, Jr. San Francisco: Jossey-Bass, 1973. <*www.uh.edu/fs/TITF/history.html*> (24 September 2006).

Mullenix, Phyllis. "Fouride Poisoning: A Puzzle with Hidden Pieces." *International Journal of Occupational and Environmental Health* 11 (2005): 404–14.

Pilkington, Ed. "US Free Speech Row Grows as Author Says Jewish Complaints Stopped Launch Party." *Guardian Unlimited*, 11 October 2006. <*www.guardian .co.uk/usa/story/0,,1892431,00.html*> (30 September 2006).

Powell, Michael. "In N.Y., Sparks Fly Over Israel Criticism." *The Washington Post,* 9 October 2006, sec. A, A3.

Sass, Jennifer Beth. "Industry Efforts to Weaken the EPA's Classification of the Carcenogenicity of 1,3-Butadiene." *International Journal of Occupational and Environmental Health* 11 (2005): 378.

Shenk, David. "Money Science = Ethics Problems on Campus." *The Nation*, 22 March, 1999. <*http://thenation.com/doc.mhtml%fi=19990322&s=shenk*> (22 October 2006).

Smith, Daniel. "Political Science." *New York Times Magazine*, 4 September 2005, sec. 6, 37 (column 1).

U.S. Department of Education, *Integrated Postsecondary Education Data System [IPEDS], Spring 2002 Survey* (Washington, D.C.: National Center for Education Statistics).

U.S. Department of Education, *1993 National Study of Postsecondary Faculty* (Washington, D.C.: National Center for Education Statistics). (Faculty Survey).

U.S. Department of Education, National Center for Education Statistics, *1999 National Study of Postsecondary Faculty* (Washington, D.C.: National Center for Education Statistics). (Faculty Survey).

U.S. Statutes at Large 12 (1862): 503.

Weiner, Jon. "Cancer, Chemicals and History." *The Nation*, 7 February 2005, 19–22.

——"Giving Chutzpah New Meaning." *The Nation*, 11 July 2005.

Chapter Nine

Safeguarding Uncertain Futures

Christian Gilde and Eve Spangler

"Business principles take effect in academic affairs most simply, obviously and avowably in the way of a businesslike administration of the scholastic routine."[1]

Thorstein Veblen, *The Higher Learning in America* (1994)

After looking at all the information presented in this volume, we believe that the issues addressing educational capitalism, institutional corporatization and academic commodification boil down to the following critical question which is of concern to students, parents, and educators: Are there adequate academic policies in place to safeguard the academic community from commercial intrusion? Exploring this question further, one will find that it harbors the seeds of the most prevalent educational queries of our time, concerned with such issues as the quality of education and its future development. Now more than ever, students seem to be served rather than educated, at a local training center rather than a university, by a part-time faculty member rather than a full-time educator.

VOICES FROM THE PAST

Since the early decades of the twentieth century, Thorstein Veblen and, in more recent years, George Ritzer have highlighted the problem of corporatization in higher education and the lack of any safeguards against this encroachment. More recently, we have also been applying theories of globalization, especially those developed by Immanuel Wallerstein, to the phenomenon of commercialization of higher education on a global scale. Both Veblen and Ritzer, who wrote directly about higher education, share a profound suspicion of the corporatization of higher education that is captured with the following statement: Higher education gravitates toward a business-like institutionalism in which students come to be treated like customers. What is in Veblen's case a business-like administration of the academic routine, is in Ritzer's case a standardization of university operations. These keen minds foresaw a commodification and rountinization that could eventually lead to a crisis in the intellectual autonomy of higher education.

Veblen's most obvious contribution to the field of higher education is his book *The Higher Learning in America*, which should be more appropriately titled *The Higher Earning in America* based on what it reveals about academia. Completed in 1904, the work is a harsh critique of the emergence of business values in a system reserved for learning and scholastic inquiry. Disapproving of the educational developments that started in his time, Veblen condemns the metamorphosis of the university into an organization that subscribes to a "businesslike administration of the scholastic routine."[2] He introduces a dialectic that centers on the distinction between higher learning and vocational training;[3] a dialect that is at the core of many educational controversies in today's scholastic environment. Unqualified business executives moonlighting on university boards and administrative complacency are not welcome in Veblen's world of higher education; a world that condemns the establishment of academic prestige through constructional pomposity, glorification of the academic management, and material frivolousness. Veblen's solutions emphasize a separation of university learning and professional education and a reorganization of the collegiate executive.[4] Veblen lets his readers know that he sees the university as an entity primarily focused on advancing research inquiry and higher learning with undergraduate education as a necessary but relatively less important appendage. It seems that Thorstein Veblen is skeptical about a successful performance of the current academic system and does not think it will change unless society and its economic, political, and cultural way of thinking progress to a more enlightened stage.[5]

A more recent analyst who echoes Veblen's skepticism about commercial higher education is George Ritzer, a professor of sociology and prolific scholar at the University of Maryland. Ritzer coined the phrase "McDonaldization," which he equates with the standardization and routinization of society and which penetrates various areas of social life, including higher education. Ritzer made the following observation during a paper presentation in the United Kingdom in 1998:

> Look to . . . McDonald's or Disney. Universities continue to look to industries for innovations, but the contemporary university is not primarily a means of production [anymore] and therefore has more in common with, and to learn from, the new means of consumption.[6]

And he is right! When examining the daily operations of the modern American university, institutions of higher education have truly turned into McVersities that are, literally, consumed by business. This rationalization process contributes to an environment that, as Ritzer argues, transforms modern universities into "highly irrational" places.[7] Ritzer, keenly aware of this alarming process, points out that "many students (and faculty members) are put off by the huge factory-like atmosphere in these universities. They may feel like automatons to be processed by the bureaucracy and the computers, or even cattle being run through a meat processing plant."[8]

If Veblen and Ritzer are correct in their core concern for the academic autonomy of the American university, then, at present, we must also be concerned about the impact of economic globalization on academic integrity. The work of sociologist Immanuel Wallterstein provides a conceptualization that incorporates all countries into a globally spanning and interconnected world system of economics and politics. We thought to ourselves that it would be a great idea to project Wallerstein's "world system" of core states (mostly located in the Western World) and peripheral states and the resource disparities among them onto the global educational system.[9] The world-spanning system of education can then be seen as part of a greater world-economic system that thrives, according to Wallerstein, on the "division of labor" and unequal distribution of resources.[10] The core education originates from universities such as Harvard, Cambridge, or the Sorbonne, all located in core states. These core education providers dominate less powerful, local institutions in peripheral countries. The semi-peripheral institutions struggle for survival between the core and periphery and undertake basic academic research, absorb less qualified students, and focus on the vocational areas of higher education. When taking a closer look, there seems to be an obvious match between the world-economic system that is driven by (capital) "economic domination" and an educational system that thrives on competition and profits.[11] The circumstances we lay out in the upcoming paragraphs are unfolding as we write and seem to foreshadow the likely future of the system of higher education: a global commercialization of knowledge.

One reason for the globalization of higher education is that, as research costs have increased, the support of federal and local governments has decreased. Therefore, institutions of higher education are forced to go beyond the occasional visits of and partnerships with foreign scholars and more intensely collaborate on projects and information exchange. Joint ventures between universities have been reported in business education, medicine, engineering, and the arts—a synergy between educational institutions in the core and periphery. For instance, in business, high-powered business professors are recruited from Harvard and other top U.S. schools to develop business schools in Asia and on other continents. In the field of medicine, professors from one university in Core Country X teach new surgical techniques or show how to operate medical equipment to professors of another university in Periphery Country Y. Engineering schools join hands to operate expensive and sophisticated particle accelerators and to find cheaper and more environmentally friendly sources of energy. The arts have, for a long time, transcended physical barriers and intellectual boundaries and built bridges between different institutions.

Another reason for higher education to go global is that the bounty of technological developments allows people to communicate much more easily and quickly to share the creative fruits of higher education. It enables schools all over the globe to talk to each other in real-time, help each other, and exchange knowledge. This technological proliferation also helps to break down educational borders in politically struggling, semi-peripheral countries such as the former Soviet Union and China.

But all these civic benefits arising from the globalization of higher education must not obscure the fact that they also put a strain on a system that is steeped in tradition; a system that, on many occasions, has performed central social functions in local societies. Knowledge spokes and hubs, oligopolization, enculturation, exclusivity, and organizational centralization are only a few of the dangers that come with the globalization movement of higher education and threaten to erode local educational systems.

With the increased globalization of tertiary education comes a polarization of the system into powerful and powerless institutions (poor and rich institutions). This world-wide movement creates a spoke and hub system in which a few knowledge hubs in Western countries control the market for higher education and keep small and powerless spoke institutions confined to support roles. The countries that lead education could be designated as core education providers that are equal to the economic core states described by Wallerstein. These are states that possess highly skilled labor, lots of capital, and are therefore able to exploit the peripheral education providers. Peripheral education providers, on the other hand, are countries that are unable to dominate the global market of higher education due to a lack of control and resources. Thus, they are relegated to play the role of secondary education suppliers and to sustain the core states by sending their people to get educated in these countries.

This unidirectional flow of resources and power creates a system in which the rich get richer and the poor get poorer. One could rightfully identify this system as system with too few prominent players. The dominant institutions (hubs) become more powerful through expansion and an increased influx of resources that enable them to cement their dominant position, thus, marginalizing the smaller players (spokes).

The regulation of higher education on a global basis contributes to its oligopolization and places its intellectual fruits in the hands of a few institutions. An already protective academic community at elite colleges and universities (*scholopolies*) in core states becomes even more protective and oligopolizes the knowledge it creates, thus, hindering the development of the intellectual fruits of less powerful institutions in peripheral states. In addition, only the core state universities that are in the limelight get the resources necessary to stay in business, distinguish themselves, and advance. The accreditation process and its quality standards are being influenced by these powerful institutions on a global scale and favor their interests. And, at some point in the near future the product labels that say "Made in Asia" will be replaced by labels that say "Educated in the United States."

For almost a millennium, institutions of higher education have played a pivotal role in the transformation of local societies and have executed crucial functions to guarantee the survival of these very same societies. An intrusion into local educational cultures and the standardization of these cultures has disastrous consequences and undermines local educational autonomy. What if a European Union controlled system of higher education finds that the School of Irish, Celtic Studies, Irish Folklore and Linguistics at the University College Dublin is not feasible anymore and decides to close this School? With fewer Irish people fluent in their ancient tongue, and with fewer and fewer young people interested in learning this language, a centuries-old language and the way of life associated with it would be vanishing from the cultural landscape.

Within this system of uneven distribution of educational resources the disadvantaged territories have to relinquish their cultural identities. Berger and Huntington found the following while conducting their research on globalization:

> Receiving foreign aid is, as Chinese scholars point out, not free. In order to compete for grants, researchers have to design their projects in accordance with Western academic norms. . . . As a result, Chinese scholars have ended up following Western scholarship in terms of both theory and method.[12]

In addition, Berger et al. discovered that the academic culture in Chile was overshadowed by a unique arrangement between Catholic University in Chile and the University of Chicago. This unique arrangement was created to drive the economic development and education of Chile. "The entire teaching staff and curriculum at the School of Economics and Business [at

Catholic University were] completely renovated and adjusted to approximate the University of Chicago's MBA and MA economics program."[13] In addition, Chicago graduate students were used to not only assume key positions at Catholic University but also at the University of Chile.

And what about the educational needs of the less developed countries? Should the global community really aspire to have a few leading universities with substantial resources, power and prestige educate entire countries, perhaps in ways that violate their local cultures? Does this exclusivity not stifle the intellectual diversity of higher education and make higher education accessible only to countries (people) who can afford it?

The globalization of higher education oligopolies forces many members of poor states to seek education in core states instead of their own countries. Berger and Huntington point out that there is a "fever for MBA degrees" in China.[14] And, since China does not currently possess a large enough educational infrastructure to provide the number of college-educated people asked for by its economy, "many of [the managerial elite in China] obtain MBA's or other graduate degrees from abroad."[15] Yet, many members of these peripheral countries are willing but not able to get educated due to an exclusivity created by the cores states and their elite institutions through monetary and travel barriers. In addition, this exclusivity causes a "brain drain," which encourages more and more talented, young periphery people to get their education in the core and never return to the periphery again.[16]

Organizational centralization is one of the main concerns that should be on the minds of international educators. As organizations such as the World Trade Organization (WTO) or European Union (EU) become more interested in higher education, one has to wonder what their aspirations are. If these aspirations lead to an increased commodification and regulation of academia, than these organizations should be prevented from meddling in global educational affairs. In his article "Higher Education and the WTO: Globalization Run Amok," Philip Altbach paints the following scenario:

> The WTO would help to guarantee that academic institutions and other education providers could set up branches in any country, export degrees, award degrees and certificates with minimal restrictions, invest in overseas educational institutions, employ instructors for their foreign ventures, set up educational training programs through distance technologies without controls, and so on.[17]

The developments portrayed by Altbach could be interpreted as a global privatization and deregulation effort that deprives local governments of their educational responsibilities and adds to the regulatory power of overblown and out-of-touch organizations.

The globalization, commercialization, and internationalization of higher education have to be undertaken with caution. What might be seen in core states as a service mainly provided by the private sector, might be viewed in peripheral countries as a service mainly provided by the public sector. What might be perceived in core states as a right, might be seen in peripheral countries as a privilege. These and other local scholastic differences should not fall prey to a "globalization of Western intelligentsia" and educational imperialism.[18]

EXTENDING THE ETHOS OF GUARDIANSHIP

Both Veblen and Ritzer have already pointed out some of the areas of university functioning that are vulnerable to commercialization and that seem, moreover, to have been neglected by the protective powers-that-be. Wallerstein extends their concerns to a worldwide, globalized system of higher education in which universities in peripheral and semi-peripheral countries have been rendered particularly vulnerable to the lure of corporate contributions.

The school officials and administrators who have declined to extend their protective mental of guardianship to safeguard one or more of the areas of university life that are frequently the target of commercialization efforts have much to consider. Following is a far from exhaustive list of the areas of and suggestions for safeguarding vulnerable parts of the university:

1. Corporate Moonlighting

   For this area it is important to understand the extensive network of policies that regulate the moonlighting of corporate leaders on university boards. In this context, the institutions and their officials have to make sure that the university committees nominating the boards try to create a balance between university-familiar and university-foreign trustees. Another factor that needs to be considered is that some boards are elected by the public. In addition, more transparency has to be observed when it comes to divulging the actual number of boardroom seats occupied by outsiders and the ways in which their commercial interests might shape university policies. Because universities need to secure resources from a corporatized global economy, they make too little effort to secure the autonomy of the highest positions of command and policy direction of their institutions. Take for instance the California Institute of Technology Board of Trustees; in a recent news release, the institution reports that three new trustees were appointed to this powerful institutional body.[19]

One of the new members is a managing partner of the Efficacy Capital family of biotechnology funds; the second one is the chairman and PEO of Capital Research and Management Company; the third one is chairman and PEO of Nektar Therapeutics.[20] Considering the current composition of the board (almost twice as many industry people as academic and otherwise affiliated members), one has to question whether the latest appointments to the Board of Caltech were a wise choice and really necessary in an era of academic overcommercialization.[21]

2. Copyright Policies

In recent years, since the proliferation of online education, the issue of copyrights regarding course material owned by outsider entities has become more and more prevalent. Therefore, due to its revenue potential for university-affiliated individuals, this area might be a primary target for commercialization attempts. It seems as if universities become interested in copyright issues only when substantial university resources are devoted to material that concerns copyrights. Universities have to make sure that sufficient policies are in place that allow the protection of copyright materials and the intellectual property of their constituents in the development of pedagogic materials. Precedence for the tensions between university, corporate, and individual interests already permeate work in the natural sciences, but may now spread even more broadly to the arts, the social sciences and the professional schools.

With more and more institutions requiring their faculty to provide course materials online, which are often accessible to the general public for free, one cannot really make sure that these intellectual fruits are safeguarded against exploitation. An example of this problem are the OpenCourseWare materials which are provided by the Massachusetts Institute of Technology.[22] Despite the fact that these course materials should be freely accessible to everyone with an Internet connection, who can really prevent the sale of these materials in other countries? Another example is the ideas that are published in online "Working Paper Series" (e.g., University of Bath School of Management working paper series, Boston College's e-scholarship project) that many universities maintain but which cannot really be protected against intellectual theft.[23]

3. Conflicts of Interest

When it comes to matters that concern conflicts of interest arising from university-corporate relationships, it boils down to what the institutions are inclined to do or not to do under such problematic circumstances. At the minimum, universities should adopt a conflict of interest policy for trustees and other university employees that allows the institutions to identify and address any conflicts of interest that might arise. Furthermore, employees should be required either to divulge such conflicts or fill in a questionnaire that discloses such conflicts or profitable transactions. Chapter 2 details a Harvard study which reports that "one-third of the 920 scientists who received gifts said their corporate benefactors expected to review their academic papers before publication. . . . 19 percent said that the donors wanted the patent rights to commercial discoveries stemming from use of the gift."[24]

4. Outside Corporate Membership of University Officials

Outside moonlighting of university officials has become more and more of a concern in recent years. In such cases, clearly written policies should be in place and approval should be sought from the appropriate university authorities when engaging in such an outside activity. Even though such activities might be conducted on personal time, the powers-that-be have to make sure that these ventures do not interfere with a person's loyalty commitment to the school and comply with federal and state laws. In Chapter 3, Catherine O'Neill mentions a 2004 article in *The Chronicle of Higher Education* that alludes to the mixed-up priorities of some universities officials. The article talks about when "on one campus, a faculty member complained that the campus star 'spent more time talking on other campuses than teaching on'" his own.[25] Furthermore, O'Neill reports that stars can "have a powerfully negative impact on departments and programs, described by one faculty member as follows: 'We can't afford stars who just sit around in a holdover glow from past successes or who too frequently fly off to distant lands to further shine. We can't allot a disproportionate share of the wealth just to hang a high-rep name on our marquee. We want a colleague who will work with us, not lord above us.'"[26]

5. Income Regulations

Commercial ventures are supported chiefly because of their potential to supplement university income and faculty salaries. To keep unrealistic profitability aspirations of faculty and students in line and safeguard the academic community, disclosure should be required in order to protect student, faculty, and institutional interests. In addition, it has to be made sure through appropriate regulations that academic and not commercial objectives take center stage in enterprising activities. Chapter 6, which concerns itself with the commercialization of college sports, reports that "in 2002, the alcohol industry spent more than 27 million dollars on National Collegiate Athletic Association basketball games and more than 5 million on football bowl games."[27] It is obvious that this is not the most refined way to supplement university income and, in the light of the existing problems of college binge drinking and teenage driving-under-the-influence (DUI), alternative revenue streams could be sought.

6. Limitations on Commercial Space

Universities do not seem to be particularly bashful when it comes to generating promotional revenues on the backs of a student body and academic community that is already overstimulated by commercial messages. At least, in this area it should be easy for university officials to regulate the amount and placement of advertisement within the confines of the school grounds. Colleges and universities do not have to stoop so low and bluntly advertise that they are, literally, "open for business." In the chapter on college sport commercialization (chapter 6), Michael Malec recalls a college sport event at which he saw "the *Bud Lite Daredevils* entertain a crowd during halftime of a basketball game."[28] He goes on to say that "the entertainment was provided not because Anheuser-Busch feels especially philanthropic towards higher education but because the brewery's advertising agency knows that a sports audience is composed of many people who are likely to buy beer, and it's profitable to remind these people that beer and basketball and good times go together."[29]

7. Policies Against the Release of Student Data

With the free flow of information on the Internet and other media, institutions of higher education should be worried about providing their students with the appropriate level of security to safeguard their private information (e.g., university e-mail addresses). In general, when it comes to releasing student data, institutions that "receive funds under an applicable program of the U.S. Department of Education" are bound by the Family Educational Rights and Privacy Act (FERPA).[30] However, "schools may disclose, without consent, 'directory' information such as a student's name, address, telephone number . . ." Then again, the schools have to provide parents and eligible students with the option of whether or not they want to disclose this information.[31] An example of this struggle to secure the privacy of students emerged at our institution. The institution's Information Technology Services alerted all people in an e-mail message about the enormous increase in the volume of commercial and unsolicited junk mail that finds its way into e-mail accounts.[32] Some of our colleagues and we noticed this shift from formerly receiving only a couple of stray spam mails every week to, nowadays, being the target of a couple of spam mails everyday. All efforts are being made at the Information Technology Services to increase the security level of the University's spam filter and to put a stop to this unwanted intrusion of a personal communication space. In another, unrelated matter the personal information of University of California, Los Angeles students and other university-affiliated individuals was compromised. It was reported that "one or more hackers have gained access to a UCLA database containing personal information on about

800,000 of the university's current and former students, faculty and staff members, among others."[33]

The foregoing list of concerns merely suggests the problems that beset higher education in its relationship to the corporate world. We do not say that there are any easy solutions, any quick fixes to the challenges identified in the list. This list is simply a starting point for administrators and educators to contemplate, if they wish to preserve a system of higher education that has worked and prospered for so many centuries.

GUARDING THE GUARDIANS

Who guards the guardians? This question should be raised in context of the previously discussed developments in the contemporary system of higher education; a system that seemed to have gone overboard as far as commercialization is concerned. School officials and administrators who are supposed to act as guardians (protectors) to shield students and the institutional community from commercial encroachments have, for the most part, neglected to do so in order to increase the institutional bottom line, nurture an overinflated administrative apparatus, and please their corporate donors.

One possibility to get education back on track and, thus, guard the guardians, is to exert pressure on the relevant political authorities to craft and implement appropriate policies and regulations. In her book *Academic Capitalism in the New Economy,* Sheila Slaughter identifies two examples of central legislative areas within the environment of academic research. "The first one deals with research and graduate students, the second one with intellectual property."[34] Of course, all implementations of safeguards also depend on which political party is in power (Republicans or Democrats), with the dubious freedom granted to institutions to engage in corporatization going virtually unchecked in the more conservative, market-oriented administrations.

Another approach to solve the persistent problem of failing guardianship that has attracted more and more attention in the modern discourse of higher learning is the use of a social contract.[35] In this context the following question arises: What role does a social contract play in modern academia? A social contract, by its very nature, stipulates that society as a whole is called upon to provide funding for academic endeavors, such as research, through federal monies.[36] In return, the universities and their researchers should provide research results that would be the "seed corn[s] for further scientific discovery" and would eventually lead to the creation of products that can be introduced in the marketplace.[37] In reality money is very often handed over by the government without any strategic goals and taken by universities for mere maintenance costs, without having any intention to deliver promising results. A social contract in this matter would be a starting point to remind both parties, the universities and corporate America, about their responsibilities and their commitments to education.

At this point it is necessary to revisit the question that was posed in the beginning of this chapter: Are there adequate academic policies in place to safeguard the academic community from commercial intrusion? The answer is, "We do not know!" Due to a lack of university transparency and ivory tower secrecy (administrative secrecy), it is hard to ascertain whether institutions have adequate and comprehensive policies and procedures in place. It can only be hoped that guardians (school officials) live up to their responsibility and protect the students, faculty, and academic communities from commercial encroachment.

When taking all the issues and developments presented in this chapter and in this text into consideration, we would like to leave the readers of this book with a final thought by David Baltimore, the former president of the California Institute of Technology and a Nobel Laureate in Physiology or Medicine. After reflecting on what the contemporary university might look like, Baltimore wrote the following in a letter to the Cal Tech community: "Contemporary universities are for the most part nonprofit organizations whose main concern is not the bottom line—yet they must be as fiscally savvy as any corporation if they want to survive to pursue their ideals. [But,] what is the proper balance between the ideal and the real, the exalted and the down-to-earth?"[38] Whether institutions of higher education are capable of striking this balance in the near future remains to be seen.

NOTES

1. Thorstein Veblen, *The Higher Learning in America* (London: Routldege/Thoemmes Press, 1994), 220.

2. Veblen, *The Higher Learning*, 220.

3. Veblen, *The Higher Learning*, 191.

4. Veblen, *The Higher Learning*, 276.

5. Veblen, *The Higher Learning*, 270.

6. George Ritzer, *The McDonaldization Thesis: Explorations and Extensions* (Thousand Oaks, CA: Pine Forge Press, 1998), 153.

7. George Ritzer, *The McDonaldization of Society* (Newbury Park, CA.: Pine Forge Press, 1993), 141.

8. Ritzer, *The McDonaldization of Society*, 141–42.

9. Immanuel Maurice Wallerstein, *The Second Era of the Great Expansion of the Capitalist World-Economy, 1730–1840s* (San Diego: Academic Press, 1989).

10. George Ritzer, *Modern Sociological Theory,* 5th ed. (New York: McGraw-Hill Higher Education, 2000), 163.

11. George Ritzer, *Modern Sociological Theory,* 163.

12. Peter Berger and Samuel Huntington, eds., *Many Globalizations: Cultural Diversity in the Contemporary World* (Oxford: Oxford University Press, 2002), 26.

13. Berger and Huntington, *Many Globalizations*, 286–87.

14. Berger and Huntington, *Many Globalizations*, 33.

15. Berger and Huntington, *Many Globalizations*, 26–27.

16. Berger and Huntington, *Many Globalizations*, 59.

17. Philip G. Altbach, "Higher Education and the WTO: Globalization Run Amok" *International Higher Education*, no. 23 (Spring 2001), *<www.bc.edu/bc_org/avp/soe/cihe/newsletter/News23/text001.htm>* (21 March 2006).

18. Berger and Huntington, *Many Globalizations*, 4.

19. John Avery, "Caltech Names Three New Trustees," News Release, Caltech Media Relations, 16 November 2006, *<http://pr.caltech.edu/media/Press_Releases/PR12925.html>* (17 November 2006).

20. Avery, "Caltech Names Three New Trustees," 2006.

21. "Trustee List," California Institute of Technology, 8 November 2006, *<http://bot.caltech.edu/subpages/trustees_list.htm>* (17 November 2006).

22. "MITOpenCourseWare," Massachusetts Institute of Technology, 2002–2006, *<http://ocw.mit.edu/index.html>* (20 October 2006).

23. "eScholarship@BC: A Digital Commons Project," Boston College, 2006, *<http://escholarship.bc.edu/>* (20 October 2006).

24. Sherly G. Stolberg, "Gifts to Science Researchers Have Strings, Study Finds." *New York Times*, 1 April 1998, A17.

25. Regina Warwick, "To Spurn a Star," *Chronicle of Higher Education,* 50, no. 19, 14 Jan. 2004, *<http://chronicle.com/jobs/200401/2004011401c.htm>* (19 May 2005), Quoted by Catherine O'Neill in *Higher Education: Open for Business*, ed. Christian Gilde (Lanham, MD: Lexington Books, 2007).

26. Regina Warwick, "To Spurn a Star," *Chronicle of Higher Education,* 50, no. 19, 14 January 2004, *<http://chronicle.com/jobs/200401/2004011401c.htm>* (19 May 2005), Quoted by Catherine O'Neill in *Higher Education: Open for Business*, ed. Christian Gilde (Lanham, MD: Lexington Books, 2007).

27. Michael Malec, "College Sports," in *Higher Education: Open for Business*, ed. Christian Gilde (Lanham, MD: Lexington Books, 2007).

28. Malec, "College Sports."

29. Malec, "College Sports."

30. U.S. Department of Education, *Family Educational Rights and Privacy Act (FERPA)* (Washington, D.C.: Family Policy Compliance Office, 2005), *<www.ed.gov/policy/gen/guid/fpco/ferpa/index/html>* (12 December 2006).

31. U.S. Department of Education, *Family Educational Rights,* 2005.

32. BC Information Technology Services, "Email Update: Spam and Yahoo," 17 November 2006, listserve message (18 November 2006).

33. Rebecca Trounson, "UCLA Data Breach Among the Worst of Its Kind," *Los Angeles Times*, 12 December 2006, The State, <*www.latimes.com/news/local/la -ex-ucla121206,0,751718.story?coll=la-home-headlines*> (12 December 2006).

34. Sheila Slaughter and Gary Rhoades, *Academic Capitalism in the New Economy* (Baltimore, MD: The Johns Hopkins University Press, 2004), 36.

35. Slaughter, *Academic Capitalism*, 46.

36. Slaughter, *Academic Capitalism*, 46.

37. Slaughter, *Academic Capitalism*, 46.

38. David Baltimore, "Letter from the President," *California Institute of Technology Annual Report 2002–2003*, 3, <*http://pr.caltech.edu/annual_report/annual_report _archive/ar_02_03.pdf*> (25 October 2006).

BIBLIOGRAPHY

Altbach, Philip G. "Higher Education and the WTO: Globalization Run Amok." *International Higher Education*, no. 23 (Spring 2001). <*www.bc.edu/bc_org/avp/ soe/cihe/newsletter/News23/text001.htm*> (21 March 2006).

Avery, John. "Caltech Names Three New Trustees." News Release, Caltech Media Relations, 16 November 2006. <*http://pr.caltech.edu/media/Press_Releases/ PR12925.html*> (17 November 2006).

BC Information Technology Services. "Email Update: Spam and Yahoo." 17 November 2006. Listserve message (18 November 2006).

Berger, Peter and Samuel Huntington, eds. *Many Globalizations: Cultural Diversity in the Contemporary World.* Oxford: Oxford University Press, 2002.

Baltimore, David. "Letter from the President." *California Institute of Technology Annual Report 2002–2003.* <*http://pr.caltech.edu/annual_report/annual_report _archive/ar_02_03.pdf*> (25 October 2006).

"eScholarship@BC: A Digital Commons Project." Boston College, 2006. <*http:// escholarship.bc.edu/*> (20 October 2006).

Malec, Michael. "College Sports." in *Higher Education: Open for Business*, ed. Christian Gilde. Lanham, MD: Lexington Books, 2007.

"MITOpenCourseWare." Massachusetts Institute of Technology, 2002–2006. <*http:// ocw.mit.edu/index.html*> (20 October 2006).

Ritzer, George. *The McDonaldization Thesis: Explorations and Extensions.* Thousand Oaks, Calif.: Pine Forge Press, 1998.

———. *The McDonaldization of Society.* Newbury Park, Calif.: Pine Forge Press, 1993.

———. *Modern Sociological Theory.* 5th ed. New York: McGraw-Hill Higher Education, 2000.

Slaughter, Sheila and Gary Rhoades. *Academic Capitalism in the New Economy.* Baltimore, MD: The Johns Hopkins University Press, 2004.

Stolberg, Sherly G., "Gifts to Science Researchers Have Strings, Study Finds," *New York Times*, 1 April 1998, A17.

Trounson, Rebecca."UCLA Data Breach Among the Worst of Its Kind. *Los Angeles Times*, 12 December 2006, The State. *<www.latimes.com/news/local/la-ex-ucla 121206,0,751718.story?coll=la-home-headlines>* (12 December 2006).

"Trustee List." California Institute of Technology, 8 November 2006. *<http://bot.caltech .edu/subpages/trustees_list.htm>* (17 November 2006).

U.S. Department of Education. *Family Educational Rights and Privacy Act (FERPA)*. Washington, D.C.: Family Policy Compliance Office, 2005. *<www.ed.gov/policy/gen/ guid/fpco/ferpa/index/html>* (12 December 2006).

Veblen, Thorstein. *The Higher Learning in America*. New Brunswick, N.J.: Transaction Publishers, 1993.

Wallerstein, Immanuel Maurice. *The Second Era of the Great Expansion of the Capitalist World-Economy, 1730–1840s*. San Diego: Academic Press, 1989.

Warwick, Regina. "To Spurn a Star." *Chronicle of Higher Education,* 50, no. 19, 14 January 2004. *<http://chronicle.com/jobs/200401/2004011401c.htm>* (19 May 2005). Quoted by Catherine O'Neill in *Higher Education: Open for Business*, ed. Christian Gilde. Lanham, MD: Lexington Books, 2007.

Index

About the Authors

Fredrick Chilson. After ten years of working in the private sector for a multi-million dollar company as an operations manager, Fredrick Chilson decided to enter higher education and pursue his doctorate in education. Fredrick Chilson spent some time as an assistant professor of education at Eastern New Mexico University where he focused on online education and cognitive learning in his coursework and research. Recently, Fredrick Chilson transferred to Adams State College, Colorado, where he teaches in the Human Performance Department. Professor Chilson's work has been published in numerous journals and presented at business as well as education-related conferences.

Christian Gilde. Born in Austria, Christian Gilde shuttled between the United States and Europe, and after high school he started community college in Santa Monica, California. With an Associate degree in his pocket he worked in sales management for American Airlines in Dublin, Ireland. Following his time in Ireland, he attained a Bachelor's degree in business administration from Eastern New Mexico University. To further his scholastic career, he first studied at Boston College for his Master's degree and is currently part of The University of Bath where he works as an instructor and research associate while putting the finishing touches on his Ph.D. Christian Gilde has published papers in such journals as *The Journal of Investing*, has been quoted in well-read college publications such as the *Boston College Heights*, and presented his research and work at numerous conferences. As far as his service to the academic community is concerned, Christian Gilde has incepted a scholarship program, developed a marketing research and consumer behavior course, and worked in a management position at a women's organization.

Michael Malec. Professor Malec attained his Ph.D. in sociology from Purdue University. At the graduate level, Professor Malec teaches a course in Statistics and Data Analysis and offers a seminar on Teaching. His undergraduate courses include Statistics, Sport in American Society, and Social Justice in Mesoamerica. His writing and research interests are primarily in the area of the sociology of sport. He is a past president of the North American Society for the Sociology of Sport and Alpha Kappa Delta, the international sociology honor society, and has served as chair of the ASA's Section on Undergraduate Education. For six years he was editor of *The Journal of Sport and Social Issues.* His publications include three books, *Attitude Change*, *Essential Statistics for Social Research* and *The Social Roles of Sports in Caribbean Societies*, as well as articles such as "Patriotic Symbols in Intercollegiate Sports During the Gulf War," "Gender Equity in Athletics," and "Baseball, Cricket, and Social Change."

Elizabeth G. Miller. Professor Miller received her Ph.D. and M.A. from the Wharton School at the University of Pennsylvania and a B.A. from Cornell University. Dr. Miller is currently assistant professor of marketing at Boston College in the Carroll School of Management. Her research focuses on how consumers interpret and respond to information, particularly during highly stressful or emotional experiences. Her research has appeared in leading marketing journals such as the *Journal of Consumer Research* and the *Journal of Marketing Research*, and has also been presented at numerous conferences, including the Association for Consumer Research, Society of Consumer Psychology, and Marketing Science conferences. Current projects include how people make decisions about their health (e.g., factors affecting adult decisions to obtain screening tests and how children make healthy food choices).

Catherine O'Neill. Catherine O'Neill (Ph.D., University of Louisiana) is an assistant professor of English at New Mexico State University—Carlsbad. Dr. O'Neill's research interests include composition pedagogy, writing across the curriculum, and narratology. She has presented papers and conducted workshops at the annual conferences of the College English Association, the American Culture Association, The Conference on College Composition and Communication, and the National Council of Teachers of English. Her fiction and poetry have appeared in *Louisiana English Journal, Mississippi Review*, and *Arkansas Literary.*

David Rutledge. David Rutledge is an assistant professor in the Department of Curriculum and Instruction at New Mexico State University in Las Cruces. As the coordinator of the Curriculum and Learning Technologies specialization in his department, Dr. Rutledge has had the opportunity to observe how technology integration in distance education has grown substantially since 2002. Currently, he teaches undergraduate and graduate courses in learning technologies, bilingual education, and ESL. Dr. Rutledge has experiences from living in Ecuador, Japan, and Canada that have influenced his teaching and research interest of integrating technology with language learning and international education/border studies.

Juliet B. Schor. Juliet Schor is a professor of sociology at Boston College. Before joining Boston College, she taught at Harvard University in the Department of Economics and was director of the Committee on Degrees in Women's Studies. Professor Schor's most recent book is *Born to Buy: The Commercialized Child and the New Consumer Culture* (Scribner, 2004). *Born to Buy* is an account of marketing to children from inside the agencies and firms and an assessment of how these activities are affecting children. Schor is also the author of the national bestsellers, *The Overworked American: The Unexpected Decline of Leisure* (Basic Books, 1992), *The Overspent American: Why We Want What We Don't Need*, and *Do Americans Shop Too Much?* (Beacon Press2000). She is also a coeditor of *Consumer Society: A Reader* (The New Press, 2000) and *Sustainable Planet: Solutions for the Twenty-first Century* (Beacon Press, 2002). Juliet Schor was appointed a Guggenheim Fellow for her work on consumer society, and in 2006 she won the Leontief Prize for contributions to expanding the frontiers of economic thought. She has lectured widely throughout the United States, Europe, and Japan to a variety of civic, business, labor, and academic groups. She appears frequently on national and international television and radio, and profiles on her have appeared in scores of magazines and newspapers, including *The New York Times, Wall Street Journal, Newsweek,* and *People* magazine.

Eve Spangler. Professor Spangler's main interests lie in the intersecting areas of inequality and social justice. Educated as an anthropologist at Yale (Masters) and sociologist at the University of Massachusetts Amherst (Doctorate), she began her career in the sociology of education, studying the long-term career development of undergraduates from blue-collar families. This led her, by turns, into the study of women's success in law school, and to the study of changes in professional autonomy in bureaucratic settings. In the more activist part of her career, Professor Spangler has spent many years promoting worker health and safety (and thus challenging corporate prerogatives to organize the workplace) through intersectoral collaboration in Central and Eastern Europe. She has also explored the possibility to promote health and safety from the management side in her work at Boston College's Center for

Responsible Leadership—a collaborative center established jointly by members of The Department of Sociology, The Carroll School of Management, and The Lynch School of Education. Her current work on the overcommercialization of higher education brings her full circle to her earliest interests in education, opportunity, and social justice.